DATE DUE

A HISTORY OF
THE GERMAN *NOVELLE*

A HISTORY OF
THE GERMAN *NOVELLE*

BY
THE LATE

E. K. BENNETT

REVISED AND CONTINUED
BY

H. M. WAIDSON

Professor of German at the
University College of Swansea

CAMBRIDGE
AT THE UNIVERSITY PRESS
1970

PUBLISHED BY
THE SYNDICS OF THE CAMBRIDGE UNIVERSITY PRESS
Bentley House, 200 Euston Road, London, N.W. 1
American Branch: 32 East 57th Street, New York 22, N.Y.

Standard Book Number 521 04152 X

First printed   1934
Reprinted   1949
Second edition   1961
Reprinted 1965, 1970

First printed in Great Britain at the University Press, Cambridge
Reprinted by offset-litho by Jarrold & Sons Ltd

To
ELLA, HAROLD
AND
JOACHIM

CONTENTS

From the Introduction to the First Edition   PAGE ix

Introduction to the Second Edition   xiii

Chapters

I   The Novelle as a literary genre   1

II   The Classical Novelle: Goethe   20

III   The Metaphysical Novelle: Kleist   37

IV   The Romantic Novelle   47

V   The Discursive Novelle   77
    (*a*) Ludwig Tieck's later Novellen
    (*b*) The Jungdeutschen

VI   The Novelle of Country Life   106

VII   The Novelle of Poetic Realism   124
    (*a*) Annette von Droste-Hülshoff
    (*b*) Adalbert Stifter
    (*c*) Otto Ludwig
    (*d*) Franz Grillparzer and Eduard Mörike
    (*e*) Theodor Storm
    (*f*) Gottfried Keller

VIII   The Novelle as a substitute for Tragedy   193

IX   The Psychological Novelle   206
    (*a*) Paul Heyse
    (*b*) Conrad Ferdinand Meyer
    (*c*) Towards the Close of the Nineteenth Century

viii   *Contents*

X   Novelle and Short Story   PAGE 241

XI   The Novelle in the Twentieth Century   247

Notes   301

Bibliography   310

Index   313

FROM THE INTRODUCTION TO
THE FIRST EDITION

I shall attempt in the first chapter, before tracing the historical development of the Novelle in German literature, to arrive at some sort of definition of the genre as such, basing myself upon the writings of German critics and poets and selecting from the innumerable pronouncements upon the subject those which seem to be of most importance. A very comprehensive account of the attempts made to define the nature of the Novelle as a literary genre is given in the first chapter of Arnold Hirsch's book *Der Gattungsbegriff 'Novelle'* (Germanische Studien, Heft 64, Berlin, 1928) to which I am indebted for much valuable information. So far no comprehensive history of the Novelle in German literature has appeared either in England or Germany.

The history of a literary genre is not the mere enumeration of the writers who have cultivated that genre, brief biographical notes about them, followed by a synopsis of their various works. It involves an investigation into the origin of the genre, an attempt to account for its emergence at a given period, its basic types, possibly in the literature of another country from which it is taken over, the changes and modifications which it undergoes, as the result of various influences, such as the personality of the writers who employ it, the prevailing literary fashions, the sociological tendencies or philosophical currents which affect the thought and attitude to life of successive generations. The genre is regarded as an organism which contains within itself possibilities of development, and the history of the genre must show how far and in what way

these possibilities have been realized. These are the lines
upon which this investigation has been carried out.

It is perhaps unnecessary to point out that the word
'development' is not used in the sense of improvement
or advance towards perfection, but signifies merely the
modifications which the term undergoes under the influence of the forces above mentioned. It is of course
possible that the history of a literary genre will reveal an
increasing improvement in the use of the form, so that in
the works of a given author or group of authors the form
will appear to have attained a maximum of effectiveness
beyond which no further progress seems possible or at
least beyond which none can be recorded. Thus in tracing
the development of the German Ode it is permissible to
say that, proceeding from the Middle Ages, when the
Ode first enters German literature from Latin sources,
a gradual development—in the nature of a greater poetical
effectiveness—can be traced which reaches one climax in
Klopstock and a second, heightened one in Hölderlin,
after which no further achievements of equal value can be
recorded.[1] Or in tracing the development of the German
novel (Roman) it can be said that the novel as a genre
develops during the seventeenth century under the influence of foreign models without attaining to any really
independent form of its own; that in the eighteenth century it follows a parallel development under the influence
of different models; and that at the end of the century it
suddenly reaches its climax in Goethe's *Wilhelm Meister*,
since when it has nothing of greater importance to
register. Though it might be added that *Wilhelm
Meister* establishes the 'inner form'—that of the Erziehungsroman—for the majority of important novels which

have been written in Germany since.

In this account of the history of the Novelle in German literature I have attempted to show its development from its Romance origins to a specifically German form which finds its most effective expression in a group of writers in the middle of the century of whom Gottfried Keller is the most eminent. Later writers in their treatment of the genre seem to me to have failed to achieve the same maximum of effectiveness, and the modifications which they have introduced have tended with few exceptions to undermine the specific form which had been slowly evolving in the course of the century. That the feeling exists with certain writers who are sensitive to the requirements of form, that the German Novelle has come to the end of its development, is indicated by the fact that a definite attempt has been made in various quarters to revert to the original Romance form.

Since there is no equivalent in English for the word 'Novelle' I have throughout adhered to the German word, printing it as a German word with a capital letter in order to avoid confusion with the English word 'novel'. I have likewise retained the German expressions: Stimmung, Bürgertum, bürgerlich, Bauerntum, Bauernstand, for which English equivalents, where they exist, are misleading. In particular the quasi-English terms *bourgeoisie* and *bourgeois* have had to be discarded as translations of Bürgertum and bürgerlich, since they fail to give the meaning which attaches to the German words. For the German expression 'Rahmennovelle' or 'Rahmenge-schichte' I have used, for lack of a recognized English literary equivalent, the term 'framework Novelle' or 'Novelle with a framework'. Quotations from foreign critical works are usually given in translation in the text. In nearly every instance the reference to the original quotation will be found in the notes.

I have restricted myself to an account of works of outstanding excellence or such as reveal some characteristic quality. It is impossible to enumerate the vast number of writers who have written competent Novellen which neither show marked originality nor contribute to the development of the genre. And this holds good especially of more modern writers, with regard to whom I have further restricted myself to those whose literary reputations were already established before 1920.

I owe a debt of gratitude, which I gladly acknowledge, to the following: to Geheimrat Professor O. F. Walzel of the University of Bonn, for his great kindness in placing the library of the Germanistisches Seminar at my disposal; to Professor G. Hübener, likewise of the University of Bonn, in particular for one most fruitful suggestion; to Fräulein Dr Etscheid and to Hellmuth Jäsrich for the stimulus derived from discussion of my subject with them; to my sister, E. N. Bennett, for her help with the index and the preparation of this book for the press; and to my friend and colleague, Dr Joachim Rosteutscher, for invaluable criticism and suggestion.

E. K. B.

St Valentine's Day
1934

INTRODUCTION TO THE SECOND EDITION

E. K. Bennett died on 13 June 1958 at the age of
seventy. His serene and genial personality will be long
remembered with affection and respect by his many
friends and colleagues. An even wider circle has known
him and will continue to know him through the medium
of his writings, and especially through the present book.
Bennett's *History of the German Novelle* was the first full-
length treatment of its subject to appear in any language,
although a number of studies on the German Novelle
have been published in German in the intervening
twenty-six years. It was as an undergraduate that
I made the acquaintance of this book when it first
appeared, and it was for me, as for many others, an
introduction to new, unexplored and fascinating aspects
of German literature.

Some years ago E. K. Bennett hoped to write a further
chapter to extend the story of the German Novelle from
the period of Thomas Mann's *Der Tod in Venedig* up to
more recent times. He told me about this plan, and we
discussed together a number of the personalities and
problems that might be involved in a consideration of the
place of the Novelle in the first half of the present
century. On taking up the preparation of the book for its
present edition, it seemed right for me to confine any
changes in the text almost entirely to those sections
about which he and I had exchanged views in some
detail. Chapter VI has, therefore, been rewritten and
now been renamed 'The Novelle of Country Life', and
some of the material from the old chapter X has been

incorporated into chapter xi so that discussion of Schnitzler, Mann and Hesse now takes its place in the context of the twentieth century. A brief new chapter x ('Novelle and Short Story') serves to introduce the new concluding chapter, 'The Novelle in the Twentieth Century'; these are both my responsibility, apart from the section on Schnitzler which has been largely incorporated from the old chapter x. To make room for this fresh material, the appendix consisting of analyses of narratives has had to be omitted. Some additions have been made to the Select Bibliography, and the Index of Novellen has been replaced by an index of authors' names. I hope that this new edition of a much-valued work will be a not unworthy memorial to E. K. Bennett.

H.M.W.

March 1960

Chapter I

THE NOVELLE AS A LITERARY GENRE

The attempt to define a particular literary genre presents two difficulties and dangers: to restrict it to certain very definite characteristics and to insist that these are essential to the genre necessarily involves the exclusion of a large number of works which are usually regarded as belonging thereto; to establish a formula, on the other hand, which covers all the various examples usually included in the genre is to widen the definition to such an extent, leave it in such general terms, that it will cease to be an exact definition altogether. A minimum of definition, to be elaborated in the course of this survey, is the following: a Novelle is a narrative in prose, usually shorter than a novel, dealing with one particular situation, conflict, event, or aspect of a personality; it narrates something 'new' in the sense of something unusual or striking. The shortness of a Novelle, indeed of a short story, is a very relative matter. Storm's *Späte Rosen* occupies a few pages; Tieck's *Der junge Tischlermeister* over four hundred. Both of them claim to be Novellen. The most that can be said on this score is that the Novelle, because it does restrict itself to one centre of interest, tends to be shorter than a novel, which has many.

The aim of the present chapter is to establish a definition of the Novelle, which will serve as a basis for a description of the development of the genre during the nineteenth century. A twofold method of investigation is possible: to ask whether the genre as such possesses certain inherent characteristics *a priori* which determine its essential nature: to arrive at a definition by tracing historically the origin and development of the genre. The first method may or may not yield important results. But there is always the danger of importing into an *a priori* definition characteristics which have in fact been obtained from a consideration of actual examples of the genre. It may, however, be said that with regard to many genres the specific quality is not merely in the form but also in the subject matter;[1] that certain subject matters seem to be specially suited for certain definite forms. Thus a given idea might seem to the poet to demand treatment in sonnet form. The ordinary reader gives expression to a similar belief when, hearing an anecdote from actual life, he exclaims: 'What a subject for a short story!', signalizing thereby that he recognizes both the suitability of a certain subject matter for a particular literary form, and also, however vaguely it may be, the characteristics of that literary form.[2] Such an exclamation on his part is of course no proof of the *a priori* essential nature of the genre in question. It may and probably does merely signify that from his acquaintance with a large number of short stories he has obtained a certain impression of what a short story should be, and that the anecdote in question seems to him to be likely to provide something similar if subjected to literary treatment.

All literature can be divided into three basic genres: the epic, the lyric, the drama, each of which has certain inherent characteristics which determine its form; and though there may be lyrical dramas, and dramatic epics, yet there is no difficulty in assigning any individual work to one of the three categories. But within these basic categories the difficulty of subdivision is considerably greater. What for instance are the exact distinctions between an ode, a hymn, a song—all subdivisions of lyrical poetry? Or within the sphere of epic literature how is it possible to say where a Novelle ends and a novel begins; or when a work must strictly be called a Novelle and not rather a tale? The three basic genres correspond to something fundamental in the relationship of the poet to the world outside of himself: they exhaust all possible relationships between poet (subject) and world (object).

(1) The objective world is absorbed in the subjectivity of the poet, so that the dualism between the poet (subject) and the world (object) ceases to exist: lyric poetry.

(2) The subjectivity of the poet is absorbed in the objectivity of the world: dramatic poetry. Every character in the drama may be a part of his ego, through all of them his ego speaks, but his ego as a whole never appears.

(3) The relationship between the subjective poet and the objective world is represented as existing, the presence of the two factors, the contact between them is apparent: epic poetry.[3]

That is to say, in all epic poetry we are aware of that which is told and of the teller of it; and the relationship between the two is of course capable of infinite variations and modifications. In pure lyric poetry all that is sung or said is part of the poet himself; in dramatic poetry the poet disappears entirely behind the characters which he has created. But in epic poetry the poet and the world which he is creating are both present to our consciousness; and it is part of the charm of epic and narrative literature generally that we are again and again reminded of the person of the narrator. Often indeed, especially in Novellen, the teller of the story appears as a definite character within the narrative, a method of composition to which the term Rahmen- (framework) technik is applied.

In the seventh chapter of the fifth book of *Wilhelm Meisters Lehrjahre* Goethe sets up the following distinction between the drama and the novel: 'Im Roman sollen vorzüglich Gesinnungen und Begebenheiten vorgestellt werden; im Drama Charaktere und Taten...Der Roman-held muss leidend, wenigstens nicht im hohen Grade wirkend sein; von dem dramatischen verlangt man Wirkung und Tat'. That is to say, the drama deals primarily with characters and the deeds which are the outcome of those characters; whereas the novel deals primarily with events as something which befalls, happens to persons—coming from outside upon them, not arising from within them. The hero of the drama is more active, the hero of the epic more passive. These characteristics of the novel are particularly noticeable in *Wilhelm Meisters Lehrjahre* itself. Here the hero is almost entirely passive—the meeting with the troupe of actors, the adventure in the wood, the experiences at the count's castle —all are things which happen to the hero from without. If this be true of the novel it is even more true of the Novelle—at least it is revealed in a more striking form. For the manifold events of the novel are concentrated in the Novelle in one definite, striking, fateful event, which befalls a certain person or group of persons: an event which is often of supreme importance in the life of the person concerned, and always of so much importance that the narration of the changes which it produces in his life seems to the poet worth recording. Thus in Kleist's Novelle, *Michael Kohlhaas*, the hero's horses are taken from him and justice is refused him. Out of that event which befalls him is developed the whole action of the Novelle. The event need not be a tragic one nor lead to tragic consequences. Humorous Novellen and Novellen with a happy ending are as legitimate a form as those which move towards a tragic conclusion. In Keller's Novelle, *Kleider machen Leute*, the fact that he is mistaken for a nobleman brings about a change in the fortunes of the tailor's apprentice which ultimately leads him to happiness and fortune. This Novelle again affords a good example of the passivity of the hero. Far from setting out to deceive, he resists at first the unmerited honours which are thrust upon him but then yields to the force of circumstances which shape his future fate.

By its concentration upon one event as coming from without and striking into the life of a person or group of persons like a flash of lightning—not as the outcome of their characters but as something which befalls them—the Novelle presupposes an irrationalistic view of life. It is a presentation not of character as fate as in the drama, but of chance as fate. And thus a modern critic, von Lukács, can describe it: 'Das Wesen der Novellenform ist kurzgefasst: ein Menschenleben durch die unendliche sinnliche Kraft einer Schicksalsstunde ausgedrückt'.[4]

Though it can hardly be maintained that the Novelle is an inevitable literary genre *a priori*, yet the fact is significant that by its very insistence upon the one event which, in order that it should be worth narrating, produces a great change in the life and fortunes of the hero, it tends at least to express a certain view of life, which may be described as fatalistic; and that its inner form at least is conditioned by the fact that it has to show that that which on the surface is chance is in reality fate.[5] For this very task are demanded a great severity and economy of form, which are characteristic of the Novelle. The novel can in comparison with the Novelle allow itself a great deal more freedom of movement. It presents a succession of events which affect the development and fate of the hero. The Novelle, by its concentration upon one, restricts itself to just those aspects which are immediately connected with the one event. The novel, to describe it graphically, advances in a definite direction from one point to another. The line along which it moves need not be absolutely a direct one, and indeed rarely is; it can twist and turn, pause, spread itself out, loiter, only its general direction must be towards the point which is its aim. Compared with this the Novelle is a circular line moving round a fixed point, of which centre it must not lose sight until the circle is completed.

If the Novelle be compared with the tale, it will be seen that the difference between the two genres consists in the presence of this one centre of interest in the Novelle which is not essential to the tale. The form of the tale is indeed merely that of a short novel: a proceeding from one given point along a more or less direct path to another. A tale like a novel can narrate the life history of a single person; so indeed can the Novelle. But the Novelle will narrate the history of the hero's life in relation to some central point or situation. An instance is furnished by one of the finest Novellen in German literature, *Die Judenbuche* by Annette von Droste-Hülshoff. This Novelle narrates the life of the hero Friedrich Mergel from his birth until his death, but always in relation to the one action which forms the core of the Novelle: the murder of the Jew. The twenty-five years during which he lived in exile are passed over in a paragraph, because they stand in no sort of relationship to the central event. In a novel or tale they would have been at least of equal importance with the childhood or the last days of the hero.

In the following pages various other aspects of the Novelle, as presented by different critics, are enumerated chronologically, with the intention of obtaining a definition of the genre from a consideration of the views of writers contemporary with the actual authors of Novellen to be later discussed. Friedrich Schlegel in his *Nachrichten von den poetischen Werken des G. Boccaccio* (1801) is the first theoretical writer on the Novelle in German literature. He describes it as an anecdote, a hitherto unknown story, which must be able to arouse interest by itself, without reference to the ordinary course of human culture and history. It is as it were a story torn away from any cultural background. And since it has to dispense with this background, which would lend significance to it, and nevertheless aims at arousing the interest of the audience, it must contain in its form something striking and attractive. This interest may be aroused for an anecdote, which is a mere nothing in itself, by the art with which the narrator presents it. Schlegel points out the possibility of retelling and remodelling already known stories in such a way that they acquire the charm of novelty; and hints that here the personality of the narrator may be the real attraction: 'To what narrator of individual stories without inner connection, either historical or mythical, should we listen for long, if we did not begin to take an interest in the story-teller himself?' The attitude is characteristic of the Romantic exploitation of the subjective even in a genre which in some respects is intensely objective. And he proceeds: 'The Novelle is particularly suited to present a subjective mood and point of view, indeed the profoundest and most peculiar, indirectly and as it were symbolically and especially adapted to this indirect and hidden subjectivity because it tends greatly to the objective'. That is to say, by the very objectivity with which it narrates an event, it supplies the poet with an opportunity of expressing his own subjective feelings in such a way that they are not obviously laid bare. As an illustration of this apparently paradoxical state of affairs from actual examples, Goethe's own Novelle may be cited. Gundolf denies that it is in any sense the expression of a subjective experience, and describes it as merely an example of Goethe's technical ability and desire to create an example of a given form.[6] Superficially it does not appear to be in any sense a part of his great confession, yet he himself said of it: 'Man fühlt es der Novelle an, dass sie sich vom tiefsten Grunde meines Herzens losgelöst hat';[7] and anyone who reads it through with care will easily recognize the elements of personal experience which are concealed in it. The same thing is true of Kleist's Novellen: beneath the matter-of-fact narration of the horrors which form the subject matter of Kleist's stories, vibrates his whole desperate uncertainty and questioning attitude to life, no less than beneath the action of his dramas. Again the historical Novellen of C. F. Meyer, which would appear to represent a maximum of objectivity, are another instance of the truth of Friedrich Schlegel's statement, Meyer himself having written of them: 'Je me sers de la nouvelle historique purement et simplement pour y loger mes expériences et mes sentiments personnels, la préférant au Zeitroman, parce qu'elle masque mieux et qu'elle distance davantage le lecteur'.[8] Friedrich Schlegel proceeds further in his definition of the Novelle: 'And though it tends to define the particulars of locality and costume with precision, it is content to do so in general terms, in accordance with the rules and habits of thought of a cultivated society, in which it (the Novelle) has its origin and home'.[9] The point which Schlegel makes here that the Novelle is at home in a highly cultivated society and has its origins in such a sphere is stressed also by Goethe. Finally Schlegel describes the symbolical Novelle as the summit and the real flower of the whole genre.[10]

The next attempt at a definition of the Novelle to be considered is that given by Goethe in a conversation with Eckermann in 1827 in which with commendable terseness he describes it thus: 'Was ist eine Novelle anders als eine sich ereignete, unerhörte Begebenheit?' (an event which is unheard of, but has taken place). 'This conception of it is the real one, and many a work which passes in Germany under the title Novelle is not a Novelle at all, but merely a tale or what else you like to call it.'[11] It will be observed that Goethe, true to his distinction between dramatic and epic, describes the Novelle as a 'Begebenheit'. With regard to the two descriptive words, 'eine sich ereignete Begebenheit' would seem to suggest that the Novelle must narrate an event which has actually occurred, and indeed in another place he debates whether a story which is not true can be of any interest. But perhaps it is safer to assume that he means here that the event narrated must have taken place in the world of reality and not in a purely imaginary world of fancy. Wieland had insisted that the characteristic of the Novelle consisted in the events it narrated having taken place neither in a fairyland, nor arcadia, nor *pays du tendre*, but in the real world, and that they should be, if not everyday events, at least such as might occur every day.[12] Schleiermacher too required that the Novelle should describe the actual circumstances of the bourgeois world.[13] According to all these views therefore the purely fantastic lies outside the realm of the Novelle and belongs to that of the fairy tale. It will be seen later that the Romantics did not in their Novellen regard this distinction between the world of reality and that of fancy, and continually passed from one into the other. With regard to the second adjective 'unerhörte', every definition of the Novelle contains a cognate word which expresses strangeness, unusualness, unexpectedness—the element of the strange, the unheard-of being certainly one of the essential ingredients of the Novelle. However, that element is capable of very different interpretation and treatment, and whereas the Romantics tended to exploit the wilder more fantastic possibilities of the word, later writers of Novellen have been content to present the unusual and wonderful in less startling forms. With regard to the distinction between the Novelle and the fairy tale, the latter, by the very fact that it removes the events into a world of unreality, can dispense with logical connection in their presentation and allows for that very reason more arbitrary rights to the imagination; whereas the Novelle, because it has to present the unusual, 'das Unerhörte', as having taken place in the world of reality, requires the strictest motivation and the most careful logical treatment in order to make the unbelievable convince as truth.

In this connection a remark by Paul Ernst, a theorist as well as a practitioner of shorter narrative fiction in the early twentieth century, may be cited:

The improbable, that may even be intensified to the impossible, is the very atmosphere in which the Novelle, that sister of the fairy tale, is most at home. It is perhaps the greatest pleasure for the poet, as far as this type of composition is concerned, to represent the improbable in such a manner as to give the impression of the purest probability.[14]

The next important contribution to the theory of the Novelle is that given by Ludwig Tieck in the eleventh volume of his collected works, published in 1829. In the introduction to the volume he writes:

The Novelle presents in a clear line a happening of greater or less importance, which, however easily it may occur, is yet strange, and perhaps unique. This twist in the story, this point from which it takes unexpectedly a completely different direction, and develops consequences which are nevertheless natural and entirely in keeping with character and circumstances, will impress itself the more firmly upon the imagination of the reader, in so far as the story in spite of its strangeness might under other circumstances be completely commonplace.

And he proceeds:

A genuine Novelle may be bizarre, arbitrary, fantastic, witty, garrulous, losing itself completely even in the presentation of side issues, tragic as well as comic, profound and saucy—all of these qualities are possible in the Novelle—but it will always have that extraordinary and striking turning-point (Wendepunkt) which distinguishes it from every other narrative form.[15]

It will be seen from the passage quoted above that Tieck allows in theory a great deal more latitude to the strict form of the Novelle than we should have been disposed to expect. In fact a Novelle may be almost anything provided it have that turning-point in its development ('den Wendepunkt') at which the action takes an unexpected turn and develops, to a conclusion which is unforeseen and yet logically convincing. Here and in the continuation of this passage Tieck is certainly speaking *pro domo,* as his later Novellen, which were appearing at the time at which he wrote this definition, strain the form to its utmost if not beyond the possible, so that Hebbel could write (with justice) of him:

In der Novelle dagegen vermag ich dich nicht zu bewundern. Diese reizende Form hast du erweiternd zerstört.[16]

Tieck cites, as an instance of this turning-point in a Novelle, the story of Ferdinand and Ottilie in Goethe's *Unterhaltungen,* in which the development of the action is determined by the fact that Ferdinand discovers by accident that a sharp knock against the bureau in which his father keeps his money will open the drawer without the need of a key. It is indeed not difficult to find in most Novellen a turning-point, and many writers on the theory of the Novelle have insisted upon this as a characteristic feature of the genre. The particular point is sometimes alluded to as the Wendepunkt, or the Pointe or the Spitze. It is often compared with the peripeteia, or change from good to bad fortune in tragedy, as indeed there is a definite resemblance between the Novelle and the Drama in construction, the Novelle by its very succinctness having a certain dramatic quality of tension and swiftness of catastrophe.

The next theorist of the Novelle who contributes something new to that which has already been considered

is Paul Heyse. His theory is probably the most famous, though not necessarily on that account the most profound or characteristic. Heyse was himself a writer of Novellen of considerable importance, more highly esteemed during his life than he is at present. In 1871 he brought out in conjunction with his friend Hermann Kurz a *Deutscher Novellenschatz*, and in the introduction to the first edition of that collection and in his *Jugenderinnerungen und Bekenntnisse* published thirty years later, he expounds his theory of the 'Falcon'. In a chapter of his reminiscences, *Aus der Werkstatt*, he writes:

We expect of a Novelle, to which we attribute artistic values, that it should present to us a significant human fate, an emotional, intellectual or moral conflict, and that it should reveal to us by means of an unusual happening a new aspect of human nature. The peculiar charm of this literary form consists in the event being sharply outlined in a restricted framework, just as the chemist isolates certain chemical elements in order to observe their effect upon one another and the result of their contact, to illustrate thereby some law of nature—herein differing from the wider horizon and the more varied problems of character which the novel spreads out before us Then: one must ask oneself, whether the story to be related has a strongly marked silhouette, the outlines of which expressed in a few words, would make a characteristic impression, in the manner in which the contents of that story of the Falcon in the *Decamerone*, narrated in five lines, impress themselves profoundly upon the memory.[17]

Again in the introduction to the *Novellenschatz*:

Nevertheless it would be no harm, if the story-teller should ask himself in advance...where the Falcon is, that is to say the specific thing which distinguishes this story from thousands of others.[18]

The 'Falcon' is an allusion to one of the *novelle* of Boccaccio. At the head of each of the hundred *novelle* of the *Decamerone* a short summary of the tale is given, as Paul Heyse says, in five lines. For the ninth tale of the fifth day the summary runs as follows:

Federigo degli Alberti loves and is not loved in return, and spending all in courteous fashion he impoverishes himself until he possesses only a falcon which, having nothing else, he gives to eat to his lady who has come to his house; she, knowing this, changes her mind, takes him as her husband and makes him rich.

The theory of Heyse proves under investigation to be neither very profound nor very illuminating. All that he says in effect is that a Novelle must have a definite subject matter. What he does not say, but what the extreme popularity of his theory proves, is that the connection with a concrete symbol impresses both theory and Novelle more permanently upon the memory than anything else. There seems to be no reason why a Novelle should contain such a concrete symbol, at the same time a great many Novellen do in effect contain one. Two other instances from the *Decamerone* may be cited. Both are taken from the fourth day, on which all the stories deal with lovers who have come to an unhappy end and have therefore all a certain similarity of subject matter. The summary of the first tale runs thus: 'Tancred, Prince of Salerno, kills the lover of his daughter and sends his heart to her in a golden bowl. She pours poison upon it, drinks it and dies'. The summary of the fifth tale is as follows: 'The brothers of Elisabeth murder her lover, who appears to her in a dream and indicates to her the place where he lies buried. She therefore exhumes him secretly, takes his head, sets it in a pot of basil and sheds tears upon it for an hour, until her brothers take it from her and she dies of grief'. Both these Novellen, like the Falcon Novelle, are characterized by something which belongs specifically to them and distinguishes them from each other and from all other Novellen about unhappy lovers. And in all three cases that specific something is a concrete symbol: the falcon, the heart, the pot of basil. Certainly it would be untrue to say that every Novelle has some such concrete symbol by which it is remembered, but there are many in which it does occur; the two horses in *Michael Kohlhaas*, for instance, which reappear at every important point in the story. Sometimes the author stresses this symbol even by using it as the title of his story: *Die Judenbuche, Die missbrauchten Liebesbriefe, Der Schimmelreiter, Das Amulett,* for instance. Heyse's 'Falkentheorie' is in reality only a label or pigeon-hole theory, requiring that every Novelle should have so definite and striking an element in its subject matter that it can easily be recognized by this label, and pigeon-holed in the memory.

This purely external use of a concrete symbol as supplying the characteristic of any given Novelle however draws attention to the fact that in many Novellen a concrete symbol is used to express some inner meaning, often the real essence and significance of the Novelle. 'Die Judenbuche' in Droste-Hülshoff's story fulfils both purposes: it does outwardly supply the label, it *is* the Falcon, by which the story is remembered and at the same time it represents the power of fate in the life of the hero. In Storm's *Immensee* the concrete symbol is no longer the label: the white water-lily towards which the hero swims in the night, but it contains the inner meaning of the Novelle; the same is true of the swans of which the Graf dreams in *Die Marquise von O.*; of the ring which rolls away in *Die Hochzeit des Mönchs*; of the hunting horn which is lost and recovered in *Die Richterin*. In none of these Novellen does the concrete symbol occupy so important a place in the economy of the story that it can be used as a sort of label to identify the particular Novelle; but in all of them it has an inner significance and symbolizes the action. One thing further may be said of Heyse's theory of the Novelle. He does draw attention again to the severity of form which Tieck had disregarded. He speaks of isolation of the event, the conflict, as the chemist isolates in order to experiment, by his use of the scientific metaphor anticipating some of the theoretical pronouncements of the Naturalistic school.

A characteristic of the Novelle which is stressed by Spielhagen concerns an aspect not yet considered, namely the type of character which the Novelle presents. 'It will always be the specific quality of the Novelle as distinguished from the novel (in which a development of the characters or at least of the hero takes place) that it brings into contact characters who are already fully developed, who merely reveal or as it were unfold themselves in the course of that contact.'[19] Without necessarily accepting this distinction between 'fully developed' characters in the Novelle, and characters whose development takes place in the course of the events related as in the novel, it may be conceded that the Novelle, by the very fact that it deals with one event or situation, is less capable of presenting the gradual process of development than the novel. At the same time the impact of the event upon the character in the Novelle produces certain changes and whether these changes be regarded as development of character or merely as the unfolding of qualities already inherent in the character seems to be purely a question of the point of view adopted. It is however true to say that in the Novelle the event which befalls the hero has the function of revealing what was inherent in him: and bringing out by the force of its impact qualities which were already present but more or less quiescent. Whether the event creates those qualities or merely arouses them to activity is a question to which no categorical answer can be given. Kleist seems to suggest that his Michael Kohlhaas was potentially 'einer der entsetzlichsten und einer der rechtschaffensten Menschen zugleich', and that it required merely the injustice done to him to reveal that darker quality in his apparently so law-abiding life. In *Die missbrauchten Liebesbriefe* the discovery of the falsifica- tion of the love letters serves to reveal the real character of the three persons who are concerned, but in varying degrees; in *Die Hochzeit des Mönchs* the death of Astorre's brother and the dissolution of his vow reveal qualities in himself which become fateful for him after- wards, but are very subtly indicated by the author as existing already in his hero. This Novelle by C. F. Meyer, a *tour de force* of technique, reveals nearly all the peculiar qualities of the Novelle in a marked degree.

Spielhagen points out another characteristic of the Novelle which is also mentioned by Heyse: 'that, in order that the effect of the contact should not be weakened, only few characters should be involved, so that the action pre- sented will be of short duration'.[20] This restriction of the number of characters to those who are immediately con- cerned in the problem or conflict is a natural condition of the Novellenform. Heyse points out that Goethe's

Wahlverwandtschaften, originally planned as a Novelle, has become a novel by the accretion of a number of characters who are not immediately concerned in the central problem. For the working out of this indeed only four people are required: Eduard, Charlotte, Ottilie and the Hauptmann, all the rest are superfluous to the work considered as a Novelle. So that it may be said of the *Wahlverwandtschaften* that it is in essence and intention a Novelle but has become a novel in the actual working out.

A summary of these opinions upon the nature of the Novelle gives the following general characteristics of the genre. The Novelle is an epic form and as such deals with events rather than actions; it restricts itself to a single event (or situation or conflict), laying the stress primarily upon the event and showing the effect of this event upon a person or group of persons; by its concentration upon a single event it tends to present it as chance ('Zufall') and it is its function to reveal that what is apparently chance, and may appear as such to the person concerned, is in reality fate. Thus the attitude of mind to the universe which it may be said to represent is an irrationalistic one. It must present some aspect of life (event, situation, conflict) which arouses interest by its strangeness, remoteness from everyday happenings, but at the same time its action must take place in the world of reality and not that of pure imagination. It depends for its effectiveness and its power to convince upon the severity and artistry of its form. Characteristic of its construction is a certain turning-point, at which the development of the narrative moves unexpectedly in a different direction from that which was anticipated, and arrives at a conclusion which surprises, but at the same time satisfies logically. It should deal with some definite and striking subject which marks it clearly and distinguishes it from every other Novelle. This striking element in the subject matter is frequently connected with a concrete object, which may in some Novellen acquire a certain inner symbolical significance. The effect of the impact of the event upon the person or group of persons is to reveal qualities which were latent and may have been unsuspectedly present in them, the event being used as the acid which separates and reveals the various qualities in the person or persons under investigation.

By its very objectivity as a literary form it enables the poet to present subjective and lyrical moods indirectly and symbolically. It concerns itself with a small group of persons only, restricting itself to those who are immediately connected with the problem or situation with which it deals. Its origin and home are in a cultured society.

These characteristics are as many as can be postulated of the Novelle as such. But with this general idea of the genre Novelle it is now possible to trace its origin and development in German literature.[21]

Chapter II

The word 'Novelle', as the name of a recognized literary genre, first makes its appearance in Germany in the second half of the eighteenth century. Wieland gives the first definition of it in the second edition of *Don Sylvio von Rosalva* (1772): 'The name "Novelle" is given for preference to a kind of tale which is distinguished from the long novel by the simplicity of its plan and the smaller compass of its story, and stands in the same relation to it as short plays to full-length tragedies and comedies'.[1] The word both here and in later references to it in the eighteenth century is used of French, Italian and Spanish tales, and though it gradually became acclimatized, it was not until the beginning of the next century that German writers used it to describe their own tales and stories, one of the first being Wieland himself, who in his *Hexameron von Rosenhain* (1805) describes a tale contained therein as 'eine Novelle ohne Titel'. Writers such as Kleist and Hoffmann did not call their works 'Novellen' but simply 'Erzählungen'; and it was only at the beginning of the 1820's, under the influence of Tieck whose later stories were beginning to appear, that the term became generally used. An isolated example in the eighteenth century of a writer who uses the title 'Novelle' for his own works is A. G. Meissner, who published in 1786 a volume entitled *Novellen des Rittmeister Schuster*; and it is perhaps not without significance that Meissner was the author of a translation of the *Decamerone* which appeared in 1782.

His earlier as well as his later collections of tales appeared under the title of *Skizzen*. Short stories of all kinds are naturally to be found in German literature of the eighteenth century in abundance. It is not until they attain to something approaching artistic form that it is possible to regard them as a specific poetical genre, and to trace the modifications and development of that genre in successive examples thereof.

The earliest works which can be described as Novellen in this sense are the tales contributed by Goethe in 1795 to Schiller's journal *Die Horen* under the title *Unterhaltungen deutscher Ausgewanderten*: a collection of tales set in a framework similar to that of the *Decamerone*. Goethe does not, however, describe them himself as Novellen, but through the mouths of the narrators as 'moralische Erzählungen'. Thus the situation at the end of the eighteenth century with regard to the Novelle in German literature is this: the new genre has made its appearance in the examples written by Goethe but has not yet appropriated to itself the name of Novelle. Further a provisional aesthetic of it (by Friedrich Schlegel) has appeared but has not been applied to any indigenous works. The concurrence of the examples furnished by Goethe with the theory put forward by Schlegel, however, serves to establish the genre; and from the beginning of the nineteenth century it becomes increasingly popular.

Some attempt must now be made to account for the emergence of the Novelle in German literature at this particular period, and it will be seen that the demand for short stories already existed though it was supplied by works of such inferior artistic merit that they could hardly lay claim to the title of Novellen. The type of fiction which had been most widely read during the seventeenth century was the cumbrous and elaborate baroque novel primarily addressed to an aristocratic public. This had been superseded in popularity by such novels as Weise's *Die drei ärgsten Ertznarren* (1672) and Schnabel's *Insel Felsenburg* (1731–43), both of which contain within the ostensible framework of the novel a large number of individual episodes and adventures which are in the nature of independent short stories. The general tendency of German literature during the eighteenth century was towards the creation of a specifically bourgeois literature, the expression of the growing awareness on the part of the middle classes of their social existence, of which awareness the appearance and immense popularity of the 'bürgerliche Trauerspiel' in the middle of the century are evidence. The eighteenth century in Germany sees the emergence of a bourgeois reading public, which, educated in literary matters by the 'moralischen Wochenschriften' and the works of Gellert, demanded for its literary entertainment works of fiction dealing with the actual conditions of middle-class life, in which its own interests lay. In view of the more restricted amount of leisure which was available to this middle-class reading public it was natural that the mere question of time should, as a contributory factor at least, influence the length of works intended for purely entertaining reading. At any rate from about the middle of the eighteenth century a great demand for short stories arose, and since it could not be supplied by indigenous authors, purveyors of reading matter resorted to translations from foreign languages and flooded the market with collections of tales. These were for the most part without literary merit, put together by jobbing translators who published them without acknowledgement of the original sources. Such collections were the *Abendstunden* (1760), which were continued in series after series. These collections of translated tales were followed by the *Satirische Erzählungen* of J. K. Wezel (1771), the already mentioned *Skizzen* of A. G. Meissner (fourteen volumes between 1778 and 1796), the *Moralische Erzählungen* of Sophie von Laroche (1784), and the *Straussfedergeschichten* published by Nicolai, some of which were contributed as hackwork by the youthful Ludwig Tieck. In accordance with the taste of the times these collections, as their titles suggest, consisted of tales of satirical and moralizing tone; and this moralizing tendency was at least one factor in keeping them below the level of literary excellence. Schiller's tale *Der Verbrecher aus verlorener Ehre* (1785) is given pride of place by some critics as an early example of a German Novelle of literary quality, though it has been less widely influential than Goethe's *Unterhaltungen deutscher Ausgewanderten*. Schiller treats here a theme similar to that of his first play, *Die Räuber*, and thus anticipates Kleist's *Michael Kohlhaas*. His central character, however, has little or no trace of heroism in him, and the man's career of robbery and murder is viewed as a social and psychological case-history.

There is a singular unanimity between the practice of Goethe in the composition of the stories contained in the *Unterhaltungen* and the theory of the Novelle put forward by Friedrich Schlegel; and this is due to the fact that Goethe in his practice was basing himself upon the methods of Boccaccio, and that Schlegel was deducing his theory from an examination of the same author. A few words therefore seem necessary about the *Decamerone* of Boccaccio in so far as it forms the starting-point for the development of the Novelle in Germany.

The *Decamerone* of Boccaccio, the most famous collection of tales in European literature, and the prototype of numberless other collections, consists of a hundred tales which are told on ten successive days by a group of ten young Florentines, who have taken refuge from the plague which laid Florence waste in the year 1348, and sought shelter and safety in a country house in the neighbourhood of that town. The stories therefore are set in a framework which is carefully elaborated and of considerable importance for the work as a whole. The introduction gives an account in very detailed horror of the ravages of the plague and the general dissolution of social order and rules for the decent conduct of life which has thus been occasioned. The picture of Florentine life which this introduction presents is one of social chaos, in which the most honoured and sacred customs and institutions are temporarily suspended or openly flouted.

A group of seven ladies meet one morning in a church in order to hear Mass. After this is over they fall into conversation upon the dangers and discomforts of life in Florence, and one suggests that they shall withdraw to a safe distance from the town and there pass the time in pleasant and profitable social intercourse until it is again safe to return to ordinary life. The proposal is accepted by the rest, and the invitation is further extended to three young men of their acquaintance who agree to accompany them. Arrived at the country house they decide that in order to pass the days of their—certainly very agreeable—

exile with profit and pleasure to themselves, they shall take it in turn to tell stories. A master or mistress of the ceremonies is appointed in turn for each day, is crowned with flowers, and enjoys the privilege and duty of deciding the subject matter for the stories of the day in question. Everything takes place with the utmost order, regularity and decorum and in keeping with the manners and customs of a highly cultivated social class. In contrast to the collapse of social order in Florence, a little social commonwealth is established amongst this group of refugees, to the self-imposed rules of which every member of the group willingly subjects him- or herself. The framework of the stories is consistently maintained. Each story is prefaced by a general reflection upon the subject matter; at the end of each story a slight comment is made upon it, though nothing in the nature of serious criticism is offered—which would be out of place in the circumstances. The stories are very varied in emotional content —tragic, farcical, erotic, witty; the improper stories, by reason of which the *Decamerone* enjoys a certain popularity, are only a minority. But however improper the stories may be which are related, the behaviour of the characters therein finds no counterpart in the behaviour of the story-tellers themselves. With regard to the choice of subject matter, Boccaccio does not draw upon heroic legends or fantastic tales of chivalry, but for the most part his tales are rooted in the political and cultural conditions of Italy of his day. The characters are members of the middle and upper middle classes of contemporary Italy, and the picture of life which he presents is that of the world which lay around him. That is to say, his subject matter is contemporary and realistic and is taken from the life of the individual citizen. It may even be said that the Novellen of Boccaccio are in essence gossip raised to the dignity of literature.

These stories of Boccaccio determine the form of the Novelle for European literature in general. It is therefore important to see what are the characteristics of this new literary genre as it develops in Italy in the fourteenth century. In the first place they are stories told to a cultivated circle of listeners, and the existence and presence of the story-teller are definitely assumed. Though in the Novellendichtung of Germany in the nineteenth century this aspect of the Novelle is sometimes suppressed—in the Novellen of Kleist for instance—it reappears again and again under a great variety of modifications, thus giving the form of the Rahmengeschichte or story set in a framework, in reality the basic form of the Novelle. It is used by Hoffmann, Gotthelf, Theodor Storm, Gottfried Keller and with great virtuosity by C. F. Meyer.

As in old heroic ages of the Epic—with Homer and in Northern literature for instance—one must assume a Rhapsode or Minstrel relating to a circle of princes and heroes the deeds of heroes and demi-gods, not greatly different from the listeners themselves, the attitude to life, the actions of the characters being easily comprehensible to the circle of listeners; so in the bourgeois world of Florence the story-teller relates incidents and events which in spite of an element of strangeness, which makes them worth relating, reflect a world which is familiar to the listeners from their own experience. The epic narrative has moved over from heroic society to bourgeois society. These stories are realistic in the sense that they deal with the ordinary events of contemporary life; they are conceived as a form of social entertainment addressed to a cultivated audience, and presenting the incident or event narrated in a form which is in keeping with the social code of the audience to which it is addressed. It is above all a question of the 'tone', the manner, rather than the subject matter. The most tragic events—the father who sends the heart of her lover to his daughter—the most improper can be related, but they must be related in a manner which does not offend—the audience must not be harrowed nor erotically excited beyond the limits which are bearable in good society. The circumstances of time, place, custom, landscape are given in a generalized way; just as precisely as is required for the understanding of the story, but not elaborately developed so as to appear to be an end in themselves. That is to say local and historical colour does not find a place in the Novelle.

It is in this form that the Novelle comes into German literature, in practice in Goethe's *Unterhaltungen deutscher Ausgewanderten*, and in theory with the definition given by Friedrich Schlegel. Hardly, however, has it started upon its course than it develops, as will later be demonstrated, along such different lines that it becomes almost a different genre, though it continually harks back to its original form. Its characteristic of being a form of social entertainment is almost immediately lost sight of; but as such it appeared still to Goethe, as the title of his collections suggests; and in practice all his Novellen, with the important exception of one, are presented as being either narrated or read to a group of persons for their entertainment or instruction. Thus the Baroness lays down what are, in her opinion, the requirements of a story:

You have perfect liberty in your choice of subjects for your tales; but let it at least be apparent in the form that we are in good society. Give us to begin with a story concerning a few persons and events, which is well invented and thought out, true, natural and not ordinary, as much action as is indispensable, and as much thought as necessary; a story which does not lag, does not remain attached to one spot too long, but also one which does not unduly hasten; in which human beings appear, such as one likes them, not perfect but good, not exceptional but interesting and amiable. Let your story be entertaining while we listen to it, satisfying when it has come to an end, leaving behind it a gentle stimulus to meditate further upon it.

The *Unterhaltungen deutscher Ausgewanderten* is, like the *Decamerone*, a framework story and, like the *Decamerone*, it has for a background disordered and disorganized social conditions. A number of German aristocrats are driven out of their castle on the left bank of the Rhine by the French revolutionary armies and take refuge in a country house in more secure surroundings. Here they are joined unexpectedly by friends, who are also fleeing from dangers to which an invading army has exposed them. In the country house in which they are all assembled political discussions arise between the various members of the group, opinions are divided and, on the part of one young man, expressed with so much violence that the new arrivals are offended and take their leave. The breach of social decorum of which the young man has made himself guilty is felt very keenly by the lady of the house, and she insists that in future their conversations shall concern themselves with topics which do not give rise to such painful differences of opinion. It is then suggested by the family priest, who is a member of the party, that he shall tell stories from the collection which he has made during the course of his life, and this suggestion is gladly adopted. It will be seen then that, for Goethe as for Boccaccio, the telling of stories was regarded as a social accomplishment which could be utilized for the re-assertion and preservation of a certain equilibrium in social intercourse; and the later Novelle 'die wunderlichen Nachbarskinder', which is inserted in the novel *Die Wahlverwandtschaften*, is introduced into the narrative for the same purpose: to relieve the emotional tension amongst a group of persons. From Boccaccio then Goethe derives the idea of the Novelle as a form of social entertainment, and like Boccaccio he narrates his stories with a certain coolness, objectivity and distance, and con-fines himself to general outlines as far as descriptions of place, custom and landscape are concerned. The question of the novelty of a story is debated amongst the characters of the framework; and the conclusion is reached that the element of novelty is an important one in a story, but that it may lie in the manner of presentation as well as in the subject matter itself. The six stories contained in the work are of various kinds and very varying lengths. One is merely an anecdote occupying hardly a page. For this procedure Goethe has precedent in Boccaccio; on the sixth day of the *Decamerone* the stories consist entirely of anecdotes relating witty retorts. Three of the stories are merely retellings of stories already known; one story is apparently freely invented by Goethe.

There is however one element in these stories which does not derive from Boccaccio, but from the popular collections of tales which were the favourite reading matter of the latter half of the eighteenth century, and against whose inartistic and unliterary form Goethe's own stories were to serve as a check and as an indication of the possibility of more artistic development. This element is that of the moral story. The two most successful and carefully elaborated stories in this collection, *Der Prokurator* and *Ferdinand und Ottilie*, are definitely 'moralische Erzählungen', are described as such by their narrator, and are intended to demonstrate an ethical idea. 'Only that story deserves to be called moral', says the narrator at the close of his story of the Procurator, 'which shows us that man possesses within himself the force to act even contrary to his inclination through a conviction of something better. This story teaches us this, and no moral story can teach anything else.'

The stories contained in the collection are of unequal interest and merit: *Die Sängerin Antonelli* is a ghost story, which is neither very convincing nor very thrilling; of the two stories which are retold from the *Mémoires* of the Maréchal de Bassompierre, the first has a certain sinister and mysterious interest; the second is the very slight anecdote which has been treated by various writers, latterly by Emil Strauss in a very beautiful Novelle called *Der Schleier*: a wife discovers that her husband is unfaithful to her, finds him sleeping beside his mistress, and leaving her veil upon the bed goes away without revealing in any other way her knowledge of his infidelity. It is interesting to note that in its original form, and as related by Goethe, the story develops certain fairy-tale elements, which later writers in their versions of it omit altogether. The most successful of these stories is undoubtedly *Der Prokurator*, an adaptation of the last of the Cent Nouvelles Nouvelles, a collection of French stories, imitated from

Boccaccio, which appeared in the fifteenth century. In his version of it Goethe has deepened the ethical significance of a story which in its original form was in essence only a witty anecdote. The feeling which the original story arouses is that of a certain malicious amusement in seeing how the principal character has been tricked into retaining her virtue; whilst in Goethe's version she has learned in her own person, as the narrator says, 'that man possesses within himself the force to act even contrary to his inclination through a conviction of something better'. What in the original version is merely the result of physical conditions becomes in Goethe's version the result of an ethical conviction: what was merely an ironical perhaps rather cynical reflection upon the connection between virtuous conduct and the physical state of the body is raised by Goethe into the realm where moral conflicts and decisions are the ruling factors. The story is briefly this: a young wife, whose elderly husband has gone away on a long sea voyage, falls in love with a young doctor of law ('der Prokurator') whom she sees from her window. She summons him to her presence and declares her love to him. He promises to gratify her desires, but informs her that he has made a vow to mortify the flesh for a year. He has lived on bread and water now for ten months and asks her whether she will shorten the remaining time, during which his vow must be kept, by fasting herself, for a month, with him. This she agrees to do and fulfils her promise conscientiously, only to find after three weeks' fasting that she is prepared to forgo the pleasures of a love affair and remain faithful to her husband. The freely invented story of Ferdinand and Ottilie relates how a frivolous young man discovers by chance that he can obtain money from his father's bureau and makes use of this circumstance in order to purchase gifts for the girl with whom he is in love; how he eventually realizes the dishonesty of his action and by industry and perseverance succeeds in paying back the money he has stolen, until he rises to a position of honour and affluence by his own efforts. As in the story of the Procurator the moral idea of self-mastery is the core of the little work. Technically it has not the same directness and simplicity of form as the earlier story; but it constitutes a very characteristic example both of Goethe's conception of the possibilities and aims of the short story and of his ethical attitude in general during the period in which it was written. It is noticeable that all Goethe's shorter narrative works belong to the later years of his life, and all the more important of them are expressions of some ethical idea.

A second group of Novellen are those which eventually find a place in *Wilhelm Meisters Wanderjahre*, many of which have this peculiarity, that they are narrated of characters, who afterwards appear as persons in the novel itself. In some cases the action of the Novelle is incomplete as narrated, and is rounded off later in contact with the characters of the novel: thus Goethe introduces a new variation of the framework technique, which rather tends to break down the original form, and has a certain similarity with some of the tricks of romantic irony which are used by Brentano and Jean Paul in their novels. These Novellen, all of which preserve the original intention of the Novelle as being something related for the entertainment of a definite social group, vary very much in subject matter and in quality: some are merely anecdotes, some are certainly very poor specimens of the story-teller's art.

Among the more successful are *Sankt Joseph der Zweite*—
the story of his own life is here related by a young carpenter whom Wilhelm meets on his wanderings; and *Der
Mann von funfzig Jahren*, the characters of which appear
later in the novel itself. In this story the hero renounces
his claims to the love of a young woman in favour of his
son, the deciding factor in determining his action being
the loss of one of his front teeth.

The idea of self-mastery which is the ethical content of
the earlier Novellen, forms the underlying motif of the
last of Goethe's Novellen, which he entitles simply
Novelle, as though to indicate that he wished it to be regarded as a model specimen of what a Novelle should be.
But in this work, completed thirty years after the stories
in the *Unterhaltungen*, Goethe has already moved away
from the basic form of Novelle as it appears in Boccaccio.
It will perhaps be interesting to apply Heyse's test to it,
that it should be possible to give its substance in five
lines: a princess and a young courtier are overtaken upon
their ride into the mountains by a tiger which has escaped
from a neighbouring menagerie. The courtier shoots the
tiger, whereupon the owner of the animal appears and
deplores its unnecessary death. He informs the courtier
that a lion is also at liberty and beseeches him not to shoot
the lion as well, as it can be overcome by other means,
and this is indeed brought about by the singing of a
child. Thus baldly stated the story does not appear to
contain the elements of a first-rate Novelle. And indeed
all that is important in the story is not, as Heyse requires,
apparent in the summary, but has in fact slipped through
and become lost to view, though the overcoming of one
animal by force and of the other by the power of music

seems to suggest a symbolical and ethical meaning. And it is indeed herein that the significance of the story lies. Goethe's own explanation to Eckermann was: 'It was the aim of this Novelle to show how that which is unruly and untameable can often be better overcome by love and piety than by force'.[2] But it may well be asked whether the Novelle as it appears in the *Decamerone* has any aim beyond that of telling an entertaining story.

That the question should be asked at this point is due to a change which the Novelle has undergone under Goethe's treatment—a change which is already adumbrated in the Novellen of the *Unterhaltungen.* The centre of gravity has been shifted from the external events related to the inner significance of those events. The symbolical, the allegorical, that which is postulated as one element in the Novelle by Schlegel has here become the predominant element. Already the genre Novelle has undergone a modification in the form of a Verinnerlichung; and with this change in content has come also a change in technique, which has become very subtle and, to borrow a metaphor from music, contrapuntal. This work of Goethe's, which is superficially unsatisfying, is in fact, as a close examination will reveal, a marvel of subtle technique, delicate adjustment of theme and motive, expressing in hints and suggestions, in oblique reference, in the slightest actions, in the physical attitude of the characters even, the ethical idea of self-mastery. The core of the action is the love of the courtier Honorio for the Princess, which is only hinted at and never openly stated. The lion and tiger are symbols of that which he must overcome in himself. Compared with the technique of a Novelle by Boccaccio one may describe that of Goethe's *Novelle* as one of muted strings: the important action, which is an entirely inward one, is suggested only, but the suggestion is supported and illuminated by the external events. A delicate music accompanies the Novelle throughout and asserts itself at the end triumphantly in the song of the child who leads the lion captive.

Certain other characteristics of this particular work may be noted: the pictorial quality of the composition, the frequent assembling of the action as it were into one striking picture: thus the grouping round the dead tiger; the attitude of Honorio after he has killed it; the final view of him, holding his pistol, and gazing into the sunset. Again the greater importance which is attached to the landscape and the description of nature, than is usual in the older forms of the Novelle; in which connection the use of the telescope should be noted as a definite artistic trick to bring together the two centres of the action—the market place where the menagerie has caught fire, and the mountain side on which the tiger overtakes the riders. With regard to the 'tone' in which the story is related—that suitability to the customs and rules of good society in which, as Friedrich Schlegel remarked, the Novelle is at home—it may be said that it is more meticulously observed here even than in the earlier Novellen of Goethe. But it is noticeable that this, Goethe's Novelle *par excellence*, has no framework: it is presented purely objectively without the intermediary of a story-teller, as though Goethe felt—and indeed it would seem justly—that the subtleties of composition, technique and inner meaning could hardly be appreciated by a listening audience, but would require the more careful and protracted attention of a reading audience.

One line of development of the Novelle in German literature comes to an end here. It may be called the classical Novelle, in so far as it is the nearest approach to the classical prototype of the Novelle in Boccaccio; and because it is classical also in a narrower sense, in so far as it presents a picture of human life, as seen from the point of view of the classical Humanitätsideal, of man as an ethical being, determining his own actions. But this very stressing of the ethical element marks from the beginning a certain dissimilarity from the basic type of Novelle, and the development of this element in the direction of a symbolization and Verinnerlichung, carried as far in Goethe's *Novelle* as is compatible with the genre Novelle at all—it requires only a step for it to pass over into either the romantic fairy tale or the legend—this development of it takes it even further away from the original type. When the Boccaccio Novelle is revived in German literature, at the end of the nineteenth century by Paul Ernst, it dispenses with the moralizing, ethical elements which Goethe put into it.

To sum up then: the Novelle makes its appearance in German literature under the influence and indeed in definite imitation of Boccaccio, but containing a moralizing element which is alien to the Novelle in its original form, being a legacy of the short stories of the eighteenth century. This moralizing element—or rather this ethical significance of the action related—is developed by Goethe to the furthest extent which is compatible with the form of the Novelle as a genre, and with him this particular type of Novelle comes to an end.[3]

Chapter III

THE METAPHYSICAL NOVELLE—KLEIST

Goethe speaks of the stories contained in the *Unterhaltungen* as 'moralische Erzählungen', and it is possible to see in them, in spite of this description, examples of the classical type of Novelle which has its origin with Boccaccio. Kleist proposed originally to call his Novellen 'moralische Erzählungen' (certainly they are moral tales in a very different sense from those of Maria Edgeworth), but the resemblance between them and the Novellen of Boccaccio is hard to establish. They are moral tales—not that they convey a moral as Goethe's Novellen do—but in this sense that they propound moral problems with which not only the principal characters but sometimes the subsidiary characters have to deal. Generally the problems are insoluble. They are always as different from those with which Goethe is concerned as Kleist's play *Penthesilea* is from Goethe's *Iphigenie auf Tauris*.

The Novellen of Kleist appeared in a collected edition in 1810, though some of them had been published separately at earlier dates. There are eight in all: *Der Findling*; *Michael Kohlhaas*; *Das Bettelweib von Locarno*; *Der Zweikampf*; *Die Marquise von O.*; *Das Erdbeben in Chili*; *Die Verlobung in St. Domingo*; *Die heilige Cäcilie*. They represent something entirely new in the Novelle, and have so little in common with the accepted form beyond the mere outward characteristics of the Novelle, that it is permissible to feel that the form has been violated by Kleist. They have significantly no framework: there is no indication of the presence of a story-teller. Ermatinger describes the attitude of the story-teller thus: a single individual entertains in an hour of comfortable ease a group of people by the narration of a happening which is completed at the time of narration. The effect of the circumstances in which the story is told upon the external form of the narrative is the following: 'Since it takes place in an hour of comfortable ease its aim must be to maintain the same atmosphere'.[1] Nothing of this can be traced in the Novellen of Kleist; they are not only in their objectivity, in the uncommented way in which they are presented, but also in their emotional intensity the work of a poet who is primarily a dramatist and not an epic writer; one whose business it is to stir the feelings of an audience by heightening his effects to the utmost. When Schlegel speaks of the origin and home of the Novelle as being 'die feine Gesellschaft', one can only say of these Novellen of Kleist's that their home and origin are in no sort of society whatever, but in solitude and anguish. Nor can one imagine the sort of society in which they could be narrated as a form of entertainment.

This absence of the social element in Kleist's treatment of the Novelle is certainly partly due to the character and temperament of the author who was by nature as well as by force of circumstance a solitary man among his fellow beings. But actual political and social conditions must also be taken into account. All of the Novellen were written during the years in which the Napoleonic wars were destroying the fabric of an ordered society in Germany. Goethe, in spite of the convulsions caused by the French Revolution, could still fall back upon the standard court society of Weimar, which, though small and existing in a rarefied atmosphere of culture, supplied him with an undisturbed background. In later years, after the Napoleonic wars had come to an end, Hoffmann could collect in Berlin the semblance of a cultured society and the framework Novelle comes back with the *Serapions-brüder*. Tieck's attempt in his *Phantasus* to create a cultured society for the background of his stories resolves itself into a set of abstract types of persons, each of whom represents some specific attitude of mind. Lacking the social background and the cultivated society for the entertainment of which the Novelle was in its origin intended, Kleist removes it into the wilderness in which he dwells alone, communing with his soul on the problems of the individual and fate.

Kleist's Novellen—like Kleist himself—stand on the dividing line between classical and romantic. They still possess in their outward form something of the self-contained quality which is the characteristic of classical literature. In two of them at least, *Michael Kohlhaas* and *Die Marquise von O.*, the principal characters achieve a self-mastery, the attainment of which is the ethical problem in the classical works of Goethe and Schiller. But the world in which the action of all Kleist's stories is laid is no longer the world with secure foundations which Goethe and Schiller had constructed, but one whose foundations are floating in incomprehensibility. The irrational, as has been shown, is an element in the Novelle—the event as such, which strikes into the lives of the characters from without, is irrational. But with Goethe the irrational in the event can be assimilated to the ethical world, overcome, subdued to the requirements of order: thus the self-opening cupboard in *Ferdinand und Ottilie*, the escaped tiger and lion in the Novelle. With Kleist the irrational element comes from a deeper source; it is not mere chance as it is with Goethe, but an expression of a fundamental quality of the universe: the faulty nature of the world—of the world as he experienced it, as a conflict of irreconcilable antitheses. What Kleist achieved for the development of the Novelle in respect of its content was not, as has been often said, that he made the tragic Novelle possible—already in Boccaccio there are tragic Novellen —but that he created the metaphysical Novelle.[2] All his Novellen are expressions of metaphysical problems—not psychological problems primarily, though psychology plays a part in them. In all of the Novellen the characters are confronted with a situation which shatters their belief in the world order and produces in them a state of mind which may be described as an agonized questioning in respect of the sum total of things. This is the essential attitude of mind of Kleist himself, and it appears with equal clearness in the dramas and in the Novellen. The Novellen have the same quality of having burst inevitably out of Kleist's being as the dramas have and they present the same characteristics. One of these characteristics of all Kleist's work is the harshness of conflicting antitheses, which finds expression sometimes in the character of his persons, sometimes in the situation. It is a presentation by means of concrete examples of that inherent dualism of the universe of which the tragic dramatist is so acutely aware. The characters of the dramas and Novellen alike reveal it: Penthesilea, tender lover and fury; Toni (*Die Verlobung in St. Domingo*), self-sacrificing lover and decoy; Jupiter (*Amphitryon*), God and seducer; der Graf (*Die Marquise von O.*), rescuer and seducer, or as the

Marquise herself calls him, angel and devil; Michael Kohlhaas, 'one of the most upright and at the same time one of the most terrible men of his age'.

In the situations as well as in the characters the same violence of contrast may be observed. Both in *Die Familie Schroffenstein* and *Penthesilea* scenes of idyllic grace and beauty between the lovers contrast with scenes of utmost horror and carnage: the Rosenfest and the death of Achilles in *Penthesilea* are particularly noticeable. In *Das Erdbeben in Chili* there is a scene of Eden-like beauty set between the natural horrors of the earthquake and the more revolting horrors in the cathedral when the mob lynches the lovers. The same conflict is revealed in the inner situation where the characters are driven to a confusion of feeling by apparently irreconcilable facts, or deeds which seem to them to be incompatible with any ordered universe: Alcmene, who is deceived by Jupiter into believing that he is her husband; the parents of the Marquise von O. who are required to believe that their daughter is innocent, when it seems to them that this is only possible if the course of nature be reversed; the characters of *Der Zweikampf* who must believe that the voice of God itself has spoken falsely if they are to believe in their own truth; the father in *Der Findling*, who is confronted with such baseness in the person of his foster-child, that life on earth is not enough for him to achieve his revenge. The Novellen only repeat in another form the same problem as that which lies at the root of all Kleist's dramas.

It is not in the nature of the Novelle, requiring as it does as a necessary ingredient the element of the unusual, 'das Unerhörte', or whatever term may be used to describe it, to give a generalized picture of the world. By its very nature it relates not the natural course of events, but the exception to that course of events. At the most it can be said to illustrate the natural order of things by the contrast to them which it presents, and this is perhaps the meaning of Schlegel when he says that 'die Novelle bringt eine Anlage zur Ironie schon in der Geburtsstunde mit auf die Welt'—it supplies as it were an ironical gloss on the ordinary course of events. Still, in its choice of subject matter from contemporary and familiar social conditions, the Novelle in its original form might be said to provide something in the nature of a picture of actual life. Nothing of the sort, however, can be said of Kleist's Novellen. He makes the utmost use of the liberty accorded to the writer of Novellen to deal with the strange, the unusual, the extraordinary. Earthquakes, war, revolution, murder, rape—these are the aspects of life which he presents. But though such events may be regarded as exceptional and abnormal from the point of view of the ordered bourgeois existence with which the Novelle had hitherto concerned itself—uncharacteristic events—in the world of Kleist's imagination they are symbols and typical expressions of the cleavage and internecine strife in the universe as it appeared to him. In this respect again the tragic dramatist reveals himself, for the tragic dramatist, as Hebbel points out, has specifically to deal with the abnormal conditions of life. In his choice of subject matter as well, then, Kleist breaks with the social Novelle, and introduces two new elements which are further developed by the Romantic writers of Novellen: the historical and the exotic.

It has been shown that the Novelle in its original form

and as practised by Goethe deals with the contemporary and the local, the latter in a generalized way. It gives pictures of life as known and familiar to the listeners, without any attempt to elaborate local colour. That such collections of tales as the *Decamerone*, the stories of Cervantes, even the *Arabian Nights*, have for modern readers the charm of the exotic is due to the fact that they were written not for them but for an audience of another period and country. Even in the *Arabian Nights* most of the characters belonged to the contemporary and familiar life, and the supernatural beings were a part of the belief at least of the listeners. Only the difference in time and place has given to these collections of stories the additional, perhaps fallacious, charm of the exotic and the picturesque. The equivalent of the *Decamerone* to-day would be a collection of stories dealing not with romantic subjects from Egypt or mediaeval Italy, but mainly with contemporary London and relating the methods by which Lady X. deceived her husband, or Miss Y. tricked her parents, or Mr Z. ran away with his employer's daughter. But with Kleist the subject matter is definitely shifted from the circle of familiar and contemporary things into a world which already by its remoteness seems to lend more probability to the monstrous events which he has to record. The Romantics make a much fuller use of these new possibilities for the Novelle. *Michael Kohlhaas* is really only the beginnings of the historical Novelle, which Tieck and C. F. Meyer afterwards developed with much erudition and virtuosity; the elaboration of local colour in *Das Erdbeben in Chili* is very slight compared with later Romantic works—but the beginnings at least are made by Kleist.

The word monstrous which has been used to describe the events which occur in Kleist's Novellen seems to be the most suitable one to designate with him that element of the 'unusual' which is an essential in all Novellen. Under the pressure of events surpassing their comprehension or power of credibility the characters of Kleist, who in themselves are in no way striking or out of the ordinary, develop a greatness or force which gives them a monumental quality, transforms them into exceptional beings. The simple horse-dealer Michael Kohlhaas, under the sting of injustice, acquires a significance not only in the life of the state but in his own eyes, so that he can announce himself as the archangel Michael, whose task it is to establish justice on earth. The Marquise von O. in the face of a situation which is not only incomprehensible to her but also the cause of her repudiation by her parents, undertakes a course of action, which exposes her to the mockery and contempt of the world, but re-establishes her own self-respect: 'Durch diese schöne Anstrengung mit sich selbst bekannt gemacht, hob sie sich plötzlich, wie an ihrer eignen Hand, aus der ganzen Tiefe, in welche das Schicksal sie herabgestürzt hatte, empor'.

The changes which this form of the Novelle has undergone in Kleist's treatment of it may be summarized as follows. The idea of the Novelle as a form of social entertainment is entirely discarded, and with it the sense of a narrator who is present and narrates to a society of his equals. The Novellen of Kleist come like a voice out of the void and re-echo into emptiness.

The subject matter is shifted from the contemporary and familiar (sublimated gossip) into an exotic distance of place or time. It has certainly in itself interest and power to hold the attention of the reader, but its specific quality is due to the fact that the incident in every case serves as an illustration of the metaphysical problem of Kleist's relation to the universe, which is basically that of an agonized questioning and seeking for certainty. Thus all the characters are faced with problems which shake their credibility and faith in their world order to the utmost. As in Goethe's Novelle therefore the external events have an inward significance. As regards the external form Kleist retains the characteristics of the genre: all the stories have a central idea, round which all the action is grouped, and a 'Wendepunkt' or Pointe, at which the action develops in a different direction: in *Michael Kohlhaas* the turning-point is the interview with Luther; in *Die Marquise von O.* it is the point at which the heroine resists the attempts of her parents to take her children from her and determines to act on her own initiative. The element of novelty, of the unusual, is with Kleist strained to the utmost, and the whole range which the Novelle can cover may be estimated by comparing Goethe's *Ferdinand und Ottilie*, where 'das Unerhörte' consists in a bureau opening without a key, with *Das Erdbeben in Chili*, where an earthquake is required to save the lives of two lovers who have been condemned to death. The irrational element, which is an essential of the Novelle, is no longer the equivalent of chance, as revealed in the event, but is conceived as the incomprehensible, irresponsible forces of the universe, which break into the ordered life of man and shake his faith in existence. It is clear then that the scope of the Novelle both in subject matter and emotional content has been enormously widened by Kleist; indeed to such an extent that the original intention of the genre, but not its outward form, has been completely lost sight of. Though Kleist's treatment of the Novelle is too individual to be susceptible of further development by any other poet—indeed it seems hardly possible that any development along those lines could take place without falling into caricature—it revealed the fact that the Novelle might be treated in a manner other than the traditional one. It showed the possibility of opening the genre to other themes and other treatment, a possibility which was immediately exploited by the Romantics.

Chapter IV

THE ROMANTIC NOVELLE

Kleist's Novellen, as has been shown in the former chapter, forsake the idea of social entertainment, to restrict themselves to the individual and his relation to fate. Though they are no longer concerned with the ethical code of organized society—both Michael Kohlhaas and the Marquise von O. take up a stand outside of ordered society and Michael Kohlhaas, indeed, is the avenger of the idea of justice upon society, like Karl Moor and Götz von Berlichingen—yet these Novellen are concerned with man as a responsible ethical being, capable of self-control and self-mastery and resenting precisely in the incomprehensible forces of the universe, their irresponsible nature, as something hostile to the ethical responsibility which he feels for himself. That is to say, that Kleist still holds, though upon a basis which is no longer so secure, the ethical standpoint of the German classics: the moral responsibility of man and hence his power of self-determination are still maintained. The incomprehensible and irresponsible forces in the universe batter against this centre of self-determination but they do not destroy it. It was left for the Romantics, beginning with Tieck, to introduce the element of the strange and unusual in the Novelle under a new guise. This element which in the Novellen of Goethe had appeared as chance, in those of Kleist as 'the monstrous', appears with the Romantics in the guise of the supernatural, and with the assault of the supernatural upon the human personality the dissolution of ethical responsibility begins.

With the Romantics the whole relationship of man to the universe had changed. He was no longer the centre to which everything had reference, but a mere spot in the universe in which various obscure forces crossed; and the core of his being was not that conscious self-determining will of the Aufklärung and the Classics, but as it were an irresponsible something which was akin to the irresponsible forces in the universe outside of himself: a traitor in the camp of reason, who was always ready to betray man to the forces of unreason without. Hermann Pongs in his *Grundlagen der deutschen Novellendichtung im 19. Jahrhundert* writes: 'Man does not will, the "It" in the soul of man wills. This "It" is stronger than man as a conscious being, extends in some way into the secrets of nature and the powers of fate. This is the basic form in which the Romantics experience life which creates its specific form in the Romantic Novelle'.[1] For the Aufklärung, for Goethe and Schiller, man was like an island of self-determination, defending his inviolability against the ocean of irrational and irresponsible forces which threatened the integrity of his being; but the Romantics had discovered that, in the very centre of that island, by submarine passages the ocean had found an entrance and formed an inland sea there whose waters rose and fell with the tides of the ocean without. And strange to say, it was no longer the firm land of the island, contrasting so reassuringly with the unstable, unreliable waters outside, that the Romantics prized; but precisely that inland sea, whose waters were so fluctuating, but so intimately connected with the ocean that surrounded them. The irrational elements of the universe without have been recognized as having their existence in man as well: no longer the contrast between man, the self-determining, and the irrational forces of the universe is stressed, as it appears still in Kleist's Novellen; but the similarity between the irrational forces of the universe and man, within whose being they are as powerful as in the external world of happenings. The irrational element in the universe is now seen under the aspect of the supernatural and as such has absolute power over the nature and conduct of man. The struggle against the irrational, the resistance of the self against determination from without is abandoned: the enemy is welcomed and made an ally. Clearly the Novelle, which in its very nature is concerned with the irrational elements in life, whose poetic task it is to give form to the unaccountable element of chance in its effect upon the human character, was a form specially suited for this Romantic view of life; just as the drama was peculiarly unsuited for it. In the drama man appears as self-determining, creating the event by the exercise of his will; in the Novelle he appears as the being whose fate is determined by the impact of an external event—it is only a heightening of this conception to see him as the mere plaything of external and incomprehensible forces.

With the inrush of these supernatural, daemonic forces into the life of man and the presentation of them in the Novellendichtung of the Romantics another modification of the Novelle takes place, parallel to that brought about by Kleist, but again different from it. Kleist, as has been shown, widened the scope of the Novelle both as regards subject matter and emotional content. For him the characteristic element of the Novelle, the 'aliquid novi', took the form of the monstrous, but still the monstrous within the limits of the natural: and indeed in *Die Marquise von*

O. and in *Der Zweikampf* the whole conflict within the
personality of the characters turns upon the ability to
transform the apparently unnatural into the compre-
hensibly natural. In the Romantic Novellen, of Tieck
and Hoffmann above all, the 'aliquid novi' takes the form
of the supernatural, which is in its very essence insus-
ceptible of natural and rational explanation. The supernatural forces from without take possession of the human
soul, devastate or destroy it. There is no protagonist to
set up a defence against them: the forces rage themselves
out. Where in Goethe's Novellen and those of Kleist still
the circle of the action is closed with the achievement of
comprehension or self-mastery on the part of the hero or
heroine, in the Romantic Novellen it is left open, because
no comprehension of the supernatural is possible. The
antithesis of 'closed' and 'open' form is used here not
in respect of the external form or construction of the
Novelle, but of its content: in respect of the conflict which
is the emotional core of the Novelle.

Before an account of individual writers of Romantic
Novellen is given it may be useful to summarize the
modifications which the genre undergoes in their use of
it. The idea of the Novelle as a form of social entertainment is, as with Kleist, abandoned; so too that aspect of
it which may be described as 'sublimated gossip'. Its
subject matter is no longer taken from the contemporary
and local world, but from the world of the imagination:
it is fantastic just as Kleist's subject matter was exotic.
This does not necessarily mean that all realistic elements
are abandoned: in practice it does amount to this with
Tieck but not with Hoffmann and Arnim. Further, the
incident, which the Novelle relates, will of course have

value in itself as event, as happening, capable of arousing
interest and excitement; but it will also have importance
as conveying some inner significance. Just as in Goethe's
Novellen the essence of the incident narrated was found
in some ethical idea; in Kleist in the illustration of metaphysical problems: so in the Novellen of the Romantics
the inner significance is usually to be found in the light
which the event narrated throws upon man's relation to
the forces of nature, and above all to such forces which
appear as mysterious and inexplicable. Setting out from
the connection—not the contrast—between man and the
irrational forces of the universe, the Romantic Novelle is
concerned with his relation to those forces. It therefore
assigns a much greater importance to external nature and
the description of external nature than will be found in
the earlier Novellen. In Boccaccio, for instance, all the
descriptions of nature are relegated to the framework,
but here indeed shorter or longer descriptions of the sun-
rise or sunset are given for each day. The narrator as
such feels that descriptive passages are alien to his task.
In Kleist's Novellen nature plays no part except in the
description of the morning after the earthquake (*Das
Erdbeben in Chili*); and even here the description of the
happy valley in which all the refugees are assembled is
rather a lyrical mood than a landscape. In Goethe's
earlier Novellen nature description is absent, though in
the Novelle itself it assumes considerable importance.
Again, the sharp clear-cut silhouette of the classical
Novelle—the outline which is projected by the incident
itself—gives way to less definite contours, which may be
formed not so much by the event as by the lyrical mood
or Stimmung, the conveying of which is the real aim of

the Novelle. Contrary to the accepted theory of the Novelle, which separates it definitely from the fairy tale or the legend, the Romantic Novelle, by its acceptance of the supernatural, tends to shift the action from the real world into a world of the imagination; and further it admits a much freer play of fancy, and demands a less consistent logicality in the events. In fact, as far as the original and strict form of the Novelle is concerned, it may be said that if Kleist violated it, the Romantic Novelle ignored it, retaining only the mere externals and heightening and extending the element of the unusual— by transforming it into the supernatural—to such an extent that it becomes the dominating characteristic.

The earliest example of the Romantic Novelle is *Der blonde Eckbert* by Ludwig Tieck, which appeared originally in 1796. Already in this, the most famous of all Tieck's stories, most of the characteristics above described are apparent. It is concerned with an old woman who lived in the middle of a wood, with a bird that laid jewels and pearls and sang a song about Waldeinsamkeit, and a little dog called Strohmi; with a girl called Bertha, who was brought up by the old woman, but, in the absence of her protectress one day, stole the bird, ran away and afterwards married a knight called 'der blonde Eckbert'. Years afterwards she narrates the story of her youth to a friend of her husband, who reveals the fact that he knows the whole story already, whereupon Bertha is taken ill and dies. Eckbert shoots the friend and thereupon discovers that the friend and the old woman were one and the same person and that Bertha was his own sister.

An attempt to apply Heyse's test of the Novelle to *Der*

blonde Eckbert must necessarily fail, for the events have so little logical connection that, isolated from the feeling which carries them, they appear meaningless and non-sensical. The actual silhouette or characteristic quality of the story is given better than in any summary of incident, by the single 'Stimmungs' word 'Waldeinsamkeit'.

But perhaps more than any other single Romantic work, *Der blonde Eckbert* reveals that aspect of man's nature which was the discovery of the Romantics, and dis-tinguishes the Romantic human being from the human being as conceived by the Aufklärung and Goethe and Schiller. It is with this aspect of man, the ethically irre-sponsible element in him which is akin to the irre-sponsible forces of nature without, that these Romantic Novellen are concerned—that point in man, at which, be-low the surface of his conscious self-determining self, the forces of nature alone are powerful and determining. Tieck continued to write stories of this kind, though without the same unique expressiveness, during the next fifteen years. They were then published together with other works between 1812 and 1816 in a framework Novelle entitled *Phantasus*. As far as the narrative works in this collection are concerned they consist of: *Der blonde Eckbert*, 1796; *Die schöne Magelone, Der getreue Eckart*, 1799; *Der Runenberg*, 1802; *Liebeszauber*, 1811; *Die Elfen*, 1811; *Der Pokal*, 1811. Not all of these stories are of equal importance, nor can they all, by any sort of exten-sion of the term, be called Novellen. *Die schöne Magelone* is the retelling of a mediaeval romance, interspersed very freely with romantic lyrics; *Der getreue Eckart* is a fusion of two mediaeval legends, Eckart and Tannhäuser, without great success, and certainly without that concentration upon one theme which the Novelle demands. After *Der blonde Eckbert* the most successful and most characteristic story is that of *Der Runenberg*, where again the connection between the inner life of man and the forces of nature is very definitely stressed. It is the theme, which appears again and again in Romantic literature, of the human being who has vowed himself to nature under some guise or other and is then claimed by nature when he attempts to break his allegiance. It occurs with various modifications in Hoffmann's *Die Bergwerke zu Falun*, in Fouqué's *Undine* and in Pierre Loti's *Pêcheur d'Islande*. The other stories in *Phantasus* have supernatural elements in various degrees, terrifying in *Liebeszauber*, charming and fairy-like in *Die Elfen*. The two stories, *Der blonde Eckbert* and *Der Runenberg*, are the best, no doubt because they present the characteristic attitude of Tieck to external nature as of something incomprehensible and sinister to man, with which however he is united by close though unfathomable ties. In the latter of the two stories certainly the influence of Tieck's friend Steffens, a student of Schelling's Naturphilosophie, can be traced.

A word now about the framework Novelle *Phantasus* as such. It seems clear from what has been said of the origin and nature of the Novelle that the framework fiction is not a merely arbitrary addition to the Novelle, but represents some intrinsic element: namely, the actual presence of the narrator. Novellen are stories told by somebody to a group of other persons, and this fact is never lost sight of: in the original examples of the Novelle indeed it determines its tone and form. This framework need not necessarily be so constructed as to

contain a whole group of Novellen (the cyclical framework), though this is its original form, and as such it
appears in the *Arabian Nights* and in older Indian collections of stories. It may simply be the framework for one
story, as it is frequently used by Meyer and Storm—
never by Kleist: that is to say, the fiction is employed
that not the author himself is the teller of the story but
some other person. Thus in the printed book the idea is
preserved of a story-teller telling his story to some one
person or group of persons who are also present; and
this, as has been shown, is an essential quality of epic
form: the listener is aware of both subject and object, and
watches the poet constructing his story as he listens.
That awareness on his part, that it is a story that is being
told and not a piece of life which is being placed before
him, is a condition of the modified intensity of emotion
which the epic can arouse as compared with the drama.

In the cyclical framework form, the framework itself is
capable of a variety of treatment. It may be of the barest
kind, serving merely to supply a superficial connection
between the stories told, and pass the rôle of narrator
from one person to another. In the *Decamerone*, apart
from the introduction, and the continual stressing of the
orderliness of procedure each day, it is not much more
than this; the ten young people are not very definitely
distinguished, though Dioneo who is the wag, and stipu-
lates from the beginning that he shall have the right to
choose his own subject, always tells the most outrageous
stories. But the framework can of course be elaborated
to a very considerable extent, so that it forms, apart from
the stories it contains, a story in itself. The most perfect
example of this is to be found in Keller's *Das Sinngedicht*,

which is a masterpiece of framework narrative and Novellen literature altogether. But the same elaboration of the framework can be seen in Hauff's groups of fairy tales, *Die Karawane* and *Das Wirtshaus im Spessart*, and in Tieck's *Phantasus*. But here it must be said that Tieck reveals only a modified appreciation of the framework technique. The framework itself was not written until 1811, and was merely a piece of literary job work to serve as an excuse for including a great deal of disparate matter in one volume. A number of friends meet, partly by chance, partly by arrangement, at a country house; very lengthy conversations take place and, in the course of these, it is suggested that every member of the party shall contribute something to the general entertainment. This they all agree to do, for they have very fortunately all brought manuscripts with them, which they then read aloud: and not only do they read stories, but when these have come to an end they read whole plays, some of them of considerable length. Thus with the reading from manuscript the *raison d'être* of the framework form partly breaks down. The preservation of the 'tone' proper to the society addressed, which is one of the functions of the framework Novelle, is neglected, for the story is already written when the story-teller presents it to his audience, and there can therefore be no question of his adapting himself to the requirements of the society before him. In effect, in the framework of *Phantasus* some of the listeners do protest against the unsuitability of the stories.

In his introduction to his collected works which began to appear in 1828 Tieck wrote:

After a number of years having the intention of collecting my scattered writings, the idea came to me in the leisure of my country life, to enliven this collection by the introduction of characters who carry on a conversation, in the same manner as many writers of Novellen have done. This framework, which could bring many things to discussion, was to become a novel on a small scale, by means of love, abduction, difference of opinion and embarrassments of manifold kinds and to end with the reconciliation and the marriage of various members of the group.... It was part of the plan to introduce into the connecting conversations criticism playful as well as serious of the various types of poetry, of fairy tales, love poetry, humour, the fantastic and so on.... The seven narrators have various characteristics and were intended to indicate various moods of the author himself, serious and gay, enthusiastic and humorous, descending even to the pedantic.[2]

It must be conceded that the differentiation between the various story-tellers is very consistently maintained, even to details of behaviour, and an attempt at least is made to assign to each one a story suitable to his particular temperament. But the slight love story contained in the framework is of such minor importance as almost to escape the reader's attention: whilst the conversations on aesthetic and literary questions which connect the stories are prolix in the extreme and the transitions from them to the actual stories are somewhat laboured. The Novellen of Tieck's later period, to be discussed in the next chapter, bear very little resemblance to his earlier stories, and would seem to derive to a great extent from the discursive method employed in dealing with the story contained in the framework itself, namely in a minimizing of the actual incident in favour of lengthy discussion. The effect of the best of the stories contained in *Phantasus* is not heightened but diminished by the laborious and wordy framework in which they are set.

To sum up Tieck's effect upon the form of the Novelle during this early period of his literary activity, it may be said that he widens the scope of the subject matter and emotional appeal by the introduction of the supernatural, but thereby affects the form so radically—more radically even than Kleist—as to create practically a new form, which may be described as 'open' compared with the 'closed' form of the classical Novelle. Kleist's treatment of the Novelle hardly admits of any further development along his own line; though in *Michael Kohlhaas* he initiated the Character Novelle which afterwards becomes a fairly recognizable type. Tieck's innovations however open up possibilities in various directions. The supernatural with him consists largely in the mysterious relations between nature and the irrational element in man; and these relations are represented usually as being of a sinister kind, as though man were subjected to a force which was in essence malevolent. The supernatural is exploited by other writers of Romantic Novellen; notably by E. T. A. Hoffmann and Ludwig Achim von Arnim, but with other aspects stressed; and the relationship between man and nature in less sinister form by Joseph, Freiherr von Eichendorff.

Tieck's activities as a writer of Novellen came to an end temporarily in 1811, and when he took up the genre again he had ceased to be a Romantic poet and composed works which, in many respects, were a repudiation of his earlier views. In 1808, however, Hoffmann's first Novelle, *Ritter Gluck*, appeared and from that date until the middle of the 1820's the Romantic Novelle was at its height in the works of Hoffmann, Arnim, Brentano and Eichendorff. Of all these writers Hoffmann is the most important from the point of view of the Novelle. His works, apart from the two long novels *Die Elixiere des Teufels* and *Kater Murr* (unfinished), consist almost entirely of Novellen and fairy tales and are contained in three collections: *Phantasiestücke in Callots Manier* (1814–15), *Nachtstücke* (1817) and *Die Serapionsbrüder* (1819–21). The last is a framework Novelle of considerable dimensions which owes something to the *Phantasus* of Tieck. As with the latter work the framework was constructed *a posteriori* to include individual Novellen and fairy tales which had already appeared. The title requires some explanation. A number of friends, most of whom have recognizable prototypes in the friends of Hoffmann, meet by chance in Berlin after having been separated for years by the Napoleonic wars and agree to foregather once a week in a Weinhaus and entertain each other with conversations and stories. Unlike all other framework Novellen this one introduces a society of men only—a circumstance which is not without its bearing upon the 'tone' of the Novelle and the conversations. At the first meeting Cyprian relates an experience of his own: his acquaintance with a certain Graf P. who believed himself to be the anchorite Serapion, who suffered martyrdom in the Thebaide under the Roman Emperor Decius. The Graf is so convinced of the truth of his obsession that he lives in fact the life of the anchorite, and converts the world of his actual surroundings into the world of his imagination. The anchorite, opines one of the society, was a genuine poet, he had really beheld that which he declared, and therefore his speech was convincing for heart and feeling. That no one should relate a story which he had not inwardly intensely visualized is ac-

cepted as the principle of their story-telling: 'das Sera-
piontische Prinzip'. The conversations of the framework,
which does not in itself constitute a Novelle, turn entirely
upon literary, musical, aesthetic questions and the problem of supernatural and semi-supernatural phenomena;
the conversation leading nearly always by perfectly
natural transitions to the telling of a story which illustrates
or illuminates in some way the matter under discussion.

The stories of Hoffmann may conveniently be divided
into three groups according to their subject matter: (1)
stories presenting a straightforward narrative of events
—*Das Fräulein von Scuderi, Meister Martin der Küfner und
seine Gesellen, Meister Johannes Wacht, Doge und Doga-
resse*; (2) stories dealing with supernatural or semi-
supernatural happenings—*Rat Krespel, Das Majorat, Der
Sandmann, Die Bergwerke zu Falun, Der Kampf der
Sänger, Der Elementargeist*; and (3) fairy tales—*Der
goldene Topf, Klein Zaches, Das fremde Kind, Nussknacker
und Mäusekönig, Meister Floh.*

Ricarda Huch in her book on the Romantic Movement
distinguishes between 'exotische' and 'nüchterne' tales
of Hoffmann and points out that though examples of the
latter type, notably *Das Fräulein von Scuderi* and *Meister
Martin*, are praised in histories of literature as his best
works and first-rate in their kind, though they are
superior to those of the former type in unity, severity of
form, and comprehensibility, yet the lover of poetry, like
Hoffmann himself, will always prefer the 'Exotische' as
giving the real essence of Hoffmann's being.[3] It may,
however, be pointed out here in connection with the use
of the word 'exotisch' for certain of Hoffmann's stories,
that whereas in the stories of straightforward happenings

the action is nearly always placed either in the historical past or in foreign countries, the action of the supernatural stories and the fairy tales is with few exceptions anchored in the actual world in which Hoffmann lived, from which it floats upward to develop itself in a world of pure fantasy.

Indeed, though the supernatural is not exclusively the subject matter of Hoffmann's tales, yet it plays so important a part in them that it may justifiably be regarded as the characteristic element of his imagination. Even in those works in which it does not find a place the events and characters are often of so strange and monstrous a nature as to arouse the same sort of emotional reaction as that to which the supernatural gives rise. In this respect Hoffmann resembles Kleist. In Hoffmann's finest Novelle—*Das Fräulein von Scuderi*—the principal character, the goldsmith Cardillac, is psychologically monstrous, in the sense in which we have used the word to describe Kleist's Novellen. It forms an interesting parallel—as a Character Novelle—to the *Michael Kohlhaas* of Kleist, and reveals a characteristic which illuminates the different ethical standpoint of Kleist and the pure Romantic Hoffmann: Michael Kohlhaas is the self-determining Willensmensch, who proceeds to deeds of outlawry and violence from an inner ethical and volitional principle; Cardillac is a man of instinct, who carries out his crimes in blind obedience to an obscure impulse, which, as Hoffmann takes care to explain, is due to prenatal influences. As in the characters of Tieck's Novellen, and indeed in the Romantic characters generally, it is the irresponsible element in man which is stressed; Cardillac commits his crimes because he cannot help doing so.

The supernatural in Hoffmann appears under various forms—rarely under the form of the mysterious forces of nature itself, as we have seen it in Tieck frequently as magnetization, hallucinations, automatism, divided personality, ghosts and revenants. But the most characteristic form for Hoffmann is that which is presented as connected with art, and more especially with music.

Something must be said here about Hoffmann as a personality in order to explain the world of his Novellen. He was like Kleist and Hölderlin a 'problematische Natur', and like them, though in a different way, he went to pieces in the conflict between ideal and reality. His life was tragic like theirs, but it had this quality which distinguished it from that of his co-sufferers and perhaps obscures the tragedy—the element of the grotesque. He was a little comic-looking man, and as such he appears himself in various disguises in a number of his works. The conflict between reality and the ideal begets in him the ironic attitude to life, which appearing in most of his works, yet finds its most complete expression in that dualism in his novel *Kater Murr*—on the one hand the idealistic but overstrained hero Kreisler, on the other hand the philistine self-satisfaction of the Cat. Before he devoted himself to writing as his main artistic activity, Hoffmann had been a professional musician and composer. He was for some time director of the opera at Bamberg, he was a music critic of much insight and originality, being one of the first to recognize the greatness of Beethoven's work, and possessing so great an admiration for Mozart that he adopted Mozart's second name Amadeus in the place of his own less attractive Wilhelm. He himself composed a number of musical works, including an opera *Undine*, which have some claim to be regarded as works of importance. In addition to his very special musical gifts, which entitle him to be regarded as something more than a mere dilettante, he was an artist of considerable merit, and was particularly skilful as a caricaturist. It will be seen, therefore, that art plays a very important part in his psychological make-up, and represents for him the irrational, daemonic forces in life which for Tieck and for Eichendorff, though in a different form, are represented by external nature. Art, and more particularly music, is the channel through which the daemonic, incalculable forces of the universe burst in upon the ordinary, calculable life of man, with an elemental force, and set up tremendous upheavals of the personality. It appears thus in the first two Novellen of the *Phantasie-stücke*, *Ritter Gluck* and *Don Juan*, in *Rat Krespel*, in *Der Kampf der Sänger*, and above all in the unfinished novel *Kater Murr*; in other Novellen such as *Die Jesuitenkirche zu G.* the art of painting is represented in the same way.

It is usual to consider these Romantic works as something definitely unrealistic. At the end of the Romantic period the histories of literature set the beginnings of realism as the reaction, the antithesis of the Romantic cultivation of the imaginary and fantastic. And this is no doubt broadly true, more especially in regard to the early Romantic poets such as Novalis and Tieck. Yet at least in Tieck's fantastic comedies, the element of satire, directed against the Aufklärung and the Philistertum of his contemporaries, has certain realistic qualities. It is true that in the early Novellen of Tieck there are no traces of realism: the world in which the action of *Der blonde Eck-bert* and *Der Runenberg* takes place has no counterpart in the world of actual things. But the same thing is not true of Hoffmann, nor indeed of many of the later Romantics: realistic elements are present in abundance. And it is most characteristic of Hoffmann's art and in particular of his use of the marvellous, i.e. supernatural, that he nearly always starts from a realistic basis. He describes with exactness and detail the streets of Berlin or Dresden of his day, in which the typical figures of contemporary life are seen moving about, and here in this familiar setting and to these familiar figures he allows the supernatural to happen. One of the most characteristic works of Hoffmann for an understanding of his methods is *Der goldne Topf*. Here we have two sets of happenings: that which takes place on the level of everyday life, and that which takes place in a fairy-tale world of marvels. The connecting element between the two worlds is formed by the characters themselves, who are the inhabitants of both worlds, and become transformed from ordinary men and women—the old apple-woman, the professor, the three daughters—into doorknockers, magicians, golden serpents and what not. Similar works to *Der goldne Topf* are the two fairy tales with realistic setting *Klein Zaches* and *Meister Floh*. *Klein Zaches* is the story of a little misshapen creature, who has been blessed by a fairy in such a way that everything done in his presence, which is in any way meritorious or distinctive, is attributed by all present to him. The irony of the situation is from the beginning apparent.

It has been pointed out that Hoffmann, like Hölderlin and Kleist, goes to pieces in the conflict between reality and the ideal. It is important for a proper appreciation of his art to realize that, under the grotesque and what he himself calls 'das Skurrile', tragical problems are being debated similar to those in the Novellen or dramas of Kleist. The tormented soul of Hoffmann, which is incapable of taking up the heroic pose or expressing itself in the pathos of despair, infuses its distress into the grotesque figures which move through the pages of *Kater Murr* and the Novellen, and it is noticeable that he is most successful in the drawing of the eccentric characters who in spite of outstanding gifts as musicians or artists live on the borderland of madness. So that stories of fantastic and inexplicable happenings, which would appear to be the arbitrary inventions of a purely objective fantasy, afford another example of that quality of the Novelle, which Friedrich Schlegel had already pointed out: its ability by the very fact that it tends to be objective to express a lyrical and subjective emotion in symbolical and indirect form. This is as true of Hoffmann as it is of Kleist. and different though their Novellen may be in many externals, they have this in common that they represent an attempt at an 'Auseinandersetzung' with a world which, to the tormented soul of the poet, presents problems which admit of no solution.

The characteristic form for Hoffmann—that in which his most personal and essential qualities are most clearly expressed—is the fairy tale set not entirely in a world of the imagination, but primarily in the world of reality. He requires this contrast of reality and imagination to produce his characteristic effects and to convey that sense of dualism in the world which, half tragic, half grotesque, torments him. Yet it would be a mistake to accord to Hoffmann quite the same tragic significance as to Kleist. Whereas for Kleist the monstrous is utilized merely as an extreme instance of the irrationality and irresponsibility of the universe, and applied as a test to the characters in order to demonstrate their power of maintaining themselves in the face of such inexplicable horrors; for Hoffmann the monstrous event is in itself and intrinsically a matter of interest and importance: the stress is laid rather upon the event than upon the effect it has upon the characters. That is to say, that Hoffmann, there can be no doubt, employs the monstrous also for its own sake—there is in him something of the aesthetically inferior intention 'to make our flesh creep', nor does he always escape the danger of exploiting the gruesome and the monstrous in a manner which seems to have no artistic justification. Yet he is, in spite of that, more of the artist, less of the poet than Kleist; Kleist's subjects one feels have importance for him—indeed he himself says so—only in so far as they enable him to express the feelings which are distressing him; for Hoffmann, the artist, the subjects have in themselves an interest, and he works at them, not only in order to express through them his Weltanschauung, but also with the pleasure of the artist in giving form to his subject matter.

Though there is no attempt in Hoffmann's tales to explain away the supernatural element rationalistically, it is usually open to explanation on subjective lines, and is frequently motivated in the psychology of the principal character: thus in *Der Sandmann* in which the hero's fear of reality is accounted for by certain impressions of his childhood. The fact that he falls in love with an automatic doll one may assume to be a romantic symbol of his inability to deal with the ordinary life of humanity, though it certainly has also ironic value as a satire upon the

society in which he moved. The stories abound in characters who live in a world of illusion, which is presented
with such intensity that the border-line between the
natural and the supernatural is never plain. With Hoffmann as with the early Tieck the element of the unexpected, 'das Unerhörte', in the Novelle assumes so
much importance as to become the predominant feature,
indeed, instead of being one point in the story, to have
absorbed the whole subject matter. This exploitation of
the supernatural and the quasi-supernatural then is one
of the contributions of Hoffmann to the Novelle; another
is his use of fairy-tale elements in connection with a
purely realistic background or basis; a third is his pre-
dilection for the artist—whether musician, painter or
goldsmith—as his main character, so that he is to a certain extent the originator of the Künstlernovelle which
is cultivated in our own day by Thomas Mann in *Tristan*
and *Der Tod in Venedig*. Further Hoffmann introduces a
new element, one perhaps alien to the form of the Novelle
in the strictest sense, in his use of satirical criticism of
contemporary conditions, an element which is afterwards
cultivated excessively by Tieck in his later Novellen.

Akin to Hoffmann's Novellen in some respects but
without the intensity of emotional content, the tragic-
grotesque presentation of inward conflicts, but nevertheless veiling a subjective mood in an apparently arbitrarily
chosen fantastic subject matter, is the Novelle of Adalbert
von Chamisso, *Peter Schlemihl* (1814). In this one work
by which he is still remembered the author gives in symbolical form a description of his own unrooted existence,
of the man without a fatherland who feels himself as much
an alien amongst ordinary beings as the man without a

shadow in his Novelle. Like Hoffmann, Chamisso starts from a realistic basis: his hero walks the streets of Hamburg, calls at the country house, is careful to wipe the dust from his shoes before he rings the bell—the opening of the story might be the opening of a contemporary Novelle dealing with the most prosaic facts of existence. Into this apparently everyday tale breaks the whole world of romantic fairy and folk tale marvels with the devil who offers him the never-empty purse of Fortunatus and buys from him his shadow.

The use of folk and fairy tale elements and folk superstitions is a recognizable element in the Novellen of the Romantic writers and is indeed one of the features of Romantic literature in Germany generally. It plays an important rôle in the works of Arnim, Brentano and Eichendorff. Arnim's Novellen belong for the greater part to the later period of his literary career. His most famous work in this genre *Isabella von Aegypten* appeared in 1812, *Der tolle Invalide auf dem Fort Ratonneau* in 1818, *Fürst Ganzgott und Sänger Halbgott* not until 1835. Arnim is a story-teller who is moved by no such profound motives as Kleist or Hoffmann, and has no such individual view of life to express in his stories of magic, mystery or marvel: it is the delight in the many coloured wealth of incident which stimulates his imagination and stirs his 'Lust zu fabulieren'.

In the poetical genius of Arnim there is a lack of unity, a failure to persevere in a single definite direction. He was at the same time a skilled resuscitator of the past, particularly of the past of Germany at the time of the Renaissance and the Reformation; an exploiter of the world of magic and fantastic dreams, and a writer concerned with ethical problems and the criticism of society. All these various interests and pre-occupations conflict and result in a confusion of effect, so that even in his best work, as for instance in *Isabella von Aegypten*, no single striking impression is produced. In this Novelle as in his unfinished novel *Die Kronenwächter*, he reveals the power of recreating the historic past not so much in the presentation of important events as in the detailed vision of ordinary life. Ricarda Huch says of him that he was able to manipulate the stage setting of the Middle Ages or of any such highly coloured distant period so as to construct beautiful and even moving tableaux.[4] In *Die Majoratsherren* he conjures up a world of magic and imagination akin to that of Hoffmann, but one in which the intrusion of ethical problems only acts as a disturbing factor in the basic impression. He believes, like Hoffmann, in another world which is in some sense more real and intense than the world which is revealed by the senses. But the two worlds are not identified to the same extent as they are with Hoffmann. For Arnim they remain distinct; only the imagination is the mediator between the two, and can bring messages from the one for the solace or delectation of the other. In some of his Novellen, as in *Mistress Lee* and in his novel *Gräfin Dolores*, he is entirely concerned with ethical problems, pre-eminently the conflict between marriage and the freedom of passionate love. The action of his stories is laid almost exclusively in the past—a past which for him possessed a greater variety and wealth of forms before the French Revolution reduced everything to a drab unity. In *Isabella von Aegypten* he describes the sixteenth century in Brabant; in *Raphael und seine Nachbarinnen* Italy of the Renaissance; in *Die drei liebreichen*

Schwestern und der glückliche Färber Amsterdam and Prussia at the beginning of the eighteenth century; in *Die Genueserin Angelika und Cosmus, der Seilspringer* the Rococo period in Germany. His subject matter is treated with a freedom of imagination and of external form which causes one of his critics to describe the effect as arabesque. Discussing the formlessness of the modern Novelle, Paul Ernst says: 'With regard to the Novelle the only possibility of artistic form which I personally can see is that of the arabesque, as it was first created by Arnim, as the best example of which I should cite *Isabella von Aegypten*'.[5]

It is interesting to note that Paul Heyse definitely excludes this particular story from his collection of Novellen because of its formlessness, and chooses instead *Der tolle Invalide auf dem Fort Ratonneau*, which does indeed conform more nearly to the standard type of Novelle as Paul Heyse was at pains to define it, his attention being directed mainly upon outward form and construction. Both these stories of Arnim are stories of fantastic happenings, the former enriched by episodic folk-lore incidents: mandrake, Golem and Bärenhäuter, and having seemingly no justification beyond its own power to charm and hold the attention by its sheer fantasy. In *Der tolle Invalide*, however, the incidents serve as an illustration to the idea which is then expressed in words explicitly at the end of the story: 'Liebe treibt den Teufel aus'. The half-crazy veteran who holds the fort and terrorizes the city for days on end is at last subdued by the courageous love of his wife, who exposes herself unprotected to his homicidal attacks.

Arnim's Novellen, in spite of the excessive praise which Heine awarded them, an opinion which has been repeated in more modern times by Wilhelm Dilthey, have not the same power to hold the interest of readers to-day as those of Hoffmann, for they have not the same intensity of emotional experience informing them. Nor does Arnim's prose style contribute to make them popular: it is hurried, breathless and without repose, so that the reader is quickly wearied. With the exception of *Isabella von Aegypten* and *Der tolle Invalide* they are little known. Arnim's contribution to the form of the Novelle can hardly be regarded as individual but merely partakes of the general characteristics of the Romantic Novelle. He utilizes the Romantic elements of folk tale and folk superstition; in works such as *Raphael und seine Nachbarinnen* he carries on the Romantic tradition of the Künstlernovelle, creating in this particular work a forerunner of Mörike's more delicately conceived *Mozart auf der Reise nach Prag.* His most individual trait lies in his tendency to embroider the strict narrative with a wealth of arabesque tracery.

A more purely fantastic writer than Arnim, one who belonged almost entirely to the world of dreamlike imaginations without the solid basis of reality which Arnim possessed, was his friend and brother-in-law Clemens Brentano, whose prose writings must be classed, as might be expected, almost entirely under the heading of fairy tales. Since these however lie outside the scope of this work, we are left with one Novelle, *Vom braven Kasperl und vom schönen Annerl* (1817), which still enjoys a considerable popularity and has points of interest for the literary historian beyond its intrinsic charm. It is essentially a work of Stimmung, the incidents recorded being subdued to the mood, half other-worldliness, half

poignant grief of the old woman, who relates the story
of the misfortunes of her grandson and goddaughter to
the poet in the night watches which precede the execution of the unhappy Annerl. The state of mind of the old
woman, the sense of the urgent need for action on the
part of the poet, felt as a presentiment long before it is
clearly pronounced, is conveyed in masterly fashion and
disturbed only once by a divagation on the professional
writer's vocation. (Similar divagations, more definitely
satirical in character, frequently interrupt the narrative in
the fairy tales.) Significantly enough for the part editor of
Des Knaben Wunderhorn and the enthusiastic collector and
imitator of folk songs, the story itself is based upon folk-
song subject matter; and the incident of the executioner's
axe which stirs in its case in the presence of a person
destined to be beheaded, though its inclusion is questionable on aesthetic grounds, belongs also to the world of
folk-lore and folk superstition. But it serves to heighten
the sense of impending and inavertible fate which hangs
over the story. Regarded from the point of subject
matter only, without reference to the poetic impression,
which is due to the treatment rather than to the facts
recorded, Brentano's story may be considered as an early
example of the Dorfgeschichte, the emergence of which
as a definite genre will be discussed later.[6]

The most lyrical of all the Romantic Novellen writers
is Joseph, Freiherr von Eichendorff, whose graceful
stories are so akin to his nature lyrics that they seem to
be a mere recasting of poems in prose form. With him
the incident is almost entirely dissolved in Stimmung and
seems to be no more than a symbolical solidification of
the varying moods of nature, as perceived by a poet ex-

quisitely sensitive to every aspect of romantic landscape. Moonlight and the magic of the forest brood upon the action of the stories and call into being strange figures of unearthly and enthralling beauty who are perilous in their attraction: old figures of pagan deities who exert their nocturnal fascination and fade away at daybreak. The folk legend of Tannhäuser and Venus with various modifications forms the basis of the action in *Die Zauberei im Herbste*, a preliminary sketch as it were to the more successful *Das Marmorbild* (written in 1817 but not published until 1826), and, with an exotic and tropical setting, in *Eine Meerfahrt*, a late work, which never received its final polish, and has only lately been published. In *Die Glücksritter* (1841) and *Schloss Durande* (1837) Eichendorff attempts a more solid background of historical circumstance, the Thirty Years' War in the former and the French Revolution in the latter. Both of them are tragic in their endings, but like the other Novellen they live in the memory not by their incident but by the atmosphere which envelops the action. *Das Marmorbild* has some claim to be regarded as the masterpiece of Eichendorff's narrative works were it not for the perennial charm and freshness of his best-known work, *Aus dem Leben eines Taugenichts* (1826). Though it would be pedantic to deny to this work the title of a Novelle, it is in effect as far as its form is concerned rather a novel of adventure writ small—the harshness and violence of incident of such works being toned down to harmless adventures in which only the very naïve hero could possibly see any danger to himself. The whole story is presented with a lightness of touch, an exquisite sense of the ever-changing aspects of landscape, a gaiety and a delicate irony which saves it from becoming at any point unduly sentimental.

Eichendorff is, with Tieck and Hoffmann, the most original and individual of the Romantic writers of Novellen. He excels in the presentation of lyrical moods. Yet he never achieves the same intensity and sinister effects as those which were at Tieck's command. Though he may conjure up malevolent forces their power is not unassailable, and the heroes of his stories who have withstood their magic return to the serene light of day after the night magic has faded. But, apart from these darker aspects of nature mysticism, his presentation of the various moods of nature is more subtly perceived, more exquisitely rendered than anything Tieck can achieve. He has not Hoffmann's power of drawing characters, above all eccentric and grotesque figures, nor the same quality of ironic criticism. None of the characters who pass through the action of his stories is sharply realized and presented as an individual. None, with the possible exception of the Taugenichts, who withholds his name but reveals so much of his feelings, remains in the memory as a recognizable personality. The persons of his stories are themselves lay figures, bearers of lyrical moods; just as his landscapes are lyrical moods and not descriptions. Irony with him has divested itself of its more trenchant qualities and has become no more than a playful touch which corrects at once any tendency to sentimentality.

'Ein Roman nach der lyrischen Seite gebildet' was Schelling's definition of the Novelle, and Friedrich Schlegel had stressed the lyrical quality inherent in the genre as such. With Eichendorff this aspect of the Novelle is exploited to the full. No further development along this line is possible or the characteristic outline of the Novelle must inevitably be lost in the mist of lyricism. The creation of Stimmung, which has already been noted in Tieck and Brentano, becomes with Eichendorff the predominant feature of the Novelle and, by its very predominance, cries a halt to this line of development. Where it reappears in the works of later writers, it is as one element only amongst others, until Theodor Storm in his early works makes it again the prevailing one.

Of the other Romantic writers of Novellen none was of sufficient originality to develop new aspects of the genre; they were content to carry on the traditions already in existence and produced works which were for the most part pale imitations of what had already been done with greater originality, charm or force. An exception may perhaps be made in favour of Friedrich de la Motte Fouqué's *Undine* (1811) in which the fairy-tale motif of the water-sprite who can acquire a soul only by marriage with a mortal is treated with considerable naïve charm. Lacking in Fouqué, however, was the power which Tieck and Eichendorff possessed of interpenetrating nature forces with human feeling. *Aslaugas Ritter* and *Sintram und seine Gefährten* (inspired by an etching of Albrecht Dürer), the best known of his other stories, are based upon Norse mythology, a source of subject matter which Fouqué exploited without any real success.

Wilhelm Hauff, the Swabian poet, wrote a number of competent and readable Novellen, without however attaining to originality or independence, so that the effect which they make is always that of derivative works. Thus *Othello* and *Die Sängerin* are clearly influenced by Hoffmann; as is also his most successful story, a fantasy rather than a Novelle, the *Phantasien im Bremer Ratskeller* (1827). *Das Bild des Kaisers* (1828), describing the political situation in Germany at the time of the Bur- schenschaften and contrasting the various attitudes to the figure and fame of Napoleon, would seem in its attempt to present prevailing attitudes of mind to be influenced by the later Novellen of Tieck. *Jud Süss* (1827) is an historical Novelle which gives a stirring and succinct ac- count of the fate of a political schemer with whom a later and more meretricious work of fiction has acquainted the novel-reading public.

Finally Leopold Schefer may be mentioned whose Novellen began to appear in 1825, a writer who achieved considerable popularity in his time with highly coloured stories whose subject matter is taken largely from Italy and the Orient.

The Romantic Novelle had almost disappeared by 1830. The relation of the Romantics to the genre is a paradoxical one. It was Friedrich Schlegel who drew their attention to this definitely Romance genre which by the simplicity and severity of its form is particularly unsuited to the Germanic formlessness of northern Romantic art. Yet cultivated by Romantic writers and modified by them to such an extent as to be almost a new genre it becomes the most popular and successful form of nar- rative literature of that age. But already in the 1820's, before its Romantic resources had been exhausted, it was being subjected to new modifications and exploited with entirely different aims.

Chapter V

THE DISCURSIVE NOVELLE—TIECK, THE WRITERS OF JUNG DEUTSCHLAND

The Romantic writers beginning with Tieck had considerably enlarged the scope of the Novelle both in regard to its subject matter and its content. If the Novelle in its original form would seem to be essentially a literary development of the anecdote, it reveals also in its insistence upon the extraordinary and unusual element a kinship with the fairy tale, and Paul Ernst has described it as 'a sister of the fairy tale'. It was this aspect of it, with the possibilities therein contained, which was seized upon by the Romantics. In the works of Tieck and Hoffmann the 'marvellous' spreading from the critical point of the story comes to be the characteristic of the whole story, and the Novelle so completely changes its character that far from being an account of everyday events which are just distinguished from the everyday, by an unexpected twist given to them, it is, with the Romantics, an account of events, of which the most striking characteristic is that they do not belong to the ordinary world. Even though Hoffmann builds up his fantastic world upon the world of reality, the effect of his method is to make the reader feel that the fantastic world is the real one, but obscured by the world of everyday, through the mere appearance of which only such happily constituted people as Anselmus in *Der goldne Topf* are able to penetrate in order to attain to reality.

Friedrich Schlegel mentions the potentialities of the Novelle for the indirect presentation of subjective moods and points of view, and this aspect of it is likewise exploited by the Romantics with a greater freedom and directness than Schlegel originally intended. It would no doubt be possible to construct a character of Boccaccio from a consideration of the Novellen in the *Decamerone*, which would certainly reveal him as a Lebensbejaher, an enemy of all hypocrisy and false affectation; a kindly ironist, and above all a believer in the healthy gratification of the senses. But the Novellen of Kleist and Hoffmann reveal the characters of their authors with much greater intensity: and what must be carefully put together from the prevailing objective nature of Boccaccio's Novellen obtrudes itself in the prevailing subjective nature of the Novellen of the Romantic writers. Metaphysical, psychological, ethical elements which, though potentially present in the classical Novellen, are subdued, assume the most important place in the Novellen of the Romantics.

The Novelle is a Romance form; it becomes naturalized in Germany with the Romantics: that is to say, it assumes specifically German characteristics which distinguish it from its Romance prototype. And this naturalization takes place, broadly speaking, when the interest is transferred from the events related to the inner significance of those events, whether that significance be found either in metaphysical, ethical, psychological ideas or even in the conveyance of a mood, a Stimmung. Goethe's 'Novelle' developed the idea of the Romance Novelle as far as possible, and stands on the border-line between Classical and Romantic: the ethical significance is the real content of the Novelle but it is subdued to the narration of external events, which still ostensibly form the *raison d'être* of the story. In Tieck's *Der blonde Eckbert*, written thirty years before, the transition has already been effected and the specifically German characteristic of the Novelle established: the events narrated are so arbitrary in their connection one with another that baldly presented—as the writers of classical Novellen present them—they would fail to convince, perhaps even to interest. It is the dark current of sinister nature mysticism on which the incidents are carried which impresses, rather than the incidents themselves, and makes of *Der blonde Eckbert* a Stimmungsnovelle, just as Eichendorff's *Aus dem Leben eines Taugenichts* is a Stimmungsnovelle—the difference in the emotional effect of the two Novellen representing the difference in the attitude of the two poets to the world of nature.

It may be noted in passing that a similar change to that which the Novelle undergoes in becoming naturalized German, occurs with other literary forms which are adopted by German poets from Romance languages. Thus the adventures and marvels of chivalry in Chrétien de Troyes are merely adventures and marvels; in the German courtly epics the same incidents are all fraught with inner significance.

It can be said then that the Romantic writers established the Novelle as a German genre. To deplore the fact that, in so doing, they destroyed the classic severity of form and clearness of outline, is simply to deplore the existence of the German Novelle as such. Here clearly the gain is greater than the loss. Kleist shows its capacity for dealing with metaphysical problems, and establishes in *Michael Kohlhaas* the type of the Character Novelle; Tieck de-

velops further its irrational elements and makes it the
channel for the conveyance of Stimmung; Hoffmann
draws the whole realm of the supernatural into its circle;
Arnim and Brentano make it the expression of the free
play of fancy; Eichendorff all but dissolves it in lyricism.
All of them heighten its subjective character. A much
greater freedom of subject matter is claimed, and the
anchoring of the events in a contemporary and everyday
world is not necessarily carried out. In most of the
Romantic writers the distinctions between Novelle and
fairy tale are disregarded. All these new elements, though
for the time being they led to a great confusion and in-
definiteness in the form of the Novelle, considerably
widened its scope and deepened its potential significance,
and later writers of Novellen were able to profit by the
gains which the genre had made during this period. But
by the end of the 1820's the Romantic Novelle had come
to an end, except in the works of unimportant imitators
of Hoffmann and Eichendorff and some isolated works of
Eichendorff himself.

This modification in the form of the Novelle made by
the Romantics is due at least to some extent to the influence of another writer, Miguel de Cervantes, an influence which extends beyond the works of such writers
as Hoffmann to the later Novellen of Tieck. For the
early Romantics, with their ideas of poetry as a universal
expression of the life of man to which every nation contributed its characteristic qualities, Cervantes came to be
the representative writer of the novel, in much the same
way as Shakespeare became for them the supreme dramatic poet of modern times. When it is further considered
that Friedrich Schlegel established the novel as the speci-

fically Romantic literary form, it will be evident that he could not fail to assign very great importance to Cervantes as the author of *Don Quixote*. Further, in his distinction between ancient and modern poetry, he specifies the quality of self-consciousness as the character of modern poetry in opposition to the work of ancient art which came into being as an organic growth. Thus he sees in Cervantes above all the conscious artist, and finds in his writings that irony which was for him one of the most valuable qualities in modern art. With Dante, Shakespeare and Goethe, Cervantes becomes for him the characteristic modern writer; and it is in contact with *Don Quixote* as well as with Goethe's *Wilhelm Meister* that he develops his theories not only of the novel but also of Romantic poetry generally. In Cervantes' preface to *Don Quixote* indeed many of the Romantic ideas are anticipated. The influence of *Don Quixote*, translated by Tieck, upon the Romantic novel is a question which lies outside the scope of this book, but it may be mentioned here that Friedrich Schlegel's conception of that work—a highly individual and one-sided one—affected the novel-writing of the Romantics to a very considerable extent.

More important for the development of the Novelle in German literature was the interest aroused by the *Novelas Ejemplares* of Cervantes. Already in his *Nachrichten von den poetischen Werken des Johannes Boccaccio* Friedrich Schlegel had mentioned them as being of an excellence equal to those of Boccaccio: and though he stresses the subjective tendency of Boccaccio's works as a whole it is in respect of Cervantes' Novelas that he enunciates his theory that the Novelle is especially suited to present a subjective mood and point of view indirectly and as it were symbolically. He proceeds:

> Why are some amongst the Novelas of Cervantes definitely so much more beautiful than others, though all of them are beautiful? By what other magic do they stir our innermost being and take possession of it with divine beauty than by this, that everywhere the feeling of the writer, the very innermost depth of his most individual peculiarity gleams through them visibly-invisibly, or because, as in the 'Curioso impertinente', he gives expression in them to opinions which by reason of their very peculiarity and depth could not be expressed or only in such a form?[1]

It is not without significance that whereas a subjective tendency is postulated by Schlegel for Boccaccio's works as a whole and his Novelle are somewhat arbitrarily envisaged from this standpoint in order to support the general argument, it is the Novelas of Cervantes which are then put forward as confirmation of the theory that the Novelle presents a subjective mood indirectly and symbolically.

This aspect of the Novelle in German literature is so frequently stressed and influences the development of the inner form so greatly that it may well be argued that the German Novelle owes more of its specific quality to Cervantes, as the originator of the subjective Novelle, presenting 'visibly-invisibly' the points of view, and attitude to life of its author, than to the less recognizably subjective Novellen of Boccaccio.

The *Novelas Ejemplares* of Cervantes were first published in 1613 and consist of twelve stories of varying length and very diverse character. In his Prologo to the first edition Cervantes definitely states:[2]

I have bestowed on them the name of 'Exemplary', and if thou dost look well to it, there is not one of them from which thou couldst not derive a profitable example.... One thing I shall adventure me to say: that if by any chance it come to pass that the reading of these Novelas could tempt anyone, who should peruse them, to any evil desire or thought, rather should I cut off the hand wherewith I wrote them, than bring them out in public.[3]

The form of the Novelas varies considerably; but with the exception of *La Señora Cornelia*[4] there is not one of them which bears any resemblance to the novelle of Boccaccio or of any of the Italian Novellisti. *Rinconete y Cortadillo* is a genre picture of the life of thieves in Seville; *El Celoso Extremeño* is a study in the psychology of a jealous husband; *El Licenciado Vidriera*, which Friedrich Schlegel cites as the most beautiful and witty of the stories which are essentially jokes and witty retorts, differs from the similar stories of Boccaccio, in that it contains a whole collection of witty retorts, whereas Boccaccio's stories in this kind always lead up to one point. This particular Novela falls into two halves, the first of which, the account of the travels of the hero, is quite separate from the second, in which his replies to impertinent questioners are recorded. So little of the formal quality of the Italian novella does it possess, that Icaza can say of it: 'For me... *El Licenciado Vidriera* is nothing but a pretext for Cervantes to publish his apophthegms'.[5] *El Coloquio de los Perros*—according to Icaza, with *Don Quixote* the most original, interesting and perfect work of imagination of that time[6]—is richer and more varied in subject matter than any other of the Novelas, containing genre pictures of the life of butchers, shepherds, the constabulary, sketches of the poet's and the actor's profession, reflections upon humility and evil speaking, together with a macabre episode in which the principal character is a witch. And this very wealth and variety of its subject matter separates it formally from the classical Novelle of Boccaccio. As in *El Licenciado Vidriera* the treatment of the story is ironical in the highest degree.

If a general characteristic of the Novelas of Cervantes be sought which distinguishes them from the formally more severe novelle of the Italian writers, it may be described as the unfettered play of the imagination and the universality of interest in all forms of life which Cervantes reveals in his choice of subject matter. These particular aspects of Cervantes' Novelas together with the ironic treatment of his themes might be expected to appeal to the Romantics, for whom the sole law to which the imagination was subject was the law of its own absolute liberty. Yet though the influence of *Don Quixote* was considerable upon the novel-writing of the Romantics, the Novelas do not appear to have affected the form of the Novelle to the same extent—though one or two exceptions must be made.

Tieck became acquainted with the works of Cervantes already in his school days; but though references, more specifically to *Don Quixote*, can be found in his early works generally, his early Novellen show no signs of the influence of the *Novelas Ejemplares*. After carefully sifting the evidence with regard to Kleist, Bertrand in his *Cervantes et le Romantisme Allemand* comes to the conclusion that what resemblances there are between the two writers are due not to an artificial imitation but to a profound kinship of temperament.[7] It is true that a similar theme,

that of the woman who is ravished during a state of un-
consciousness, is treated in *Die Marquise von O.* and in
Cervantes' *La Fuerza del Sangre*, but the similarity exists
only in the subject. Hoffmann's tale, *Das Gelübde*, has
the same central incident. In Eichendorff's prose fiction
the influence of Cervantes is apparent only in the novel
Ahnung und Gegenwart,[8] and possibly in the Novelle *Die
Glücksritter*.

Hoffmann is the only one of the major Romantic
writers who reveals quite openly the influence of the
Novelas Ejemplares, in support of which statement it suf-
fices to cite the Novelle in the *Phantasiestücke, Nachricht
von den neuesten Schicksalen des Hundes Berganza*. In this
work Hoffmann continues an account of the adventures
which the dog Berganza had related to his companion in
Cervantes' *Coloquio de los Perros*. In spite of the ampli-
fication of the witch episode in the Spanish original, the
new adventures of Berganza differ in substance and significance from those related by Cervantes, and Hoffmann's
tale resolves itself into a piece of ill-disguised autobiography. Nevertheless Hoffmann, like Cervantes, makes
the dog pass through various phases of human life, which
he judges and describes satirically; and in the course of
his adventures the new Berganza, like the old, makes all
sorts of moral observations, which he sets forth in long
digressions.[9]

It is precisely this last element in Cervantes as in
Hoffmann, which is taken up and elaborated excessively
by Tieck in his later Novellen; and though there can be
no doubt that the greater freedom in the use of the form,
the unfettered play of fancy, the masterly use of irony, all
of which are characteristics of Cervantes, contributed to

the development of the Romantic Novelle, it is the discursive, digressive element in Cervantes consisting in the description of certain states of society, in reflections upon abstract themes or special aspects of life and in moral observations and satirical comment, which determines very largely the form—or lack of form—of the later Novellen of Tieck.

In the 'twenties of the nineteenth century Tieck entered upon the second period of his literary career, a period lasting for some twenty years, during which time his principal poetical output was in the form of prose fiction, which he himself described as Novellen. He was for the first part of that time living in Dresden, the centre of a literary circle there, and a literary personage of considerable importance. He had definitely outgrown his Romantic predilections and found himself to a certain extent in conflict with a circle of literary people in Dresden —the so-called 'Pseudo-Romantiker', who represent a continuation of Romanticism in a debased form. Half-way between these epigones of an exhausted Romanticism and the younger writers of the Jung Deutschland movement, with their demand for a literature placed in the service of political and social tendencies, stands the Tieck of these years, belonging to neither school.

The Novellen which Tieck wrote at this period of his life are not easily accessible. The last complete edition of them was published in 1853, and of the thirty-nine which make up the twelve volumes, only three or four have since been reprinted among the selected works, from which it may be reasonably argued that they have no very great or living poetical interest. Further, in the history of the German Novelle they do not represent a fruitful line of development. They stand alone—the greater number of them—the monument of a mistaken conception of what the genre can achieve, and for this reason they had no successors except in some minor works of the Jung Deutschland writers, which like the Novellen of Tieck himself have fallen into oblivion.

In the introduction to the eleventh volume of his collected works published in 1829 Tieck had given a definition of the Novelle stressing the necessity of a Wendepunkt in its construction; and in his further remarks on the same subject he assigns to the genre other characteristics, which are obviously put forward in support of his own methods at the time. Referring to the Novelas of Cervantes, to which his own later stories are definitely more akin than to the *novelle* of Boccaccio, he writes: 'But all ranks of society, all circumstances of modern times, their conditions and peculiarities are certainly to the clear-seeing poetical eye not less suited for poetry and a noble presentation than his own time and surroundings were to Cervantes'. Later in the same introduction: 'It will also occur that attitudes of mind, disposition and opinion develop themselves in the contrast, the conflict between the persons involved in the action, and thereby become converted into action themselves'. Later he speaks of the opportunity which the form of the Novelle offers for argument, judgment and variety of opinions.[10] The gist of these demands on behalf of the Novelle is that it may deal with contemporary events and conditions, and that it is capable of treating controversial ideas and of presenting them in the form of discussion. Thus the stress is again shifted from the event as such, to the ideas, for the presentation of which the event itself and almost inevitably the characters are merely the occasion and have no real, living justification. Tieck introduces then what is known as the Reflexionsnovelle, which contains all the germs of Tendenzdichtung. In this type of Novelle the source of inspiration is not the event which is the basic core of the Novelle in its purest form, but the discussion of some abstract idea, or more frequently some topical question of the day, some literary or social tendency. The characters and incidents are then constructed to illustrate the ideas, usually to demonstrate the ill-effects of the tendency which is being attacked. Thus in the Novelle *Die Gemälde* (1821) he attacks the false cult of art; in *Die Vogelscheuche* (1835) the intrigues and ineptitudes and exaggerated self-importance of the Pseudo-Romantics; in *Der Mondsüchtige* (1831) he breaks a lance on behalf of the aged Goethe, who is the subject of attack by such writers as Pustkuchen and Menzel; in *Eigensinn und Laune* (1835) he gives a realistic picture of female degeneration, which is represented as the result of the emancipated ideas with regard to the status of women which the Jung Deutschland writers were making popular. As may be expected the characters are more or less schematic representatives of ideas: 'Programmfiguren', says one writer, of 'Deutschtümelei, religiöse Schwärmerei, Konvertitenwesen, Weltschmerz, Nazarenertum, Teegeselligkeit Berlins'.[11]

As far as the external form is concerned it tends to be extremely diffuse—some of these so-called Novellen run to three and four hundred pages—and this is no doubt an inevitable result of the subject matter. In a great many of them the element of actual discussion and debate is so predominant that practically the whole Novelle is in the form of conversational dialogue. The epic form is broken through, and instead of either narrative or description—which are the two legitimate functions of the epic writer—Tieck gives dialectics, a characteristic perhaps of dramatic literature but not of epic. So important a part indeed does the dialogue play in these Novellen that Kimmerich divides them into two groups: 'Erzählungen mit eingelegtem Dialog; und Dialoge mit eingelegten Erzählungen'.

These Novellen have lost their interest for later generations to such an extent that they have never been reprinted since the collected edition of 1853; they were, however, at the time the most popular form of prose literature, though some contemporary writers—for instance, Grillparzer and Hebbel—deplored them as being incompatible with the formal requirements of literature. The reasons for their contemporary popularity and their present neglect are the same. Tieck was at that time the literary authority of Germany, the greatest name after Goethe: he has ceased to be of any living importance today, and even his purely Romantic works are seen to be inferior to those of Novalis for instance. Moreover his subject matter concerned itself with contemporary problems, which stood in the centre of public interest in his day, but have now long been superseded and were of so specialized and time-conditioned a nature that the Novellen can no longer be understood without a knowledge of the cultural conditions of the age in which they were written. Further, the treatment of these problems in a rather *dégagé* conversational tone—without any attempt at stylization—has deprived them of that permanence which formal beauty and distinction can lend to subject matter which is in itself second-rate. By an easy careless tone of narration and conversation Tieck gained immediate popularity at the cost of future and enduring respect. However, though the purely human content of these Novellen is too slight and the style too little *soigné* to have secured for them an enduring place in German literature, their importance from the point of view of the history of German culture must not be overlooked. They give us a valuable picture of the cultural conditions and interests of educated society in the larger towns.

The following brief survey of these Novellen arranged in groups is based upon the arrangement made by Jakob Minor.[12]

(1) *Zeitnovellen*—that is, pictures of contemporary life, generally ironical or satirical in tone—attacking morbid tendencies of Romanticism (excessive religiosity, the cult of the marvellous, a mystical attitude to art) which were prevalent at that time. These Novellen belong mainly to the period 1820–30 and include such stories as *Die Gemälde* (1821), *Musikalische Leiden und Freuden* (1823), *Der Geheimnisvolle* (1823).

(2) *Künstlernovellen*—composed between 1825 and 1835—written not merely to present the character of the artist, usually the poet, but also with a certain didactic tendency. The best known of these—one which is reprinted in most of the Selected Editions—is *Ein Dichterleben* (Part I, 1825; Part II, 1829), which deals with the figures of Shakespeare, Nash, Kyd, and describes the death of Marlowe. Some of the speeches placed in the mouth of Shakespeare are a repudiation of Romantic theories. Other Novellen of this kind are *Das Fest zu Kenilworth* (1824), and *Der Tod des Dichters* (1833)—the

last-named dealing with the death of the Portuguese poet, Camoëns.

(3) *Historische Novellen*. To this group belong some of the best achievements of Tieck's later years, namely, *Der Aufruhr in den Cevennen* (1826), an account of a religious rising in the early years of the seventeenth century, in which the underlying theme for discussion is religious bigotry, *Der wiederkehrende griechische Kaiser* (1830), *Hexensabbath* (1831).

(4) *Tendenznovellen*, attacking 'das junge Deutschland'—written during the 'thirties; including *Der Mondsüchtige* (1831), *Der Wassermensch* (1834) and *Eigensinn und Laune* (1835). Tieck's position is now reversed. Whereas in the 1820's he had been attacking Romanticism and so appeared as a potential ally to the Jung Deutschland movement, he is not prepared to go the whole way with them in the acceptance of their principles, whether social or literary. They, on the other hand, find a lack of seriousness in his easy talkative style, and require that literature shall be placed in the service of political agitation. In his rejection of this point of view and his attacks upon the Jung Deutschland tendencies in his later Novellen he is frequently driven back upon Romantic subject matter.

(5) *Spuk- und Zaubernovellen*. These include *Pietro von Albano* (1825), *Das Zauberschloss* (1829) and *Die Wundersüchtigen* (1831), in which, however, the apparently supernatural elements are rationally explained.

(6) *Spitzbubengeschichten*. Stories dealing with the adventures of thieves and rogues. Amongst these *Der Jahrmarkt* is clearly influenced by Cervantes' Novela, *Rinconete y Cortadillo*.

Two other Novellen, *Der junge Tischlermeister* (begun 1819 but not published until 1836) and *Des Lebens Über-fluss* (1838), do not fall into any of the above groups. *Der junge Tischlermeister*, the longest of the Novellen, is largely concerned with the social conditions of the time, gives an elaborate description of the trade of a carpenter and discusses at length the question of guilds and corporations. *Des Lebens Überfluss*, the most readable of all these later Novellen, is an illustration of the idea that most of the things which are regarded as the necessities of life can under the force of circumstances be dispensed with as luxuries. Mention must also be made of *Die wilde Engländerin*—a Novelle within a Novelle, since it is related by one of the characters in *Das Zauberschloss*. In this succinctly presented psychological Novelle, Tieck exhibits an unusual skill in construction and gives a striking example of the Wendepunkt, which he had himself postulated as the essential element in the Novelle.

In a general estimate of Tieck's later Novellen it can be said that only those works have taken a permanent place in the development of the genre which are, on the whole, free from Tendenz: the Künstler and historical Novellen, and both types have their origin in the works of earlier writers (Kleist and Hoffmann). In the historical Novellen Tieck definitely contributed something to the development of a special form, which reaches its summit in the works of Conrad Ferdinand Meyer. The Novellen, however, which are essentially presentations of prevailing social and literary conditions with satirical intention— the Tendenznovellen—have long since ceased to be of interest, as they are in essence alien to the form of the Novelle. It may indeed be maintained with some justi-

fication that Tieck's literary and poetical gifts were
peculiarly unsuited to the Novelle as a genre. Tieck was
a facile writer, and, as with most facile writers, he possessed a mind of no great profundity. What he has to say,
he says with great ease, with a specious poeticalness and
unfailing loquacity. Further, he was by nature as well as
under the influence of Romantic theories regardless of
the purity of form. All these things are characteristic of
his early works—*Franz Sternbalds Wanderungen, Kaiser
Oktavian, Genoveva, Prinz Zerbino*—works which are
wearisome by reason of their length, the shallowness of
their poetical quality, and the continual oscillation between epic, dramatic and lyric form[13]: they are the antithesis of those qualities which are demanded of the writer
who practises the severe artistry of the Novelle. Again,
though a certain amount of reflection may be conceded as
a permissible element in the Novelle, it is only tolerable
when it is the reflection of a mind of originality or profundity such as Cervantes. Tieck had considerable critical
ability and his *aperçus* on art and poetry and the art of life
are often marked by real acumen and artistic perception,
but his reflections upon questions other than aesthetic
ones are not the outcome of a deeply philosophic mind.
The result is that the action of his Novellen is overlaid
and suffocated with reflections of negligible importance.
Nor is the action itself, when unearthed, of such interest
as to hold the attention of the reader.

Tieck brought the Novelle back from the exoticism of
the later Romantic writers into the circle of contemporary
subject matter. He set it to deal with the world of actu-
ality, with social, literary and political conditions but in
a form which was unsuited to its specific nature, and his

treatment of the genre had no real or lasting influence upon its development, except in so far as it revealed to the Jung Deutschland writers the possibility of using the Novelle form for their own tendencious purposes.

In spite of certain misgivings on the part of Heinrich Laube as to the artistic propriety of the later Novellen of Tieck and the suitability of discussional elements for the form of the Novelle as such,[14] the writers of the Jung Deutschland movement as a whole derived their theory of the Novelle from Tieck, regarding him as the originator of a new type: the Tendenznovelle. Laube still makes the distinction between the Novelle which is a short succinct narrative, and the Novelle with a definitely tendencious aim; the latter he regards as an extraordinarily important discovery of a modern form.[15] But it is with Theodor Mundt that this new conception of the Novelle finds its most uncompromising expression; and the following passage from his *Moderne Lebenswirren* (1840) will indicate clearly enough the rôle which the Novelle is to play in modern literature: the Novelle being, according to Mundt, particularly adapted to carry political propaganda unobtrusively and convey it without arousing the notice of the censorship. He asks:

Which literary form is most in keeping with the trend of the times? It is the Novelle...the Germans must be caught by means of the Novelle. The Novelle makes its nest in rooms and amongst families, sits at table with the family and overhears the evening conversation, and then is the opportunity to insinuate something under the night cap of paterfamilias, or whisper to the son whilst he is comfortably smoking his pipe, a train of ideas which may possibly in time

affect the future of the whole nation. The Novelle is a mag-
nificent harvest field for political allegory.

He then suggests that he will write historical, comic, i.e.
satirical Novellen whose subject matter is taken from
contemporary conditions. 'They shall fly out over the
present age like bees, each one equipped with a sting.'[16]

This conception of the Novelle is repeated by Mundt
in his *Geschichte du.· Literatur der Gegenwart* (1842):
where the element of reflection directed upon some contemporary tendency is postulated as essential to the
genre, *apropos* of which however he points out that this
particular element is hostile to the plasticity of its form.[17]
Side by side with this entirely arbitrary and tendencious
view of the genre as possessing an extra-aesthetic aim
goes the doubt as to its artistic validity. Thus Gutzkow
writes in 1834 that it is artistically not fully valid as a
genre, and that it is only its connection with public
affairs and its satirical possibilities which recommend it
to a certain extent to ambitious young writers.[18]

Actually during the 1830's the Novelle—largely under
the stimulus of Tieck's later works—was the favourite
form of prose fiction. Periodicals and newspapers were
full of so-called Novellen and countless collections of old
and new ones appeared. That these works were almost
entirely undeserving of the title Novelle, in so far as it
designates a severely artistic form, goes without saying
in view of the prevalent idea that the genre was a particularly suitable vehicle for conveying tendencious ideas.
And in effect there are no works of first-rate artistic
merit to be recorded. What is true of the Novelle is valid
also for other literary genres. For the writers of Jung
Deutschland literature was primarily a means of spread-

ing revolutionary ideas. Thus Gutzkow in an article 'der deutsche Roman' states frankly the function of literature as conceived by the generation of writers, who were in revolt against the conventions and restrictions of that period of political, social and religious reaction: 'die Literatur müsse der Revolution der Sitten immer vorausgehen'. The novel is the dark lantern of the smuggling of ideas.[19]

The Jung Deutschland movement was characterized by the two qualities of revolutionary ferment and pessimistic misgiving. It was a period of transition similar to that of the Sturm und Drang. And just as the Sturm und Drang movement in revolt against the rationalism of the Aufklärung prepared the way for the more solid ideals of German idealism, the Jung Deutschland movement, shaking itself free from the idealism of Classicism and Romanticism alike, was the forerunner of the Poetic Realism of the middle of the century. But that very element of misgiving, together with all its revolutionary fervour, distinguishes it from the more virile revolutionary movement of the preceding century. Out of its feeling of impotence in the face of the political and social forces arrayed against it grows the Weltschmerz which characterizes so many of the writers of that period. It becomes conscious of itself as a generation torn between conflicting forces and tends to coquet with its own inadequacy and ironize its sufferings. It is the age which established the popularity of Byron in Germany. The catchword 'die Zerrissenen' is coined to describe those who are over-sensitive to the spiritual and intellectual problems of the time. Literature and journalism were the weapons which it found to hand to carry on its war against obscurantist ideas in politics, religion and morality. But in view of the rigid nature of press and book censorship then exercised by the various governments in Germany and Austria, the war itself could be carried on only by subterfuge. Every writer of the Jung Deutschland movement suffered under the censorship ban.

The decree of the Bundestag in 1835, prohibiting the publication of books by all the writers designated under the title of Jung Deutschland, marks a definite period in the production of these literary revolutionaries. Though up to that date none of them had doubted that the only important element in literature was the transmission of tendencious ideas, regardless of literary form, after 1835 a greater importance is attached to the form itself, a change of attitude which is particularly noticeable in Laube. At the same time, even in the later period of their writings, formal excellence was rather a recognized desideratum than a real achievement. For the severe artistry of the Novelle none of them possessed the necessary poetic equipment, and their conception of the genre was from the beginning falsified by the belief that it was one which having no precise form could be utilized for every ulterior purpose.

The characteristic of the Novellen of the Jung Deutschland writers, more especially in the earlier period of their literary activity, is, together with the extra-aesthetic motive of 'idea smuggling', the tendency to present, instead of a clearly outlined incident, a picture of certain cultural conditions, of representative groups of individuals, of 'attitudes of mind, disposition and opinion', as Tieck writes, seen always from the point of view of the Jung Deutschland reformer. Thus Gustav Kühne in his *Wartburgfeier* (1831) gives a description of the state of public feeling after the wars of Liberation; Theodor Mundt in his *Madelon oder die Romantiker in Paris* (1832) draws a picture of the young generation of French poets; E. A. Willkomm (the author of a novel *Die Europamüden* (1838)) writes a so-called Novelle in two volumes, *Julius Kühn* (1833) describing the life of a typical Jung Deutschland literary man; Ungern-Sternberg, a writer of no great intrinsic importance, presents in his Novelle *Die Zerrissenen* (1832) a picture of the generation of that period, which felt itself inwardly torn in the conflict of ideas. As late as 1853, even, Gutzkow describes in *Die Nihilisten* a type of intellectuals which the Jung Deutschland movement had brought to the fore, who brandished in the face of philistine opinion their freedom from the recognized conventions of society. It must be conceded, however, that by this time Gutzkow's attitude to the characters of his story is more critical than admiring. In his *Quarantäne im Irrenhause* (1835) Kühne makes use of the fiction of a young man being mistakenly detained in a lunatic asylum to give a picture of the world in which the so-called sane are represented as mad, the mad as sane. All these works as well as other Novellen by Kühne—*Die beiden Magdalene* (1833), *Klosternovellen* (1838)—and by Mundt are mainly concerned to ventilate problems of the age, consigning the actual 'novellistic' element of incident and character to a position of minor importance.

Amongst the writers of superior, though not of first-class merit, who were associated with the movement, Heinrich Laube and Karl Gutzkow contributed Novellen of more permanent value than those already mentioned, though it is to be remarked that their better achievements belong to a period in which the Jung Deutschland ferment had subsided. As has already been suggested the year 1835 marks the close of the more militant aspect of the Jung Deutschland literary activities. With Laube the change of attitude is almost immediately apparent in a more resigned state of mind as well as in the greater attention which he devotes to considerations of form. The period in which he was most productive as a writer of Novellen lies between 1832 and 1842; after this he turns to the drama and takes up the Novelle again only in the 'eighties. Gutzkow's Novellen, apart from his early works at the beginning of the 'thirties, culminating in *Der Sadduzäer von Amsterdam* (1834), belong mainly to the 'fifties, especially to the period in which he was editing the magazine *Unterhaltungen am häuslichen Herd* (1852–61). Like Laube he was deflected for a time towards the drama, which became his principal form of literary expression during the 'forties.

Laube's *Reisenovellen* appeared in six volumes between 1834 and 1837. In their contents as in their title they betray the influence of Heine, and would have been more suitably entitled 'Reisebilder' or 'Reiseabenteuer', for they have little or no connection with the genre Novelle. The Reisebild was a bastard genre invented by Heine. Its ill-defined form was especially suited for the purposes for which Heine required it, namely as a receptacle for such disparate elements as political or literary satire, travel description, personal experiences largely of an erotic nature, and reflections and observations of a general kind. Laube's aim was to narrate stories which, in their subject matter, were specifically characteristic of the various districts through which he travelled and illustrated the manners and customs, the landscape, the type of inhabitants of each individual place. In effect the *Reisenovellen* consist to a very large extent of travel description, accounts of other travellers, and of Laube's own real or imagined amorous adventures. Though the author himself, in editing these early works for inclusion in a complete edition, attempts to stress the Novelle element in them in order to underline his independence of Heine's *Reisebilder*, any strict chronicler of the genre must reject them as lying outside the province of the Novelle both in subject matter and literary form. Only occasionally does Laube separate from the mass of description and personal adventure a self-contained narrative which even superficially bears some resemblance to the form of the Novelle, and these narratives—*Die Novelle, Eine Tiroler Geschichte, Gebirgsnovelle, Die Maske, Die Novelle in der Theaterloge*, for instance—are either merely sketches, embryonic Novellen one might call them, or are lacking in that artistry which is an essential of the genre.

Laube's superficiality, his facility in writing and his fundamental vulgarity are most evident in these *Reisenovellen*. His positive assets as a writer are vitality, liveliness of mind, wit, though certainly inferior to that of his model Heine, and a certain highly coloured quality. As has already been suggested he begins about 1835 to develop a feeling for the importance of form, and the dedication of his Novelle *Die Schauspielerin* (1836) (to Varnhagen von Ense) may be regarded as a confession of former guilt in regard to this question and a promise of betterment in future, as also a rejection of the idea that literature is merely a vehicle for the conveying of tendencious ideas. With special reference to the genre Novelle he singles out two qualities which have had a deleterious influence upon contemporary production in the genre: the lack of taste and the violence which has been done to the form by making it the vessel for polemical discussion.[20] Nevertheless, in spite of the praiseworthy intentions with regard to form and the determination to avoid polemical treatment of his subject matter, it cannot be said that the later Novellen of Laube attain to any real distinction. Neither *Liebesbriefe* (1835) nor *Die Schauspielerin* (1836) nor *Das Glück* (1836) rises above the commonplace in subject matter or treatment. None of them reveals that 'sharply marked silhouette' which Heyse requires of the genre. The incidents which form the core of the narrative are without originality, the characters are uninteresting, the style flat, and the continual intrusion of trite reflection is tiresome and unedifying. In all these stories love plays an important part, and the subject is never approached by Laube without a certain tone of vulgar amorousness, and it is perhaps not too much to say that he always betrays himself as fundamentally the philanderer. The best of Laube's stories is *Die Bandomire* (1842), in which, forsaking contemporary life and problems, he gives an historical picture of Courland at the beginning of the eighteenth century. But though the story has a vigour and precision of character-drawing lacking in the others, it exceeds the limits of the Novelle in the diffuseness with which it spreads itself over historical events generally. Laube himself called it 'eine Erzählung'.

Of a more serious temperament than his friend Laube, Karl Gutzkow is equally prolific though less facile as a

writer. For him, as for all the writers of Jung Deutschland, literature was in the first place the vehicle for the
propagation of ideas of social and political reform, and
even when his early reforming zeal had cooled, he continued to occupy himself mainly with the discussion of
contemporary social problems in his novels and dramas.
Much of his narrative work is of a purely ephemeral
nature and his short stories, contributed largely to newspapers and journals, are in the nature of sketches. Rarely
does he attain the distinction of form which justifies the
description of his stories as Novellen. Among his early
writings the only one which calls for comment is *Der
Sadduzäer von Amsterdam* (1834), in which his personal
experiences are presented in the fate of the apostate Jew
Uriel Acosta (afterwards dramatized in the blank verse
tragedy bearing the name of its hero). The sufferings
which his own abjuration of orthodox religion had
brought upon himself, the hostility thereby incurred and
the loss of his fiancée, give to the Novelle a greater intensity of emotional content than his other works possess.
But the Novelle is fundamentally a Tendenz work, attacking intolerance in religious matters.

After 1835 he was mainly concerned with novels and
dramas, but in 1849 a volume of 'Neue Novellen' appeared and from that time onward, more especially during
the years 1852 to 1861 during which he was editing his
journal *Unterhaltungen am häuslichen Herd*, in imitation
of Dickens' *Household Words*, the short story became his
principal and most successful form of literary expression,
the more so as his popularity as a writer of dramas was
steadily declining. Of the Novellen contributed to his
journal *Die Nihilisten* (1853) has already been mentioned

as an instance of the inclination in writers of his school to present groups of characters, typical of prevailing intellectual tendencies, rather than the fate of individuals. *Die Nihilisten* is rather a short novel than a Novelle in the strict sense of the term. In *Der Emporblick* (1852), originally entitled *Ein Mädchen aus dem Volke, Novelle aus dem Volksleben der Grosstadt*, he breaks new ground in drawing his chief character from the city proletariat. The potentialities of the Dorfgeschichte had by this time been fairly well exploited and the genre as such was well established and had, in spite of much adverse criticism, become widely popular.[21] It would seem that its popularity suggested to Gutzkow the possibility of using the life of the poorer classes in the cities as a new source of subject matter in the same way as Gotthelf and others had drawn upon the life of the village. One of the characters in the Novelle, relating the earlier adventures of some of the persons concerned, asks for indulgence for what he calls 'eine städtische Dorfgeschichte', and continues: 'Glücklicherweise haben wir es in unserm Geschmack dahin gebracht, uns für die kleinen Abenteuer von Bauern, Milchmägden, Viehhirten, Rekruten ebenso zu interessieren, wie man sich sonst für Undine und Kühleborn, Schlemihl und seinen Schatten, Goethes Eugenien und Theresen, Natalien und Ottilien interessierte'.[22] He proposes calling his story *Die Weihe der Arbeit*, a title which, as the incidents reveal, is ironical in intention.

Amongst the numerous short stories written at this time and later (*Die Diakonissin* (1855), originally written as a drama; *Aus dem Schwabenland* (1856), a village story; *Der Werwolf* (1871), an historical tale) one calls for special mention, as approaching more nearly than any other work of this kind to the stricter form of the Novelle. This is *Die Kurstauben* (1852), a psychological study of considerable subtlety, in which the peripeteia is the result of a deliberate psychological experiment made by one of the characters upon another. The climax of the story, which approaches very near to bathos, is akin to that of Boccaccio's story of the Falcon. In both Novellen the turning-point is a meal of roast birds, which were not originally intended for human consumption; but whereas in Boccaccio's story the falcon is eaten, in Gutzkow's the carrier pigeons do not appear upon the table. A comparison between the two stories cannot fail to reveal the superiority of the society of fourteenth-century Italy to that of nineteenth-century Germany as Gutzkow knew it.

Neither Gutzkow nor Laube was suited by temperament to be a writer of Novellen. The tendencious element in literature which was for them, at least in their early years, an article of faith prevented them from the start from appreciating justly the formal requirements of any poetical genre, of the Novelle in particular. Where Laube was inclined to be trivial and vulgar, Gutzkow tended to be ponderous, slipshod in his style and lacking in any sort of distinction. Their subject matter had in some instances the specious and ephemeral interest which attaches to the latest topical problem; when that interest was lacking there was no profoundly human one to take its place.

One other writer must be mentioned here, Georg Büchner, in virtue of an unfinished Novelle, *Lenz* (1835 ?). Büchner, though not a member of the Jung Deutschland group, was acquainted with Gutzkow and was a revolutionary of a more uncompromising type than his literary contemporaries. In his dramas, notably *Woyzeck*, he anticipates the ideas and methods of literary movements which came into existence sixty years later. *Lenz* is a psychopathological study of the Sturm und Drang poet, at a time when he was already on the verge of insanity. The Novelle is practically without incident, consisting entirely of a subtle and delicate analysis of Lenz's state of mind, anticipating in its form the psychological Novelle of the end of the century, and in its prose style expressionistic methods.

The Jung Deutschland writers following the lead given by Tieck had brought the Novelle back from the exoticism of the Romantics into touch with reality, to the treatment of subject matter taken from the everyday contemporary world, but by their stressing of 'Zeitprobleme' had set it a task with which it was unable to cope. The Novellen of the middle of the nineteenth century are almost without exception realistic, but with a realism which in its finest expression does not exclude Romantic elements. This realism in the Novelle, however, does not derive so much from Tieck and the Jung Deutschland writers, as from the Dorfgeschichte. It is the amalgamation of Dorfgeschichte with the Romantic deepening of emotional content which produces some of the finest specimens of the Novelle in German literature.

Chapter VI

THE NOVELLE OF COUNTRY LIFE

This chapter is not concerned with any specific modification of or addition to the formal possibilities of the Novelle as a genre, but with the entry of a fresh thematic emphasis into German prose literature. In the 1830's and 1840's life in farming communities in Germany, Switzerland or Austria began to be more widely appreciated as a basis for imaginative literature. It is as if, realizing the inevitability of industrialization, some writers sought to preserve in literary form a rural way of living which would soon be threatened by the advances of technology.

Though the life of the village and of peasants forms the subject matter of certain works of literature in medieval Germany, it is not actually until the eighteenth century that it is treated sympathetically and presented as something having intrinsic interest and not merely as matter for satire. The idylls of Voss and Maler Müller were aiming at a representation of country life which should be true to nature in conscious opposition to the graceful and unreal idylls of Salomon Gessner. Maler Müller, especially in the two idylls in dialogue form, *Die Schafschur* (1775) and *Das Nusskernen* (written earlier but not published until 1811), gives pictures of village life which can hardly, it is true, be called Novellen, but nevertheless contain the germ of the village story in the anecdote which is related and debated by the peasants at their work of sheep-shearing or nut-shelling. In its

simplest form the village story is the Kalendergeschichte
—that is to say, popular stories in the nature of an
anecdote, generally of a moralizing character, which
found a place in the almanacs issued for the use of
peasants. Matthias Claudius in the late eighteenth
century is an example of a literary man who by means of
his almanac, *Der Wandsbeker Bote*, sought to bridge the
gap between intellectual and less educated readers.
Johann Peter Hebel's *Der Rheinländische Hausfreund* in
the early years of the nineteenth century reflected its
editor's gifts for racy, direct writing upon themes that
would appeal to the countryfolk of Baden. These 'literary'
contributions to the annual almanacs formed practically
the only secular reading matter of the peasants. The
subject matter, since the stories were intended for the
consumption of peasants, was devoted to the description
and narration of events drawn from the same social
milieu as that to which the readers belonged; and this
idea that the story is intended not for an educated, but for
an uneducated public is not entirely dropped even when
the story of rural life becomes a recognized literary type
—about the middle of the nineteenth century—with the
result that it tends to retain a moralizing, paedagogic
tone.

Michael Kohlhaas may perhaps be described as an
'unintentional' village story. The source of inspiration
for Kleist was a chronicle of the eighteenth century in
which he found a character of daemonic force of will and
obstinate adherence to an idea. That this man was a
peasant was not a matter of prime importance. What
interested Kleist in him was not, it is safe to assume, his
social standing—whether farmer, middle-class townsman

or noble was immaterial—but his qualities as a personality, pure and simple. Nevertheless the incidents of the story, the injustice to which Kohlhaas is subjected, depend precisely upon his social standing as a peasant-farmer whose rights can be flouted and disregarded by a simple Landjunker who finds protection at court. In so far, therefore, as the events which befall Kohlhaas are conditioned by the fact that he is a peasant-farmer, and as such is subject to a set of circumstances which are characteristic for the peasant life of his day, Kleist's Novelle may be called a tale of country life—an 'unintentional' one, because Kleist was not really concerned to give a picture of the injustice to which a certain class of society was subjected, but to illustrate in the personality of an individual certain ethical and metaphysical ideas. A more genuine example of the village story is furnished by Heinrich Zschokke, whose Novelle *Das Goldmacherdorf* (1817) became very popular in its time and is still so far read that it is frequently reprinted in cheap editions. *Das Goldmacherdorf* has no very great claims to be regarded as a work of art. It is essentially a tract, and its aim, beneath the 'novellistic' form, is to raise the educational and ethical life in the village. Like *Michael Kohlhaas*, it represents only certain aspects of the tale of country life, and cannot claim to be a fully accredited example of the new literary tendency. Nor can Brentano's story, *Vom braven Kasperl und vom schönen Annerl*, which appeared in the same year. Though it is a story of peasant life, its inspiration is a folk-song, and it is in essence a Novelle of atmosphere, belonging definitely to the world of Romanticism, in spite of the fact that its characters are drawn from everyday life, and a certain attempt at realism in the presentation is apparent. Perhaps in view of the Romantic predilections for folk literature, the peasants whose fates it records should be regarded as representatives of the Romantic 'idea' of the people rather than of actual peasant life.

The novel and Novelle of country life first makes its full impact on German literature in the work of Jeremias Gotthelf, the pseudonym which Albert Bitzius assumed in his writings. Gotthelf's monumental work, controversial from the time of its first appearance, has come to represent the definitive expression in the German language of literature which takes its themes from peasant society. His vitality and visionary sweep, his intimate realism, his humour and his burning sense of moral responsibility have a power that has dwarfed any of his contemporaries such as Auerbach and any of his successors in this field, from Anzengruber to Wiechert, when their work is compared to his. His life's work has been compared to a huge granite block that has found its way into the meadows of German writing, to be misunderstood and distorted, or to be admired and loved.[1] Gotthelf had the advantage of being able to approach his peasant material both with the close familiarity of long knowledge and with the ironic detachment of a sophisticated observer. Like his fathers before him, he was by profession a Protestant pastor. As a boy he grew up in a country community where the minister of religion could not but be intimately concerned with the problems of farming people, responsible as he was not only for their spiritual well-being, but for the secular education of their children. He studied theology at the university of Berne and spent a year at this time in Göttingen and North

Germany. His first extensive piece of writing, not published until long after his death, was a *Reisetagebuch*
(1821) which anticipates in some measure the slant of
Heine's satire in *Die Harzreise*. If his later work contains attacks on literature as a profession, it is not
through ignorance of the classics of antiquity nor of the
German classical-romantic movement, but through a
conviction that the direct portrayal of everyday life
around him, interpreted through the vehicle of his own
religious and political ideas, was of more importance and
of greater reality, at least for him and his public. His
political views reflect the course of events; during the
revolution in Berne in 1830 he was a liberal and an
active participant in the movement against the 'Restora-
tion' régime, though by the time of the Sonderbund
War (1847) his particular form of liberalism, having
stood still, found itself in conservative opposition to the
radical cause which the younger Gottfried Keller was
then supporting in Zürich. While being an opponent of
much that the Young German school stood for, he
shared with this movement the conviction that literature
should be linked with social and paedagogic purpose. At
the same time, Gotthelf was no cosmopolitan in his
literary tastes nor in his aspirations to influence. His
first two novels, *Der Bauernspiegel* (1837) and *Leiden und
Freuden eines Schulmeisters* (1838–9), were written with a
first purpose of drawing local attention to social abuses in
Canton Berne—the maltreatment of orphans and the
lack of respect and reward given to the teaching profession. Contemporary with these two novels are two
Novellen, the titles of which indicate clearly enough their
specific moralizing purpose: *Wie fünf Mädchen im Brannt-*

wein jämmerlich umkommen (1838) and *Dursli der Brannteweinsäufer* (1839). Gotthelf did not expect these works to have any impact further than the borders of his own canton, and they are strongly interlaced with Bernese dialect and with references to local politics. The influences that formed these narratives were primarily Swiss too, they included the paedagogic fiction of Zschokke (who had settled in Switzerland from Germany), the autobiographical account by Ulrich Bräker, *Der arme Mann in Toggenburg* (1789) and the educational writings of Pestalozzi. During the years 1839–44 Gotthelf was also editing and writing the *Neuer Berner Kalender*, a traditional almanac which contained peppery political satire and a variety of short stories. Of these latter, *Das arme Kätheli*, with its dream-vision set in the harsh reality of the sufferings of an ill-treated child, anticipates Hauptmann's play *Hanneles Himmelfahrt*. But the impulse that drove Gotthelf to writing was not simply philanthropic, it was an imaginative urge which was an inner fulfilment and a release from the frustration he felt in the vicarage of Lützelflüh. Writing in 1838, he said:

Thus I was hemmed in and kept down on all sides, I could express myself nowhere in free action.... You must realize now that a wild life was moving within me which no one suspected the existence of, and if a few expressions forced their way out of my mouth, they were taken as mere insolent words. This life had either to consume itself or to break forth in some way or other. It did so in writing. And people naturally don't realize that it is indeed a regular breaking-out of a long pent-up force, like the bursting forth of a mountain lake. Such a lake bursts out in wild floods until it finds its own path, and sweeps mud and rock along in its wild flight. Then it gets cleaner, and may become quite a pretty stream. My writing too has broken its own path in the same way, a wild hitting-out in all directions where I have been constricted, in order to make space for myself. How I came to writing was on the one hand an instinctive compulsion, on the other hand I really had to write like that, if I wanted to make any impression on the people.[2]

Gotthelf's fully mature writing begins with the novel *Wie Uli der Knecht glücklich wird* (1841), the work which extended his reputation beyond Switzerland into Germany and further afield. From now until his death in 1854 followed a prolific outpouring of fiction; within eighteen years he wrote twelve large-scale novels and some forty Novellen, apart from the short stories from the five years of his activity as almanac editor, some prose works on social and religious subjects, and various fragments. After *Uli der Knecht* came what are probably his best novels, *Geld und Geist* (1843–4) and *Anne Bäbi Jowäger* (1843–4), where the Emmental peasantry become vehicles for detailed and penetrating psychological study. Among his later novels *Uli der Pächter* (1848), the sequel to the farmhand Uli's material and moral progress, and *Die Käserei in der Vehfreude* (1850), one of Gotthelf's most amusing longer works, are outstanding. The Novellen, many and varied as they are, were a sideline to the novels, which occupied most of his energies as a writer. From the point of view of artistic merit, the shorter tales both gained and suffered as a result of being treated by their author as minor products of his pen. A few of them are certainly ephemeral in purpose, such as the political satire *Ein deutscher Flüchtling* (1851) or *Hans Jakob und Heiri oder Die beiden Seidenweber* (1851), with its teaching of the uses of savings banks, while others fail to come up to their creator's best standard, such as the peasant story *Die Erbbase* (1849) or the legend *Servaz und Pankraz* (1850). But the more concentrated form of the Novelle compelled Gotthelf to limit his narrative within severer confines than was the case with his novels; didactic asides are less frequent in the shorter works, and if the characterization has not the epic breadth of the novels, the Novellen frequently gain from the tauter manner of exposition.

In the tales which are set among the peasant-farming community of Gotthelf's own time, or a generation or so earlier, lively humour and sharp realism are the principal attractions. The author sometimes takes one theme and uses it as a basis for several stories. Thus there are three tales concerning a young man's search, with varying degrees of cunning, for a suitable wife; *Wie Joggeli eine Frau sucht* (1841) is a slight prelude to the delightful comedy of *Wie Christen eine Frau sucht* (1844) and *Michels Brautschau* (1849). Rural intrigues play a part too in *Hans Joggeli, der Erbvetter* (1848), where a series of grasping relatives or would-be relatives are satirically sketched in their vain efforts to deflect the old farmer from remaining loyal in his affection for two servants. Emmental peasant life is shown as based on a prosperity derived from hard work, simple and plain in many respects, but on the whole pervaded with an attitude of willing acceptance on the part of most of the characters. The old man Hans Joggeli and the quiet, affectionate maid Bäbeli are among the most attractive of Gotthelf's Novelle characters. If the sunny side of peasant life is shown in *Hans Joggeli, der Erbvetter*, a pendant story *Harzer Hans, auch ein Erbvetter* (1848) shows miserliness developed into obsessive, destructive evil, while *Segen und Unsegen* (1851) portrays the gradual decay of a farmer both in material prosperity and personal character. The stark ruthlessness of the first version of *Ich strafe die Bosheit der Väter* (1852) was too much for the publisher who had requested the tale, and the author allowed himself to be persuaded to supply a more reconciliatory ending. *Barthli der Korber* (1852) combines the temptations of meanness and the hopes of inheritance in further variation, while the shorter *Der Besenbinder von Rychiswyl* (1852), which was to attract Ruskin's attention, relates in terms of idyllic content the simple, uneventful life of a broom-maker. *Die Frau Pfarrerin*, Gotthelf's last completed tale, has a spirit of character evocation similar to that of *Der Besenbinder von Rychiswyl*; there is a lyrically expressed resignation which has its parallels in many of Stifter's Novellen. *Der Oberamtmann und der Amtsrichter* (1853) is a bustling, humorous tale of a quarrel between two rural administrators, where the interest is primarily focused on the plot; *Der Besuch auf dem Lande* (1847) is somewhat similar in texture, though approaching more closely to farce. The gentle idyll *Der Sonntag eines Grossvaters* (1852) is scarcely a full Novelle; *Das Erdbeeri Mareili*, a haunting portrayal of a simple 'strawberry-girl', has something of the quality of a Romantic 'Märchen'. Idyllic too is *Der Besuch* (1854), which portrays an apparently trivial theme, a young wife's difficulties in settling in a strange district with its differing manners and speech, with an insight that blends poetry and realism. *Hans Berner und seine Söhne*, originally published as a Novelle in 1843, was being rewritten as a large-scale comic novel shortly before Gotthelf's death.

In his concern for the historical past and the legends of Canton Berne, Gotthelf was an heir to Romantic tradition and to the work of Scott. His original intention was to write a unified cycle of Novellen illustrating episodes from the history of his canton, but this purpose was never fulfilled in the way that Keller later composed his *Züricher Novellen*. However, a number of tales were successfully finished, including the outstanding *Die schwarze Spinne*. Artistically a number of these Novellen are less attractive than the tales of peasant realism, though Gotthelf's treatment of daemonic, archetypal figures and of material that belongs to myth rather than history, is original and reveals a further complex strand in his imaginative powers. If Gotthelf did not find accredited sources, he was fully capable of inventing legendary phenomena of massive, gigantic proportions. The priest, as leader of a Helvetic tribe, dominates *Der Druide* (1849), and his wisdom is acknowledged by the tribe after it has disobeyed him and met defeat from the legions of Julius Caesar. *Die Gründung Burgdorfs* (1846), ostensibly set in Merovingian times, expresses in sombre symbolism a fierce conflict based on sexual passion. *Kurt von Koppigen* (1844) is a tale of a young man's development from the wildness of youth until his rebellious spirit is broken in and a new and morally, if not aesthetically, satisfactory start is made. Here the vitality of Gotthelf's contemporary realism is transferred to a thirteenth-century setting, with little loss to the narrative force in the process. *Elsi, die seltsame Magd* (1843) is a tale of frustrated love which culminates in tragedy as a consequence of the French invasion of Switzerland in 1798. The heroine, deeply ashamed of her father's fall from prosperity to bankruptcy, takes on work as a maid in a district where her family is not known. She rebuffs the advances of a man who comes to love her deeply, until in desperation he seeks death in battle; Elsi goes to share his fate on hearing of his action. This Novelle is quietly effective in its combination of muted elegy and tension.

In the nineteenth century Gotthelf was known first as the author of *Uli*, and even Keller, whose critical discussions of Gotthelf's work were the most percipient to be made during that century, does not mention *Die schwarze Spinne* (1842), the Novelle for which Gotthelf is now most widely known. This work successfully combines the two principal strands in Gotthelf's Novelle writing, humorous realism in a contemporary setting and the grandiosity of myth. But it should not be regarded as the prototype for all aspects of his art; here there is no place for gentler serenity nor for the working out of a love story, nor for the more sensitive approach to religious experience which is so well exemplified in the novel *Geld und Geist*. *Die schwarze Spinne*, however, belongs to Gotthelf's happiest and most fertile creative period, and its artistic mastery is indisputable. The framework tells of a christening festival on a sunny Ascension Day at a farmstead a few miles away from Gotthelf's house and church at Lützelflüh; the gathering together of the relatives, the walk to the church and the subsequent repast are recounted in an atmosphere of easy-going warmth and security that is in deliberate contrast to the grandfather's narrative of the medieval plague-legend. Here the reader is plunged into a quick-moving, concentrated tale of exploitation, oppression and suffering that bring out the worse qualities of the down-trodden, until a pact with the devil, that is to be made at the cost of an unbaptized infant's life, is sealed. Christine, the strange woman from Lindau, alone dares to confront the Green Huntsman, whose kiss initiates the plague and subsequently transforms her into a monstrous spider bringing death to peasants and overlord alike. The sequence of the episodes causes the tension to mount inexorably until the creature is exorcized. Evil is depicted starkly in this figure of horror. The grandfather's second story, of the spider's return some centuries later, drives home the further moral that peaceful happiness may decline into materialistic vanity and then be exposed to destruction by daemonic forces. This second plague-legend, although less extended than the first, is by no means a mere pendant or afterthought; the form of the whole work is certainly unusual, but artistic skill and dynamic vitality permeate it at every stage. The sum total of Gotthelf's works gives a picture of Bernese peasant life—a world in itself—which is Homeric in its objectivity, solidity and plasticity.[3]

Berthold Auerbach made his first appearance as a writer of village stories with *Der Tolpatsch* in 1842, the same year that saw the publication of Gotthelf's *Die schwarze Spinne*. Though he turned away from the village story afterwards in favour of problem novels, he returned to his first successes in 1876 with the publication of four new village stories under the title *Nach dreissig Jahren*. In Auerbach's tales of country life, the point of view is that of the literary man, to whom the incidents and characters are copy, but copy which, as a literary man, he feels must be touched up a little in order to make it really interesting. So he strengthens the sentiment in one place, heightens the dramatic tension in another, underlines oddities of psychology in a third.

The subject matter of the story of country life can be grouped round three or four main themes of interest: the farmhouse ('der Hof'), and all the problems connected with it; the whole village community; the contrast between village and town life; some exceptional passion or vice in an individual peasant. Auerbach's stories illustrate all these possibilities, but he is perhaps most successful in the stories in which he draws highly individualized psychological types—especially degenerate or criminally inclined characters: this very fact proving that he is in essence a literary man rather than a recorder of peasant life. It has been objected to his peasants that they are drawing-room peasants, projections of a literary mind, having ideas which are foreign to their station; and certainly compared with those of Gotthelf they appear to be much more sophisticated. 'His peasants are turned out so smartly, and are so polished, they have the ideas of an Uhland and an Auerbach and are quite adapted for the world of refinement, but—they are no longer Swabian—they are Swabians transfigured'.[4] This is a characteristic attitude to Auerbach's peasants. He himself said, in defending his method of presenting his characters: 'I know perfectly well that the peasant has muck sticking to his clothes and boots, but that I don't reproduce'.

Auerbach's best-known stories are *Barfüssele*, *Die Frau Professorin* and *Diethelm von Buchenberg*, though they are not necessarily his best stories. *Barfüssele* is the story of a village Cinderella, rather sentimental but not

without its charm; *Die Frau Professorin* deals with the
contrast between village and town: a village maiden
marries a young student who afterwards becomes a
professor, and the difference between their ideas leads
ultimately to tragedy. This story was dramatized by
Charlotte Birch-Pfeiffer under the title *Dorf und Stadt*,
and for fifty years at least was one of the most popular
plays in Germany. The third of the stories mentioned,
Diethelm von Buchenberg, is Auerbach's finest achievement and perhaps the only one of his stories which
deserves a place among the masterpieces of Novellen
literature of the nineteenth century: the tragic story of a
peasant whom threatening financial disaster drives to
crime.

The Novelle of country life brings a whole new type of
subject matter in place of the fancies of the later Romantics and the topical problems of the Jung Deutschland
writers. It opens up the whole world of the Bauerntum, a
self-contained world characterized by its own laws,
customs and traditions reaching back into the Middle Ages
and having still abated nothing of their rigidity at the time
in which it becomes the object of literary exploitation.
There is no equivalent to the Bauerntum of Germany in
the England of the nineteenth century. Two main types
of writers of village stories may be distinguished: the
writer who is country born and bred, and though himself
not a peasant in the strictest sense of the term, is in such
close contact with the life of the peasant that the circumstances of his subject matter are part of his immediate
experience; and secondly the town-bred writer, the literary
man by profession, who discovers the peasant world as a
source of subject matter, which can be drawn upon with

fruitful results. To the former type belong Melchior Meyr and Peter Rosegger, to the latter Friedrich Spielhagen and Hans Hopfen.

Melchior Meyr's *Erzählungen aus dem Ries* began to appear in 1856 and were continued in 1860 and 1870. His stories centre upon his native village of Nordstetten in Swabia, and were written as he himself says 'to pay his debt of poetical gratitude to his homeland in the descriptions of its village life'. The underlying theme of all of them is the conflict between the rigid class conventions of the peasant world and the natural instincts and emotions of the individual characters, the conflict being invariably presented in the form of a love story in which the union of the lovers is hindered and delayed by the fact that one of them is poorer and occupies a less honoured position in the village than the other: thus *Ludwig und Annemarie*. Like Auerbach, Meyr tends to sentimentalize his peasants and to subdue the harsher features of farming life, and with him too the element of moral reflection obtrudes considerably. But he possesses a welcome sense of humour and power of characterization, and makes skilful use of dialect to heighten the realistic effect of his stories. A certain easy-going spaciousness of narration deprives his stories of that formal excellence which would entitle them to be regarded as Novellen.

What Gotthelf did for the Emmental, Auerbach for the Black Forest and Meyr for his district of Swabia, Peter Rosegger, the son of peasants, a shepherd boy, afterwards a journeyman tailor, and an entirely self-educated man, did for Styria. His numerous works of fiction, novels as well as shorter stories, made him the interpreter of the landscape and people of his native mountains to the whole of Germany, and acquired for him a popularity which passed over from being a literary one to become a more personal one. His best collections of stories are *Sittenbilder aus dem steirischen Oberland* (1870), *Geschichten aus Steiermark* (1871) and, most popular of all, *Schriften des Waldschulmeisters* (1875). In spite of his realistic descriptions of country life, he holds to an idealistic view of the beauty of a life more in accordance with nature amongst the mountain farms than is the life of the cities, and attacks the growth of industrialism which was threatening the purity of country manners. Rosegger's moralizing, paedagogic tendency, like that of Gotthelf, is the outcome of a definitely religious attitude of mind.

Akin to Rosegger both in his underlying religious convictions and in his hostility to the invasion of modern industrialism in the simpler world of agricultural life is the Catholic priest Heinrich Hansjakob, whose special province is the district of Baden on the shores of Lake Constance. His stories—*Schneeballen* (1892), three volumes; *Der Vogt auf Mühlstein* (1895)—attract by their simplicity of feeling and style, a succinct power of characterization, and an individual sense of humour of a somewhat dour type, seasoned by the usual element of moralizing reflection.

North Germany as well as South Germany has its writers of village stories. The life of the Hanoverian peasant is the subject matter of Heinrich Sohnrey's stories. Sohnrey was for a long time the editor of the *Deutsche Dorfzeitung* and devoted his life to the amelioration of the peasant's lot. In his collections of stories, of which *Die Leute aus der Lindenhütte* (1886) is the best

known, he reveals himself as a writer with natural gifts of
story-telling, but without great conscious artistry. Finally,
among the more naïve writers of village stories, Timm
Kröger may be mentioned, like Theodor Storm a native
of Schleswig-Holstein, though his attitude to life is more
optimistic than that of Storm. His best-known collections
of stories are *Eine stille Welt, Bilder und Geschichten aus
Moor und Heide* (1891), *Leute eigener Art, Novellen eines
Optimisten* (1904), *Um den Wegzoll* (1905).

Amongst the town-bred writers who discover country
life as a literary subject matter, Friedrich Spielhagen,
whose main province is the problem novel dealing with
contemporary social and political questions, deserves
mention for his Novelle, *Die Dorfkokette* (1868). The
story, which does not show that immediate knowledge of
some special district which is characteristic of the writers
of the first class, is nevertheless an effective piece of
narrative, revealing the art of the skilled literary man.
Town-bred like Spielhagen was Hans Hopfen, who was
originally a member with Paul Heyse and Emanuel
Geibel of the Munich school of poets. Hopfen is a story-
teller possessing freshness and humour, and his Bavarian
peasants are drawn with truth and convincingness. His
writings comprise the *Bayrische Dorfgeschichten* (1878),
Kleine Leute (1880), and a much later work *Der Böswirt*
(1903), a forerunner of the Bavarian stories of Ludwig
Thoma. Of greater eminence than Hans Hopfen, both as
a creative writer and as a literary artist, is the Viennese
poet and dramatist Ludwig Anzengruber. Though he
began his career as a writer of sketches and stories his
main claim to fame lies in his peasant dramas, almost
equal to which in excellence are the two peasant novels

Der Schandfleck (1877) and *Der Sternsteinhof* (1884). His village stories are contained in the collection *Dorfgänge* (1879). Anzengruber's attitude to the life of the peasants as subject matter is akin to that of Auerbach, for whom he expressed a great admiration; and like Auerbach he has a conscious intention to enlighten and reform, especially to substitute for the rigidity of peasant prejudices a wider, more tolerant morality based upon more humane ideals.

It will be seen from this brief summary of some of the writers of village stories during the second half of the nineteenth century that the moralizing, didactic tendency of the Kalendergeschichte remains one of its characteristics, even when the subject matter passes into the hands of professional literary men. In the history of the development of the Novelle the literary discovery of rural life plays an important part in enlarging and modifying the subject matter with which the Novelle is able to deal. The opening years of the present century saw in Germany a revival of interest in fiction dealing with themes from country life. After Naturalism had emphasized in drama the life of the urban working classes, as seen with detailed photographic realism, other writers, led by Adolf Bartels and Gustav Frenssen, advocated the application of these techniques, though with a differing political slant, to rural society. The Heimatkunst movement initiated a widespread revival of interest in regional fiction during the first half of the twentieth century, one of the best-known writers in this sphere during this period being Ernst Wiechert. But the imaginative world of Gotthelf still towers massively above the efforts of all later German writers on country themes, just as Thomas Hardy's work is outstanding in English fiction of this type.

Chapter VII

THE NOVELLE OF POETIC REALISM

The fifth decade of the nineteenth century marks the beginning of the great period of the German Novelle: the period in which it attains to its distinctive form as a specifically German literary genre and finds expression in a number of works which are masterpieces of their kind and, considered as a genre, represent the highest achievements of German literature during a period which may be said to last until 1890. The other literary genres during these fifty years offer on the whole only isolated examples of greater works, and do not consistently maintain a high level. The great period of German drama was over, and no outstanding dramatic poet or group of poets dominates the middle years of the century with the one, certainly important, exception: Friedrich Hebbel. Coming after Gotthelf, Keller's contribution to the novel is limited to *Der grüne Heinrich* and the later, less interesting *Martin Salander*: Stifter's *Nachsommer* is more important than his *Witiko*; the novels of Raabe and Fontane mark the late close of this mid-nineteenth century period. The fifty years beginning round about 1840 show the Novelle occupying a dominant position in German literature.

The period coincides also with the emergence and development of a new type of literature. Sturm und Drang, Classicism, Romanticism, Jung Deutschland are followed in the fullness of time by the 'Poetische Realismus'—a title invented by Otto Ludwig, who is one of the most characteristic exponents of this new movement. Poetic

Realism is the prevailing literary movement for the whole of the middle of the nineteenth century, having as a rival during the next fifty years only the bloodless imitation of German classicism represented at its best by the Munich school of poets. Both the writers of Poetic Realism and the epigones of German classicism with their cult of pure form are superseded by the Naturalists of the 1890's, whose ideal of literature was the exact antithesis of that of the Munich poets and the logical development of certain aspects of Poetic Realism.

The essence of Poetic Realism consists in its complete description of reality, the attribute 'poetic' signifying that it is not concerned with a pessimistic dissection of life, but rather that it accords to it positive value. When translated into the world of literature, life appears as 'poetical', that is to say, as something which has intrinsic worth, and their conviction of this intrinsic worth is the basic characteristic which unites all the realistic writers of this period. This conviction distinguishes them from the earlier and later naturalistic writers, and more especially from those who belong to the immediately succeeding generation at the end of the century. The characteristic of Poetic Realism, therefore, consists in the manner in which it describes reality, which is not one of analysis, investigation, examination from the standpoint of some philosophico-moral or sociological theory, but is content to be pure description. It is in essence optimistic, finding positive values in life without reference to transcendental sanctions. Poetic Realism follows immediately upon the Jung Deutschland movement and reaches its height in the development and clarification of the ideas of the earlier movement; though to begin with its difference of attitude to the world around it, an attitude of acceptance rather than of revolt, was noticeably prominent. In the history of literature of the nineteenth century Poetic Realism occupies a position analogous to that of Classicism in that of the eighteenth century. It gives poetic expression to the view of life of a mature period of culture, of which the Jung Deutschland movement with all the exaggeration of a revolutionary period, full of unclarified ferment, was the herald. It owes something on the side of philosophic content to the materialistic philosophy of David Friedrich Strauss and Feuerbach; but at least as much on the literary side to the Romantics' discovery of the value of Stimmung and the importance of imagination and feeling. At the same time it rejects the extreme subjectivity and the fantastically marvellous of Romanticism.[1] It is essentially a middle-class movement; its subject matter is drawn from the bürgerliche world, considered in its widest sense as comprising middle-class society from the leisured classes to the handworker and the peasant, but excluding the proletariat; and its view of life and ethical code is a bürgerliche one. The characteristic and most successful expression of this new literary movement is the Novelle.

Such works as Otto Ludwig's play *Der Erbförster* and Gottfried Keller's novel *Der grüne Heinrich* are, of course, equally products of the movement, and if one writer can be singled out as representing the movement in its finest and most perfect form, that writer is Gottfried Keller. This line of argument would seem to lead to the conclusion that the German Novelle reaches its greatest heights in the works of Keller. But before coming to these works it is necessary to trace the development of the Novelle within the limits of Poetic Realism.

The Jung Deutschland writers had produced no actual Novellen which can claim to be of first-rate importance, for those of Laube, Gutzkow, Mundt, Kühne, Ungern-Sternberg are only of inferior merit. Nevertheless, they had manifested a great interest in the genre, and precisely during the years in which they had dominated German literature there had been numberless collections of Novellen published.[2] It was, as Mundt had pointed out, the most popular and fashionable literary form, partly no doubt because it could be so easily and unobtrusively utilized for social and political propaganda. The demand that literature should concern itself with the actual conditions of life had been answered rather in the sense that it plunged into polemical discussion of existing abuses and prevailing tendencies. It was essentially a literature of the town and of a sophisticated public. With the advent of the Dorfnovelle it had discovered, in the place of a negative critical attitude, a more positive subject matter. The extension of writing to an appraisal of rural environments substantially widened the range of German prose. But Gotthelf had emphasized too sharply and polemically the contrast between the artificiality of town life and the newly discovered reality and naturalness of the life of the peasants. The contrast is developed rather too schematically by Auerbach, whose writing may be said to be characteristic of the transition from Young Germany to the attitude of Poetic Realism towards its new subject matter. Later writers are content to concentrate upon the reality of country life without necessarily having to bolster up their point of view by reference to the antithesis town-country.

An early example of the transition to Poetic Realism is

exemplified in the work of Immermann, *Münchhausen, eine Geschichte in Arabesken*, which may serve as a starting-point for a consideration of the development of the Novelle within the limits of Poetic Realism. Immermann was a critic of his age, and his two novels *Die Epigonen* and *Münchhausen* describe the decay of a sophisticated society, which had become a prey to falsehood and outworn conventions. *Münchhausen*, published in 1839, falls into two parts, a negative and a positive one. The negative side of the novel deals with the lying charlatan Münchhausen, and is intended to expose all the hollow shams of the aristocratic and industrial society of that period. It is an example of the genre 'Zeit- oder Tendenzroman', which deals generally in satirical form with the abuses of the age. But into this novel Immermann has woven an almost independent story, which represents as a contrast to the falsehood and unreality of social life, the truth and reality of country life amongst the peasants of Westphalia. These chapters were afterwards extracted from the original novel and, having been put together, formed the Dorfgeschichte or Novelle *Der Oberhof*, which has survived as a piece of imaginative literature, whilst the rest of the novel has long since ceased to be of interest except to literary historians.

Der Oberhof is only by courtesy a Novelle, for it remains a story torn out from its context, and not entirely comprehensible except by reference to that context. It cannot, therefore, lay claim to that severity of form which is required as an essential feature of the Novelle. Further, it contains many of those romantic and unreal elements which betray its inner connection with the decay of Romanticism. Nevertheless, it gives a vivid and sincere

picture of peasant life in Westphalia, accurately observed
and described, and presents in the figure of the Hofschulze
one of those characteristic peasant types, which appear
again and again in the literature of village and country
life.

On a much higher plane, indeed one of the masterpieces
of German Novellen literature, is the Novelle of Annette
von Droste-Hülshoff, *Die Judenbuche*, published in 1842.
If *Der Oberhof* stands half-way between Jung Deutschland
and Poetic Realism, and still with some rags of undis-
carded Romanticism hanging about it, Droste-Hülshoff's
Novelle can be said to represent Poetic Realism in a
form which is hardly surpassed by anyone except perhaps by Gottfried Keller. In the great period of Novellen
literature it is a fine work which combines all those elements which constitute the distinctive type of the German
Novelle; all that Goethe, Kleist and the Romantics had
contributed to the creation of a new form: realism enriched by poetical depth and symbolical significance.

Annette von Droste-Hülshoff was in the first instance
a lyrical poetess, whose descriptions of Westphalian landscape have a quality which no other German lyrical
poetry possesses. Her prose writings are few, and consist only of sketches and descriptions of Westphalia, its
landscape, people, traditions and customs. *Die Judenbuche*
is her only narrative work in prose, though she wrote
also a number of ballads and short epics. She calls it ' ein
Sittengemälde aus dem gebirgigen Westphalen', though
in her first reference to the project of writing it she describes it as ' eine Kriminalgeschichte, die sich in Pader-

born ereignete, von rein nationalem Gehalt'—the word
'national' having here the significance of 'local', belonging essentially to the district in which the events take
place. The point is significant because it introduces a new
factor in the Novelle of this period, a factor which is absent from the Novelle in its original form, namely the
utilization of local colour as an important ingredient in
the events that form the subject matter. It goes hand in
hand with detailed nature description which occurs to a
much greater extent in the Novellen of Adalbert Stifter
and Theodor Storm. The more or less detailed elaboration
of the setting—the Milieuschilderung—now becomes a
permanent element in the Novelle. It is noticeable that
the most important writers of this period—Droste-Hülshoff, Stifter, Gotthelf, Storm and Keller—nearly always
make use of definitely localized settings for their stories
—Westphalia, the Bohemian Forest, Thuringia, Schleswig-Holstein, Switzerland—and that the incidents and
characters of the stories are so closely connected with
the definite locality in which they are set, that their very
existence appears to be conditioned by it.

The source of *Die Judenbuche* is an incident which
occurred in a village in Westphalia in the middle of the
eighteenth century. Records of the incident existed in
the family archives of the author's family, and had been
edited and published by her uncle under the title *Geschichte
eines Algierer Sklaven*. In most critical editions of Droste-
Hülshoff this original version is published as an appendix,
and it is extremely interesting from the point of view of
the technique of the Novelle to see the alterations which
the poetess has made in the original story. The change
in the title itself is significant: that aspect of the story—

the years which the hero spends in slavery—is passed over by Annette as of no importance from her point of view.

Heyse's test applied to this Novelle yields the following result: a young peasant murders a Jew to whom he owes money and, having concealed his body under a beech tree in the forest, disappears from the neighbourhood. Twenty-eight years later he returns in disguise, and after living for some time in his native village hangs himself on a branch of the tree under which the body of his victim had been concealed. This synopsis suggests something of the essential quality of the Novelle; but it is much less adequate as a synopsis than the five lines which Boccaccio uses to describe one of his Novellen. The events are certainly more important in themselves than the events of Goethe's *Novelle*, for instance—which were submitted to the same test—but Droste-Hülshoff's story is a piece of realistic literature far removed in style and intention from the abstracter methods of Goethe's later classicism. It is and purports to be 'eine Kriminalgeschichte' and the events which it relates are such as will hold the attention independently of any additions in the way of symbolization or Stimmung which the poetess may add. The description of Friedrich Mergel's childhood, his drunken father and humiliated mother, the poaching and illegal traffic in timber, the midnight raids and scuffles—all these things have intrinsic interest. But the real 'Falke', to use Heyse's expression, is the tree itself; which has ceased to be merely a piece of scenery, and has become a symbol: a symbol of some more primitive conception of justice than the laws which the modern state has devised. The roots of the Judenbuche are in the Old Testament, in the days when the rule of an eye for an eye, a tooth for a tooth, was valid. Its branches overshadow the whole story with the sinister, long-enduring sense of retribution. After the death of their co-religionist, the Jews of the village bought the tree and carved into it with an axe a Hebrew inscription. This is printed in the text of the Novelle in Hebrew characters. At the end of the Novelle, when the dead body of the hero Friedrich Mergel is discovered hanging in the branches, the translation of the inscription is given: 'Wenn du dich diesem Orte nahest, so wird es dir ergehen, wie du mir getan hast'. The translation of the inscription at the very end—at least for those who are unable to read Hebrew—produces in the reader something in the nature of a thrill, in so far as it casts a light back upon the whole sequence of events and underlines, as it were, the real significance of the story. The same method, though infinitely more crude and sensational, is often employed by modern short-story writers—when they keep throughout the story a secret which only the last line reveals. But the Novelle does not as a rule descend to these melodramatic surprises at the end, which lie rather within the province of the short story. In the Novelle the Pointe or surprise or Wendepunkt, as it is variously called, is usually of a less sensational nature, and in the Novellen which are now to be considered almost disappears.

One point is worth observing in the technique of the story: when Friedrich Mergel returns to his village after an absence of twenty-eight years, he gives himself out to be someone else—a cousin of his who had disappeared at the same time as himself—and is not recognized by the villagers as the murderer. The reader is not told whether he is Friedrich Mergel or not; indeed he is led to believe that it is the cousin, who relates what is in reality a fictitious account of Friedrich's death. So there is no possibility of psychological analysis—no account of the process of remorse which goes on within him and drives him to suicide. After living in the village for some time he disappears: by chance some time later the body is found, already half decayed, hanging in the tree—and with that discovery the reader is for the first time assured that it really was Friedrich who came back to the scene of his crime. By this means the poetess can produce her startling effect at the end.

A comparison of *Die Judenbuche* with two early Novellen —the two earliest which fall within this survey: Goethe's *Der Prokurator* and Tieck's *Der blonde Eckbert*—will show how the genre has developed from the original form, and what similarities it has retained. It is, to begin with, quite clear that *Die Judenbuche* is very much more akin to Tieck's Novelle than to Goethe's. Goethe's story is placed in a purely generalized setting—which indeed he calls Genoa, but takes no pains at all to describe; whereas *Die Judenbuche* depends for its particular effect upon the description of the exact locality, its people, customs and landscape. It has, however, this point of contact with *Der Prokurator* that it deals with a moral problem, that the principal character is in both instances a responsible moral being who recognizes the validity of moral laws and his or her own subjection to them. In Tieck's Novelle the characters are moved by blind impulse and instincts, and what they do and what befalls them is part of the un- accountable nature of the universe just as natural forces are. Both Tieck's and Droste-Hülshoff's Novellen are

Stimmungsnovellen—with this difference that in *Der blonde Eckbert* the Stimmung pervades the whole story, whereas in *Die Judenbuche* the Stimmung is a retrospective one—is not engendered until the end of the story when it flows back and envelopes the whole series of incidents in memory. Both the Romantic and the later Novellen owe a great deal to irrational elements; but in Droste-Hülshoff's work the irrational is not exploited for its own sake with the deliberateness which Tieck employs, but asserts itself as it were inevitably, as an ethical factor, appearing as the force which drives the murderer back to the scene of his crime and compels him to expiate it by a voluntary death. It may be pointed out that this irrational element is very much heightened by the fact that the reader is never told that the murderer has any stings of remorse, and that therefore he never sees the rational and logical steps which lead him to suicide. Unlike Tieck's Novelle, *Die Judenbuche* does not deal with a purely fantastic world but with the world of reality. It is again in essence a piece of gossip, raised to the level of literature, but with differences: (1) it is now a piece of village gossip, rather a sensational piece, it is true, and one which embodies an exceptional event; (2) it is not merely an incident and its effect upon a person or group of persons which is related, but the preliminary events which lead up to the central incident are also carefully recorded—the account of Friedrich's father and his first marriage; (3) something has been added by the poetess which may be called Stimmung or poetical vision or symbolical value, and this shifts the centre of interest from the mere events narrated, as in a Novelle of Boccaccio, for instance, to the ethical content.

(b) ADALBERT STIFTER

In the writings of Adalbert Stifter the actual incidents are reduced to a minimum of importance, and if Heyse's test were applied to them the result would in most cases be extremely disappointing, for the element of the exceptional, the extraordinary or the sensational is almost entirely lacking. Indeed, in Stifter's Novellen, the form has so fundamentally changed that it is at least doubtful whether they can really be classed as Novellen. Nor did the author himself call them thus, but rather Studien or Erzählungen. But they have at least as much claim to be regarded as Novellen as the later stories of Tieck, and are intrinsically of much greater literary and poetical value.

Stifter was born in a small village in the Bohemian Forest; and it is as important a fact about his writings as the fact that Droste-Hülshoff was born in Westphalia, and Theodor Storm in Schleswig-Holstein. His first story was written when he was thirty-five years old—in 1840. His writings consist of two sets of Erzählungen, which were published under the titles *Studien* and *Bunte Steine*. The *Studien*—thirteen in number—were written between 1840 and 1845; the *Bunte Steine*—six stories—appeared in 1852. There are further seven Erzählungen written at various times between 1844 and 1866 which are not included in either of the above-mentioned collections. In addition to these works Stifter wrote a novel *Der Nachsommer* which appeared in 1857, of which Nietzsche said that it was one of the finest pieces of prose in the German language; and an historical novel, *Witiko*, which appeared in 1867.

The epic writer has two possible functions, to narrate and to describe: 'berichten' and 'schildern'. Narration deals with the sequence of events in time; description with the juxtaposition of things in space. Both functions are present in all epic works, but sometimes one, sometimes the other predominates. When the former predominates the work becomes more dramatic, more exciting: when the latter predominates the effect is more contemplative. Kleist is the type of the epic writer as narrator: the whole stress is laid upon the events which succeed each other in point of time so swiftly that there is no opportunity for mere description, which by its very nature has a retarding effect. Stifter is the type of the epic writer as describer: the whole stress is laid upon the descriptions of nature in which the events merely appear as episodic disturbances —hardly more. Where, in Kleist, all is movement and swiftness, in Stifter all is tranquillity and leisureliness. They stand as far as the Novelle is concerned at the opposite poles of epic art: half-way between them, but with a distinct bias towards the descriptive side, stands Gottfried Keller. And just as in Kleist the incidents recorded are exceptional in their violence and wildness, so in Stifter they are of the simplest most ordinary kind. The tension is everywhere of the slightest; the dramatic moments are rare, and when they occur they are lacking in intensity because the author is clearly not concerned to make the most of them. His interest is in other things.

The actual subject matter of most of his stories deals with everyday domestic events: two children cross the mountains in the winter and lose their way in the snow, but by a piece of good fortune discover a cave in which they pass the night and so are preserved from death

(*Bergkristall*); a youth goes on a visit to his uncle, an eccentric old bachelor, passes some months with him, and by his candid nature wins the old misanthropist back to a certain degree of human affection and belief in humanity (*Der Hagestolz*); a married couple who have long been parted meet again after years and are reunited through the danger of death to which their son is exposed (*Brigitta*). But this concentration of Stifter upon the everyday, the unexceptional, is a definite artistic procedure with him. In the preface to *Bunte Steine* (published in 1852) he explains and justifies his methods: 'It was once remarked in criticism of me that I describe only that which is small, and that my characters are always ordinary characters. If that is true I am now in the position to offer my readers something that is still smaller and more insignificant'.[3] (The attack upon him to which he here refers is probably that of Hebbel, to whom Stifter's whole art was distasteful. Later on when Stifter's novel *Der Nachsommer* appeared, Hebbel defied anyone to read it to the end. In effect, Hebbel's art is the exact antithesis of Stifter's.) That which is 'still smaller and more insignificant' to which he refers are the stories in *Bunte Steine*, which are all concerned with children. He proceeds:

But since we are talking of that which is great and that which is small, I will expound my views on this point, which probably differ from those of many people. The stirring of the air, the rippling of water, the growth of corn, the movement of the sea, the growing green of the earth, the glowing of the sky, the shining of the stars are what I consider great: the thunderstorm that approaches in splendour, the lightning which destroys houses, the tempest which drives breakers before it, the volcano in eruption, the earthquake which overthrows whole countries, are for me not greater than the phenomena mentioned above. Indeed I consider them smaller, because they are merely effects of higher laws. They make their appearance in isolated instances and are the results of special causes. The force which makes the milk in the saucepan of a poor woman rise up and overflow is the same as that which drives up the lava in the volcano and makes it roll down over the slopes of the mountain. These phenomena are merely more apparent and attract more forcibly the attention of those who are uninformed and unobservant.[3]...

It will be noticed that in the list of things which Stifter describes as great, every phenomenon is a permanent state, not a passing startling event; and that it is the former things which he considers worthy of observation and description, not the latter. In view of the essential nature of the Novelle, which consisted in the striking event, the Begebenheit, the something startling and exceptional which, falling like a bolt from the blue, befalls the characters, it may well be asked whether Stifter's whole conception of what is worth recording does not in itself constitute a rejection of the Novelle as a form. In any case it must be admitted that he strains the form to its utmost limits, by elaborating the nature description to such an extent that the events—which are the essential core of the Novelle—are almost lost sight of. Generally speaking, in the development of the Novelle as a form in German literature, there has been a tendency to minimize the importance of the actual event—'die unerhörte, sich ereignete Begebenheit'—which in Romance literatures receives the main, often the exclusive attention, and to stress instead some other element—it may be ethical significance or the supernatural or symbolical value or Stimmung. Here in Stifter another example of the same tendency is apparent—the actual events in his case being sacrificed to the description of nature. And it is from this side that Stifter must be approached as a writer. These permanent aspects of nature—such as he enumerates them in the preface to *Bunte Steine*—are his real subject matter. In most writers, in whose works external nature plays an important part, it is there as a background, often a very important background, for the human beings who carry on the action of the plot. They may be profoundly influenced and conditioned even by the nature in which they live, so that they are incomprehensible and meaningless taken away from their particular setting—compare, for instance, the characters of Storm's Novellen or of Thomas Hardy's novels in England—but they are nevertheless the foreground, the element with which the author and the reader are mainly concerned. However dynamic nature may be in such works in its effect upon the human characters, it still remains merely background. But with Stifter this is not the case. The real subject matter of his stories is not the doings of a person or group of persons who pass across the surface of nature, but nature itself is the subject matter—in its permanent states, and in its gradual changes through spring, summer and winter. The characters are *merely* foreground; moving points against the enduring grandeur of the landscape. In nature, then, for Stifter that is great which is permanent, enduring, undisturbed—states, not incidents; the ordinary, not the exceptional; and so too in human nature. In the preface to *Bunte Steine* he continues:

As it is in external nature, so it is also in man's inner nature. A whole life devoted to justice, simplicity, self discipline, reasonableness, activity within its own circle, admiration of beauty, completed by a serene and calm death is what I call great; powerful emotional disturbances, fearful outbreaks of anger, the lust for revenge, the excited mind which is eager for activity, tears down, alters, destroys and in its excitement often flings away life itself; these things I do not consider greater but smaller, as they are just as much the products of individual and special forces as tempests, volcanoes, earthquakes. We are concerned to discover the gentle law whereby the human race is guided.

Thus in the sphere of human nature as in that of external nature there is an exact parallel with regard to the things which Stifter considers worthy of observation and description: states, not incidents, though the latter may be more exciting and startling: the life devoted to justice and charity, rather than the outburst of hatred or anger: the enduring, not the episodic. And here too the subject matter is unsuitable for the Novelle, whose very essence it is to present the exceptional incident. So that Stifter forces the Novelle as a form—with a very gentle force certainly—to do the very opposite of that which is its function: to reproduce permanent states of things instead of the interruptions to those permanent states. Stifter would make the Novelle describe a long uneventful summer day, the sky cloudless from morning to evening, passing imperceptibly from one shade of colour to another. But actually it is the business of the Novelle to describe the thunderstorm, which arising unexpectedly shatters suddenly the calm and serenity and then passes away leaving crops beaten down and houses destroyed by lightning. The preface to *Bunte Steine* may be regarded as a manifesto of the aims of the new Poetic Realism; for Realism is concerned with the everydayness of life rather than with its exceptional moments, and the Poetic Realism of the middle of the nineteenth century, unlike the thoroughgoing naturalism, fifty years later, looked upon life and found it good, and recorded with loving and minute care the details of existence. The same tendency exists in Gottfried Keller, though it is indulged less frequently and less circumstantially. Stifter is an extreme case both in theory and in practice. In all the other writers of this period the 'event' is accorded much greater importance, and is frequently of so striking and even sensational a character as to serve very well for the 'unerhörte Begebenheit' which is requisite for the Novelle. Nevertheless, even though it be admitted that Stifter represents the practice of Poetic Realism in an extreme and perhaps even abnormal form, it is clear that the Novelle of the middle of the nineteenth century, as the characteristic expression of that movement, has very substantially changed its form and function, and that in its choice of subject matter it is much less concerned about the extraordinary and exceptional than it was during the Romantic period.

Stifter's literary career began with two Novellen, *Der Kondor* and *Feldblumen*, which do not yet reveal his specific qualities: *Der Kondor* has similarities with the later stories of Tieck; *Feldblumen* is still under the influence of Jean Paul. With his third story, *Das Heidedorf*, Stifter enters upon his special province, the description of life and landscape in his home country, the Bohemian Forest. Most of his Novellen are set in this district. His nature description reaches its height in the description of the forest. *Der Hochwald*—one of the finest of his Novellen—has been called 'das Hohelied des deutschen Waldes'. Three of the Novellen and indeed three of the finest have however more exotic settings: *Brigitta* deals with life on the Hungarian plains; *Zwei Schwestern* takes place mainly on the shores of Lake Garda; whilst *Abdias*, the most tragic and perhaps the greatest of all Stifter's Novellen, describes life in the north of Africa, though the hero passes the latter part of his life in a valley in Upper Austria.

As is natural where the stress is laid upon description rather than narration, these Novellen acquire a greater spaciousness of form: such events as occur are recorded with a certain leisureliness which is in striking contrast to the concise form of the Romance Novelle—the inevitable result is that they are very much longer than the Novelle in its basic form. Many of them—like *Abdias*—narrate the events of a whole life-time or a considerable span of years. Where the action is concentrated round a single incident, that incident is rarely of a sensational kind, but may be nothing more than a heavy snowstorm (*Bergkristall*); a hailstorm (*Katzensilber*); a drought and its breaking (*Das Heidedorf*). These Novellen of Stifter are by no means exciting, but, for those who have time and patience to read them, they have a quiet, virginal beauty alike in their prose style, in the characters and incidents which they present, and in the spirit in which they are written.

Stifter is a writer who was for a long time neglected but is now coming into his own, and is gradually being recognized as one of the minor classics of the nineteenth century. And whilst creating a type of prose work which bears the unmistakable imprint of his own temperament and character, so that he has had no followers and no imitators, he has yet preserved perhaps more than any other writer that sense of traditional values, of the importance of all that has been gathered in the past and handed down from earlier generations. There is a great deal of Goethe in Stifter's attitude to life—not perhaps the Goethe of *Faust*, but the Goethe who was a patient and careful observer of nature in every aspect: Stifter is a more specifically bürgerliche Goethe. The two fundamental activities of his mind can be described as collecting and cherishing: the collecting of countless specimens of nature and art—his novel *Der Nachsommer* is full of collector's activities—and the cherishing, with pious care, of all that has proved its worth and value for humanity. He lived in a period in which the Bürgertum was not yet shaken and undermined in its foundations. The value and importance of possessions—of material possessions—was an article of faith in such an age. Already Goethe had recognized the poetry of inherited possessions, of the loving and patient additions made to increase the store for the next generation, whether in works of art or buildings or land. It was not the mere greed for wealth, but a finer spirit—a sense, perhaps a mistaken one, that a man's value was heightened by the possession of things which were recognized as having worth in themselves. Poetic Realism was definitely a bürgerliche movement: its greatest writers, Stifter, Keller, Storm, were characteristic Bürger, who believed in the ideals of their class and the attitude of mind to which the movement gives expression is a bürgerlich view of life. Perhaps for this reason it produced no tragedy—for the ecstasies and agonies of tragedy are sometimes alien to that view of life. The Novelle, in essence a bürgerliche poetical form, supplies the nearest substitute for tragedy in that bürgerliche age.

(c) OTTO LUDWIG

Otto Ludwig carries on in his narrative works as in his drama, *Der Erbförster*, the traditions of a realism which is closely connected with a particular locality. He is the poet of Thuringia, as Droste-Hülshoff had been of Westphalia and Stifter of the Bohemian Forest. Ludwig would have wished to take his place in literature as a dramatist, and the whole of his life was spent in unremitting but also unavailing attempts to master the dramatic form. Of the several plays which he wrote and planned only two attained to anything like artistic form—and even with regard to these, *Der Erbförster* and *Die Makkabäer*, the opinions of critics are greatly divided. As a side issue he wrote epic works also—to use his own expression, his stories 'wurden gleichsam hinter seinem Rücken geschrieben'—yet, whatever degree of excellence he accorded to them, there can be no doubt that his two regional stories secure him his place in German literature rather than his dramas. *Die Heiterethei* is a humorous, *Zwischen Himmel und Erde* a serious Novelle. These are his best achievements as a story-teller, though there are some half dozen shorter stories which have some claim to serious consideration. It may, however, be said that the specifically Ludwig quality, unadulterated by influences of other writers, is to be found in these two big Novellen only.

Whatever similarities there may be between the works of Stifter and Otto Ludwig—and these similarities are merely superficial ones, the choice of subject matter and its poetic realistic treatment—in their approach to literature and in their attitude and intention the two writers were entirely different. Both, it is true, possessed that intense reverence for art as something second only to religion in the scale of human values. Stifter writes:

Art is for me something so high and sublime, it is for me... after religion the highest thing on earth, so that I have never considered my writings as works of poetry and shall never be so bold as to consider them as works of poetry.... Yet even though all spoken words cannot be poetry, they can be something else which is not lacking in every justification of existence. It was the aim of my writings, and will always remain their aim, to provide friends of similar tastes with an hour of recreation, to send to all of them known and unknown a greeting, and to contribute a grain of good to the building of eternity.[4]

The fundamental impulse with Stifter is an ethical social one; with Otto Ludwig the fundamental impulse is an artistic one: it is the desire to give form ('gestalten'), and to master a given form. The struggle for artistic mastery, the unquenchable curiosity into the nature of poetic form occupied Ludwig all his life, and his countless studies and theoretical essays and investigations bear witness to it. In all his work there is a great deal more deliberate artistry, more conscious manipulation of the form, than in any of the other writers of the period with the exception perhaps of C. F. Meyer. And this attitude of mind—that of the conscious craftsman—though it is undoubtedly a disadvantage for the writer of tragedies, is for the writer of Novellen perhaps an advantage, for as has been stressed from the beginning, the Novelle is a form which requires a maximum of artistic treatment. And this is due to the fact that it deals with an event, apparently purely fortuitous, which has to be endowed with the inevitability of fate.

Die Heiterethei (1854) is a village comedy in which

two lovers are separated by their own pride and obstinacy until the gossip of the village old women reveals to them both the happiness they are jeopardizing. It is a village version of the problem which Jane Austen solves with so much wit and charm and humour in *Pride and Prejudice*. But the two characters, 'Holders Fritz' and 'die Heiterethei' are two living, breathing human beings compared with all the synthetic creatures which people Ludwig's tragedies, into whom he strives in vain to breathe life enough to make his tragedies convincing.

Zwischen Himmel und Erde which appeared the following year (1855) is a bigger achievement altogether. If the difference between Roman and Novelle were one of length only, it would certainly have to be included under the former rubric, for it is longer than any work yet considered with the exception of some of the later Novellen of Tieck. But there is no doubt that in form and structure, in its concentration upon one centre of interest, it is essentially a Novelle. Even the characters who are immediately involved in the central conflict, almost the only persons who are mentioned in the story, are only four in number; and its main theme, to which everything in the nature of incident is subordinated, is the preservation of the integrity of the hero's conscience. Here in the Novelle the peculiar quality of Ludwig's genius found a much more suitable vehicle than in the tragic drama which was his aspiration.

The meticulous adaptation of means to end, the exact subordination and emplacement of every trait, a certain precise niceness and orderliness in construction: all these things the Novelle can assimilate. Even though they obtrude themselves upon the reader's attention they do not detract from his appreciation. In tragedy the slightest obtrusion of artistic intention is damaging. That the presence of deliberate artistry should rather heighten the appreciation of a Novelle but hinder the surrender to the effect of a tragedy is a fact whose explanation lies in the very nature of the different genres, epic and drama, and is suggested in the two words: appreciation and surrender. That quality of conscious artistry and further the purposiveness of every incident, every trait even is a characteristic of *Zwischen Himmel und Erde*, as it is characteristic also of Goethe's *Novelle*, and in more recent literature of Thomas Mann's *Der Tod in Venedig*. All three works, widely different as they are in every other respect, have this heightened quality of style in common.

The poet Wilhelm Hauff made the distinction between the Novelle and the tale consist in this, that a tale could easily be re-narrated, merely by allowing the memory to follow the natural course of events recorded, whereas a Novelle could be re-narrated from memory only by very careful thought, because the order of events was not the natural one, but had been altered for the sake of effect.[5] That is, of course, only one particular aspect of the fact already noted, that the Novelle is a very deliberately artistic form. This particular aspect of the form of the Novelle can be observed in *Zwischen Himmel und Erde*. Let it be assumed that the natural order of events in chronological sequence is $abcde$... and so on—each letter standing for some incident or stage in the story to be related. Now observe the order in which the events are presented by Ludwig: the story begins with the end (call it e). The hero, already an old man, sits in his garden and recalls his past. (It may be noted that this is a very frequently used technique in the Novelle—and is often to be found in a writer who is given to writing 'Memory' Novellen such as Storm.) The author then narrates that past, beginning with the moment at which the hero as a young man returns from his travels (*b*). Then he takes the reader back, in the memory of the hero, to the point in time still earlier, at which those travels began (*a*), and follows them up again to the point at which he returns (*b* again); then continues for a while straightforwardly—the main stretch of narrative, which in chronological sequence must be called (*c*). At a decisive point in the story he then jumps three decades and returns to the point at which the story began, and in which it also finishes (*e*) and finally narrates what has happened in between (*d*). So that instead of the logical sequence of events *abcde*, the formula for *Zwischen Himmel und Erde* is *ebabcde*.[6] In the ordinary Erinnerungsnovelle— say *Immensee*—the formula will generally be *eabcde*.[7]

It is not easy to apply Heyse's test to *Zwischen Himmel und Erde* and obtain a result which will be very illuminating. Two brothers, slaters, of whom one is over-conscientious, the other fraudulent, love the same woman. The fraudulent marries her and becomes jealous of his brother. In an attempt to murder him he is killed. The surviving brother abstains from marrying his sister-in-law because his conscience tells him that he desired the death of his brother. That gives the moral problem which is the core of the Novelle, but it has omitted at least half of that which gives the story its particular interest: namely, the setting; the life of the slaters 'between heaven and earth' on the tower of the church, where they are engaged in repairing the roof. At one point in the story the author pauses between two exciting incidents to give an account of the slater's profession; and all that is connected with this particularized aspect of the life of the characters, namely the local colouring, assumes very great importance. As has been seen, in the original form of the Novelle, there was no room for local colouring, and all was left in generalization. In the writings of Poetic Realism generally, as indeed was inevitable from its attitude to reality, the description of what may perhaps be called attendant circumstance—the physical, material setting of the lives and incidents recorded—assumed much greater importance than it can possess in the more abstracted atmosphere of Classicism. It appears in Droste's story in the description of the *milieu* of the hero; in the stories of Stifter in the meticulous and loving description of landscape; in Ludwig's Novelle it is concentrated upon the actual *métier* of the two chief characters. Just as in some stories the characters and incidents are comprehensible only in relation to the landscape in which they exist or occur, so in Ludwig's story they have significance only in relation to their *métier*. The conflict between the over-scrupulous Apollonius and the unscrupulous Fritz acquires its whole interest from the stage upon which the action is performed, the scaffoldings between earth and sky, where the perilous trade of the slater is carried on. *Zwischen Himmel und Erde*, like Goethe's *Novelle* and C. F. Meyer's *Die Hochzeit des Mönchs*, is a very interesting work considered purely technically as an instance of the genre Novelle—revealing traditional elements and innovations in conflict one with another. All three works are, significantly enough, works in which the conscious artistry of the author is apparent. What are now the characteristics of Ludwig's story as a Novelle? It has, in spite of its great length, the necessary concentration upon one conflict—this quality it has in a very high degree, wherein it bears a certain resemblance to *Die Wahlver-wandtschaften*. Its characters are restricted to just those four who are immediately involved in the conflict. (It will be remembered that in *Die Wahlverwandtschaften* the strict framework of the Novelle was enlarged to admit a great number of other characters who did not in any way participate in the central conflict.) It has a very definite Wendepunkt or point of highest interest from which it takes a turn in a direction not foreseen—namely, the scene in which Fritz attempts to murder Apollonius and is himself destroyed; further, it possesses very marked characteristics—what Heyse calls 'eine starke Silhouette' —which distinguishes it from every other Novelle which deals with a similar theme of the love of two brothers for the same woman. Finally the artistry with which it is composed tends to force itself upon the attention. All this is true—and yet, all that gives *Zwischen Himmel und Erde* its characteristic quality is to be found in elements which are not inherent in the Novelle in its original form. First the specific setting, the elaboration of the local colour, in this case in the description of the slater's *métier*. The idea of murder—the central incident of the Novelle—is suggested to Fritz by the very fact that he and Apollonius are daily working in peril of their lives, and that a single false step may hurl them down to destruction. This is an enlargement of the scope of the Novelle due to Poetic Realism; and it may be pointed out here that it is an enlargement of its scope which is full of danger for the genre as such. When it becomes the main interest, as it does with the Naturalistic writers of the end of the century, the Novelle can no longer exist, but becomes suffocated under the mass of material circumstance. Secondly, one of the main interests in Ludwig's Novelle is the psychology of the two principal characters: of Apollonius 'der Federchensucher', as Ludwig calls him, in whom he aimed at drawing 'the type of the born moral hypochondriac', the type of the over-conscientious; just as in Fritz he aimed at drawing the type of the under-conscientious. In regard to the two characters it may be observed that Apollonius is by no means a type of over-scrupulousness, or indeed a type of anything at all, but an over-scrupulous individual; and again Fritz is not a specimen of the under-conscientious, for during the whole of the story he is tormented by his conscience for the original fraud which he had perpetrated, and it is precisely the torments of conscience which drive him to attempt murder. One other point with regard to Apollonius: he is in the ethical world what Otto Ludwig is in the aesthetic world; and if Ludwig calls him a moral hypochondriac, Apollonius might turn upon his creator and call him an aesthetic hypochondriac. For Ludwig is just as much a 'Federchensucher' in aesthetic matters as Apollonius in moral ones.

To return to the second point: the fact that a great deal of the interest of the story lies in the psychology of the hero is, on the whole, something new in the Novelle, certainly an element which was not present in the genre in its original form. Though the psychological element had been developed to some extent in earlier German Novellen—as for instance in the Künstlernovellen of Hoffmann such as *Das Fräulein von Scuderi*, where it is true the element of the abnormal and monstrous plays an important part also—it is with Ludwig's *Zwischen Himmel und Erde* that it really establishes itself as the essential content of the Novelle, as which it is then utilized by Paul Heyse and C. F. Meyer; and it is significant that Heyse was enormously impressed by the work and wrote to Ludwig to tell him 'wieviel ich Ihrer Novelle verdanke'.

It is not the business of the critic to blame an author for the type of character which he has chosen to present; but the fact that Ludwig has chosen the over-conscientious 'Federchensucher' Apollonius (though perhaps the term 'chosen' suggests a more deliberate activity on Ludwig's part than is true) has given to his Novelle an atmosphere of the arbitrary rather than of the inevitable and so detracted from a really tragic effect. Apollonius, like the characters in Hebbel's bürgerliche drama, moves in that suffocating atmosphere, which Hebbel calls 'die schreckliche Gebundenheit in der Einseitigkeit', the narrow ethical code from which they are unable to free themselves.

To sum up then the importance of Ludwig's *Zwischen Himmel und Erde* in the development of the Novelle, it may be formulated under three headings: (1) he has strengthened the significance of local colouring and given it a particular application in the description of the profession or *métier* (Gottfried Keller will make use of this form of local colouring later, though not with the same insistence as Ludwig); (2) he has discovered the element of psychology as a possible content for the Novelle; and (3) he has given the rural Novelle stylistic treatment, thus continuing tendencies in Gotthelf, for whose work he expressed his admiration. It may perhaps be objected that Ludwig has stylized the Dorfnovelle too much, and that in his use of stylistic tricks and ornaments he is creating a rather paradoxical form; a use of recurrent epithet, which in so sophisticated a subject matter and work as Thomas Mann's *Tod in Venedig* appears perfectly appropriate, may seem rather out of place in a chronicle of village life, where a greater simplicity is expected. However, with Otto Ludwig's *Zwischen Himmel und Erde* a considerable artistic achievement has been made in the sphere of regional realism, whether the work be regarded as a long Novelle or as a novel.

(d) FRANZ GRILLPARZER AND EDUARD MÖRIKE

Two isolated Novellen now come up for consideration by writers whose main claim to fame lies in some other province of literature. Both works may be regarded with some extension of the term as products of Poetic Realism, though both are such individual creations as to stand somewhat apart from the main tradition of the movement. These are *Der arme Spielmann* by Franz Grillparzer and *Mozart auf der Reise nach Prag* by Eduard Mörike.

Der arme Spielmann appeared in 1848. Already in 1828 Grillparzer had written a Novelle, *Das Kloster bei Sendomir*—a story of sensational horror which belongs still to the Romantic period in feeling. Two travellers arrive at a monastery late at night; a monk tells them the story of a faithless wife who had been murdered by her husband and reveals himself at the end of the story as the hero of the incidents he has been relating. The Novelle was dramatized by Hauptmann under the title *Elga*.

Der arme Spielmann was written at the very end of Grillparzer's career as a poet, for though he lived until

1872 he published nothing of importance after the 1840's, and the three posthumous plays which were found in his writing desk by his executors were certainly sketched out and would appear to have been completed before 1848.

There are no Romantic elements in *Der arme Spielmann*, and it may quite legitimately be included under the rubric Poetic Realism, with however a more definite tendency to the individual-psychological than is usual in most works of this school. The general tendency in Grillparzer's dramas is towards a greater psychological realism in his character drawing, which reaches its summit in the character of Kaiser Rudolf in *Ein Bruderzwist in Habsburg*. Friedrich Schlegel had said of the Novelle that it was particularly suited to convey a subjective mood and point of view indirectly and as it were symbolically. It is this subjective element in *Der arme Spielmann* which gives it a particular interest. The author meets an old fiddler on a fair day and gives him a coin. The fiddler uses a Latin tag which arouses the author's interest, who seeks him out in his attic and hears his story. Some time later on the news of floods in the neighbourhood of the town he seeks out the fiddler again and finds that he has been drowned in attempting to save his landlord's property from destruction. But that is merely the framework—the whole interest of the Novelle lies in the psychology of the old fiddler as he reveals it himself in his account of his own life. He is the most touching and naïve representative of that type of character which Grillparzer under some form or other continually draws: the character who is unable to adjust himself to life—the last and extreme expression of that timidity in the face of reality which was characteristic of Grillparzer himself. It appears in the plays in the characters of Sappho, Bancban, Medea, Kaiser Rudolf, Libussa, and is always represented as due to some superior quality—it may be poetical, prophetic gifts, or philosophical insight, or excessive conscientiousness, but in every instance it is a disguise of the poet's own lack of adjustment to reality. In *Der arme Spielmann* it is represented not as the result of superior gifts but as the result of excessive simplicity and timidity. It would seem rather that Grillparzer had at last arrived at the truth about himself, and recognized that the quality in himself which prevented him from finding his proper place in the world of reality was not a virtue but rather a weakness. But together with this simplicity amounting to lack of intelligence goes also in the character of 'der arme Spielmann' that other simplicity which is synonymous with purity of heart. 'Der arme Spielmann' is one of the 'poor in spirit' who are mentioned in the Beatitudes. His timidity, stupidity, clumsiness are nothing compared with the shining quality of innocence and goodness which radiates from him. And this effect is achieved with singular skill, for the poet does not comment upon the Spielmann's story at all nor interpret for us the incidents related. The fiddler in the story of his life is far from wishing to impress his visitor: rather he is telling the story of his failures and incompetence in every situation in life in which he has found himself, and the total effect is not that we have been listening to the life of a fool, but that we have been listening to the life of a saint—who is unaware of his saintliness.[8]

In Grillparzer's later works he inclined more and more to dramatize himself, even to endowing his heroes and heroines with his own individual predilections—this is particularly true of Kaiser Rudolf in *Ein Bruderzwist in Habsburg*. Here in his Novelle he has done the same thing in giving to his old fiddler his own love for the purely sensuous beauty of sound, apart from the logical connection of individual sounds to form a melody. The story is full of individual touches of what may justifiably be called Poetic Realism—amongst which a particularly striking one is the action of the old man in drawing a chalk mark on the floor of the attic which he shares with two labourers to mark off his particular province, within which he preserves an island of neatness and cleanness in the midst of the disorder and dirt of the rest of the room.

The element of the unusual, 'das Unerhörte', in *Der arme Spielmann*, does not exist in the events, but in the psychology of the principal character. The incidents—the death of his father, for instance—are in no way arresting or startling, and the changes they bring about are of importance only in so far as they affect his inner life. The turning-point in the story is the scene in which the humble Barbara, who loves him with a maternal affection, brings him the washing she has mended for him, and then leaves him because she is going to get married. *Der arme Spielmann* is certainly one of the most exquisite Novellen in German literature, and without doubt the most perfect of all Grillparzer's works: that is to say, that less than any single drama it affords an opening for the criticism that the form and the content do not exactly coincide.

If the incident in Grillparzer's story is of little importance and partakes in no wise of the quality of the startling or sensational, this is even more true of Mörike's little novelistic masterpiece, *Mozart auf der Reise nach Prag*, published in 1856. Mörike's chief claim to fame is as a lyrical poet; but he also wrote a number of prose works, including a novel, *Maler Nolten*, to the writing and re-writing of which he devoted many years of his life. In addition to this he published a number of stories, none of which however would have received much attention had they not been the work of an already known poet, with the exception of two: *Mozart auf der Reise nach Prag*, and the fairy tale *Das Stuttgarter Hutzelmännlein*, with its subordinate story *Die Historie von der schönen Lau*. The latter, delightful as it is, does not fall within the limits of this survey, since it belongs quite definitely to the genre fairy tale. It is the story of a water-sprite and forms a humorous pendant to Fouqué's fairy tale *Undine*.

Apropos of this Novelle, *Mozart auf der Reise nach Prag*, Hebbel wrote to Mörike that he admired the art with which the poet had caused a whole world to evolve out of a grain of mustard-seed. Adolf von Grolman, more concerned about the strict form of the genre than Hebbel, says: 'Precisely in *Mozart auf der Reise nach Prag* the event which should specifically be the essence of the Novelle is as it were entirely absorbed by the broadly human and historical attendant circumstances in spite of the considerable charm of the whole story'.[9] Little therefore as *Der arme Spielmann* fits into the strict idea of what a Novelle should be, Mörike's story does so still less. The two works must be regarded as a special type, in which the aim of the author is to reveal the characteristic qualities of a certain person, to give a character picture, not by means of description—which would certainly be outside of the province of the Novelle—but by showing the reaction of the character to a number of events which are not in themselves either unusual or startling, but have merely so much importance as to set the springs of action in motion. It is true that in Mörike's story the incident is even less important than in Grillparzer's and more restricted in point of time. Where Grillparzer gives us a picture of a character by the account of his whole life, Mörike is content to give us a very short section of his life, and to reveal all the characteristic qualities of his hero within that restricted period. But the aim of both authors is the same: to present a complete picture of a given character by means of his reactions to a number of events. Substantially it is the procedure of the Novelle in its basic form, with two modifications. Instead of one striking event which reveals the character as it were in a flash of lightning, there are a number of smaller events which light up the character less vividly perhaps, but by their repetition more comprehensively. The second modification is inherent in the change from the single startling event to the succession of more ordinary events: the interest is shifted from the external event to the personality of the character which it helps to illuminate—another example of the general tendency of the Novelle in Germany to shift its point of interest inwards.

The subject matter of Mörike's Novelle is of the slightest: Mozart with his wife is on his way to Prag to conduct a performance of *Don Juan*. On the journey they stop at an inn and whilst Madame Mozart rests, Mozart wanders into a park, enters a summer-house, and in a fit of abstraction picks an orange from a tree. On the appearance of a gardener who accuses him of having spoiled a choice plant belonging to the Count, he sends a note to the owner of the house, apologizing for his action. It is the betrothal day of the son of the house, and the orange

tree was to be presented to his fiancée Eugenie. On the
receipt of the note the Countess sends for Mozart, and
his wife is fetched from the inn. They are entertained and
fêted during the evening; the duet that Mozart has just
composed in the summer-house is sung by the betrothed
lovers, and Mozart sits down at the piano and plays the
finale of *Don Juan*. The travellers spend the night at the
castle and the next morning continue their journey in a
coach which the Count presents to them. Eugenie locks
the piano upon which Mozart has played and hides the
key; looking over the music which lies upon it, she
notices with a sinister presentiment a song, the words of
which seem to prophesy the early death of Mozart.

Here there is hardly any incident at all—certainly nothing that could possibly be described as 'eine unerhörte
Begebenheit'. The turning-point of the story is Mozart's
picking of the orange in a fit of abstraction. Such an
incident might be related as a characteristic instance of
absent-mindedness on the part of a great composer, but it
would, on the face of it, hardly seem to be adequate to
form the kernel of a Novelle. But out of it as from a grain
of mustard-seed, as Hebbel said, Mörike has developed
not only a picture of Mozart himself but also a picture of
the rococo world of his time.

It is interesting to compare the different standpoints of
Hebbel and the other critic of the Novelle quoted. For
Hebbel the incident is merely the occasion for the development of a picture of the world—this is the dramatist
speaking, of whom it is required that he shall present a
picture of the world. For the other critic—who is the
greatest purist in respect of the form of the Novelle—the
incident is the important thing, 'der eigentlich novel-

listisch sein sollende Vorgang'—and this incident, which ought to be the centre of interest, is absorbed by the more generally human aspects and shades of local colouring. It is merely a question of the point of view. Certainly too strict and narrow a conception of the form of the Novelle would mean the rejection of many works of great charm and beauty. But it is noticeable that all the finest examples of the Novelle in German literature stand on the very boundaries of the form and strain it to the utmost. It is perhaps permissible to make the generalization— taking other genres into consideration as well—that the German genius achieves its finest and most characteristic effects not in the strict observance of a given form, but in straining a form to its utmost possibility—in complete antithesis to the Romance genius, which always achieves its maximum of effectiveness in a complete acceptance of the form.

(e) THEODOR STORM

Theodor Storm, like Gottfried Keller, is pre-eminently a writer of Novellen. That is to say that, though both writers achieved excellence in other literary forms as well, in the Novelle they seem to express their most individual qualities. Both of them have their special characteristics; both of them contribute something definite to the genre, impress their definite stamp upon it; both of them stand at the end of a development. It has been shown how the genre has been enriched, enlarged by the assimilation of elements which successive schools and generations have contributed; Storm and Keller benefited by these additions. But of that which they themselves contribute there is no succeeding generation to derive the benefit. The Novelle reaches the maximum of excellence in them; with them its utmost possibilities have been exploited, and those who come after them can only repeat that which has gone before, or experiment in forms which constitute a dissolution of the genre. The Naturalism of the 'nineties produced no Novellen of first-rate quality; it could not by the very nature of its theories. The psychological Novelle beginning with Otto Ludwig continues with Paul Heyse and Conrad Ferdinand Meyer, but as it becomes more and more analytical and subtle in its presentation of character and event, it loses the possibility of a definite outline, which is one of the essentials of the Novelle.

A glance back over the history of the development of the genre during the nineteenth century will reveal the fact that those writers who destroyed the original form by the addition of new elements, which were incompatible with it, were building up at the same time a new form; but it is likewise true that those who were bringing new elements for the construction of that new form were also preparing its destruction. In the hundred years between the publication of Goethe's *Unterhaltungen* and the last of Storm's or Meyer's Novellen, the genre has passed through all possible developments of its form; has been modified, expanded, enlarged; has assimilated all the elements which it is possible for it to assimilate and still remain itself. It is significant that at the beginning of the twentieth century with the appearance of a neo-classical movement in German literature, the Novelle too returns to its original strict form in the works of Paul Ernst and Wilhelm Schäfer.

Theodor Storm belongs in every aspect to the movement of Poetic Realism. His Novellen may be divided into three groups: the early ones up to about the year 1870, of which the most popular and characteristic is the very early work *Immensee*; a second group, the Chronicle Novellen, of which *Aquis submersus* may be taken as the finest achievement; and a third group which contains the Novellen dealing with ethical problems. Every Novellendichter has his own characteristic form, but in no one is it more marked than in Theodor Storm. In spite of the changes which his treatment of the Novelle underwent, the fundamental type with him is the Erinnerungsnovelle, as it appears already in *Immensee*: an old man recalls an experience, or the experience of his youth. This is the basic schema for all Storm's early works, and though the figure of the framework varies the technique is substantially the same—the underlying idea is the juxtaposition and contrast between the present of the framework and the past of the story related, by means of which a sentiment of melancholy, of mutability, of the passing of youth and happiness is evoked.

Storm comes to the Novelle by way of the lyric; and the lyrical attitude of mind is apparent in nearly all his works: they are, more consistently than the works of any other writer of Novellen, Stimmungsnovellen; and for that very reason they tend to be more sentimental, softer than the Novelle in its original form can possibly be. This is more a characteristic of the earlier stories than the later or rather latest ones; but so late a story as *Aquis submersus* with its tragic subject matter exhales a softer, more pathetic and sentimental atmosphere than the austere one of tragedy. Even a Novelle as uncompromising in its realism as *Hans und Heinz Kirch*—one of his very last—

makes use of sentimental episodes and situations. It is therefore not unjustly that Storm as a Novellendichter is associated with the idea of a certain elegiac melancholy which pervades all the work of his earlier years and appears even in his later more severe style.

Storm himself claimed for the Novelle a place beside the drama, indeed conceived of it as a substitute for the drama in a generation for which the severity of great tragedy was lost. In an unpublished preface to one of his collections of stories he attacked the idea that the Novelle was a genre of minor importance. The writer Georg Ebers had unwisely, in publishing a short story, stated that the writing of Novellen was a suitable occupation for a man who was convalescing after an illness. This evoked from Storm the following pronouncement with regard to the Novelle:

The Novelle, as it has developed in modern times more especially in the last decades and as it now appears in individual works as a more or less finished achievement, can deal with the most significant subject matter, and it only depends upon the poet for the highest achievements of poetry to be attained even in this form. The Novelle is no longer what it once was, 'the succinct presentation of an event, which attracts by its unusual nature and reveals an unexpected turning-point'. The Novelle of to-day is the sister of the drama and the severest form of prose fiction. Like the drama it treats of the profoundest problems of human life; like the drama it demands for the perfections of its form a central conflict from which the whole is organized and in consequence the most succinct form and the exclusion of all that is unessential. It not only accepts but actually makes the highest demands of art.[10]

This statement of Storm is neither so novel nor so profound and illuminating as he no doubt imagined: indeed it reveals a certain amount of unjustifiable self-satisfaction. Severity of form had been from the beginning —even in the days when the Novelle was 'eine kurzgefasste Darstellung...einer fesselnden Begebenheit'—an essential element in the Novelle, and presupposed that centre from which everything was organized. Indeed, the severity of form was more apparent in the Novelle in its original form than it was among the works of Storm himself and his contemporaries. But it is true, and perhaps he is the first one to recognize it, that the content of the Novelle had substantially changed, as has become apparent in following the development of the genre, and that necessarily with the change in the content there had gone hand-in-hand a change in the form. For the 'presentation of an arresting event', which had been the original content of the Novelle, Storm now claims that it can deal with the 'deepest problems of human life'— Storm's further claim that the Novelle is the sister of the drama, and has indeed assumed the function of the drama in modern times, is supported by him by quite inadequate and superficial reasons. At the same time there would appear to be a great deal of truth in the statement itself, though the explanation is to be sought in other causes than in those which he suggests.

The relation between the Novelle and tragedy is a very interesting one and has been debated from Storm onwards by a number of writers. It is no doubt not without significance that, in the second half of the nineteenth century when Novellendichtung in Germany was at its height, there was no tragic drama. As has already been suggested, tragedy is not the characteristic poetical expression of a bürgerliches age, such as the second half of the nineteenth century undoubtedly was: the most characteristic writer of the period is Gottfried Keller, whose specific form of expression is the bürgerliche Novelle. Storm writing on June 26th, 1880, to Keller says: 'At any rate it is an article of my artistic creed, that a Novelle constructed upon tragic lines, if it is as it should be, should arouse tragic and not pathetic emotion' ('erschüttern und nicht rühren soll'). But the claim which Storm here makes for the tragic Novelle is scarcely fulfilled by any of his own works, since the effect of even his most unhappy stories is on the whole one of Rührung rather than of Erschütterung. It may be pointed out that in the very Novelle which was intended to demonstrate the tragic possibilities of the genre, *Der Herr Etatsrat*, there is no trace of tragic emotion aroused by the presentation of the pitiful fate of the two children, incapable of resistance to a brutal and perverse father. The emotions aroused are those of mingled pity for the unhappy victims and disgust at the character of the father.[11]

Storm writes of his own Novellen:

My art as a writer of Novellen developed out of my lyrical poetry and at first yielded only 'Stimmungsbilder' or such individual scenes, in which the incident to be presented seemed to the author to contain a particular stimulus to poetical presentation. Connecting links woven in as allusions gave the reader the opportunity to picture to himself a larger complete whole, the whole destiny of a human being with the causes that set it in motion and its course to the end.[12]

The lyrical Stimmung element in his Novellen is most pronounced in the early works. Not that it is a creation of Storm's, but rather a legacy of the Romantic movement. A comparison between Tieck's *Der blonde Eckbert* and Eichendorff's *Aus dem Leben eines Taugenichts* reveals the range of which Stimmung is capable: nothing could be further removed from the sinister tone of *Der blonde Eckbert* than the gay lightheartedness of Eichendorff's story. The weakness with Storm is that his range is extremely narrow, and that the prevailing feeling which all his early stories arouse is that of a gentle melancholy, a sense of the mutability of things. He was by nature of an elegiac turn of mind, with an intense attachment to the place of his birth, to the actual material things which surrounded him, to the customs and habits amongst which he had grown up.

His first attempt at a Novelle was a little sketch entitled *Marthe und ihre Uhr* written for a local publication, the aim of which was to record representative aspects of the life and customs of Schleswig-Holstein. In this early sketch the two elements of Storm's attitude of mind are already implicit; the two factors which make up poetic realism: an accurate observation and description of reality, and the imagination of the poet which plays upon them and evokes from them their poetic value. These two factors are necessarily inherent in all the writers who can legitimately be described as poetic realists—only in each one the realistic observation and the poetical transfiguring of reality will assume different forms according to the temperament of the individual author. A consideration of Stifter will reveal that his subject matter is mainly the eternal aspects of nature, the enduring qualities whether of external landscape or of human character, and his poetical transfiguration of these realities consists in seeing them precisely as enduring, permanent things, subject to and conforming with eternal laws. (In Stifter's novel

Nachsommer the realistic factor is concerned not so much
with the sublime aspects of nature, as with nature under
the hand of man—the cultivated nature of the garden—
and with works of art, even down to furniture and house
utensils, and all these things are seen also under the aspect of things created and maintained by conformity with
permanent laws of being.) With Storm the realistic observation is directed upon nature in a more restricted,
localized sense than with Stifter: Storm hardly ever moves
away from the neighbourhood of his native town Husum.
When the scene of the action is shifted for a time to a
university town—almost the only alternative to the narrower background of Husum (Husum used here as an
ideal name for the usually unnamed small town in Schleswig-Holstein in or near which the action of all his Novellen
takes place)—the background is perfunctorily sketched in.
External nature for Storm is the small grey walled town
—'die graue Stadt am Meer' of his poems—set between
a grey sea and a wide expanse of heath. In addition to
the world of external nature, there is the world of indoor
inanimate things, which Storm draws with the same
loving care for detail as is found in the little Dutch
painters. Lukács says of these interiors of Storm that
every piece of furniture is enriched by the glance of an eye
that has lingered upon it lovingly.[13] Internal nature is
represented by the citizen of that town going about
his everyday tasks methodically and conscientiously—
whether it be farming, housekeeping, shopkeeping, doc-
toring or practising as a lawyer or magistrate.

The poetical transfiguring of this reality consists with
Storm, in exact antithesis to Stifter, in seeing all these
things under the aspect of mutability, as things which are

not enduring, but subject to the laws of decay and dissolution. So the prevailing Stimmung of Storm's Novellen is one of melancholy—but of melancholy combined with resignation. For the characters whom he draws are not beings of strong will: rarely do they take active steps to combat the misfortunes which threaten them; they remain passive and watch the clouds gathering which are afterwards to engulf them; they yield themselves up to the fate that overtakes them and suffer it with calm and resignation. In this respect it may be said that they are particularly suited to the form of the Novellen, which deals with events that befall people rather than actions which they undertake. In *Immensee* this aspect of Storm's characters is already apparent—indeed *Immensee* is in almost every respect a comprehensive example of Storm's whole methods—for the principal character appears to have failed to grasp happiness simply from a kind of lethargy of mind, a passive endurance of things, where he might have altered the course of events to his advantage by energetic action.

The effect of this prevailing Stimmung—however poetical and attractive it may be in a single Novelle—is to beget a certain feeling of monotony, of unrelieved similarity, if a number of Storm's Novellen are read one after another. And this is true even of the Chronicle Novellen, the six of which are published together under the title *Vor Zeiten*. They all tend to run one into another, so that it becomes difficult in memory to distinguish them one from another. Nearly all Storm's Novellen—a few of the later ones must be omitted from this generalization—are variations on the same theme: the theme of two people who love each other but fail to achieve happiness, or achieve it only after dangers and difficulties have been surmounted. In effect the scope of Storm's ideas is extraordinarily restricted. Ermatinger says of him:

His thought-experience is the ethical form of the German family. Neither the state which nevertheless interfered trenchantly in his life, nor the universe as a whole exists for him as a poet, though they exist for him as a human being. The cosmic experience which was so extraordinarily fruitful for Hölderlin (in *Empedokles*) became thinned out with Storm to a sense of insecurity, to the apprehensive question as to the survival of the individual, which is answered in the negative. But all that builds up the family, maintains it or destroys it constitutes the basic problem upon which his Novellen are constructed.[14]

And in another place: 'How narrow is the circle of ideas of Storm'—he is comparing him here with the width and wealth of interest of Gottfried Keller.

For Storm as a creator the concept life shrinks down to the narrow province of German married life on the basis of the enlightened positivistic morality of the nineteenth century. The problem with which he is concerned is that upon which marriage is built up, namely love in all its forms and conflicts. That which maintains it physically and morally: health, truth, loyalty, purity. That which can destroy it: dangerous disposition. Thus the family stands in the centre of his attention. For him as a poet the subject matters: art, science, religion, the state, industry and commerce do not exist. His whole feeling, thinking, creating circles round the ideal of marriage as the guiding star of his life's belief.[15]

This judgment of Ermatinger is essentially true of all of Storm's Novellen, with the exception of the last one, *Der Schimmelreiter*, which has a strength and force which no other work of his possesses. Even here, though the main theme—unique in Storm's works—is that of the strong, active, self-reliant man, defying the forces of nature, working on behalf of society, even though that society takes up a hostile attitude to him, yet it is interwoven with the domestic interests, which Ermatinger characterizes as the centre of Storm's Ideenkreis. But apart from this one exception, the generalization is correct: hardly anything touches Storm's creative imagination outside of the relationship of human beings to each other within the limits of the family. In the centre of his emotional experience is the unity of the family and round this centre all his interests revolve. Clearly a vast number of relationships, situations, problems are possible within that circle and these are utilized by him to the full. But he never ventures out into the world of wider interests. His range is 'ein bescheidenes Hausgärtchen'. It is even rare for him to draw characters in which the destructive force of passion, considered as an elemental force, is represented. When he goes to the past for his subject matter, in his Chronicle Novellen, he is not concerned with the past as history; he is still dealing with the same personal relationships, and all that distinguishes these stories from his stories of contemporary life is the colouring of the past—it would be inaccurate to call it historical colouring—and the deliberate archaic style of language which he adopts. Of what different treatment a Chronicle Novelle is capable can easily be seen by comparing Kleist's *Michael Kohlhaas* with Storm's *Eekenhof* or *Zur Chronik von Grieshuus*. In Kleist's work the action of the Novelle is shifted right into the centre of historical happenings and connected with them at every point; in

Storm's work the action is just as domestically encircled and isolated from the world of historical events as it is in any of his contemporary stories of life in Husum.

Speaking to Heyse in the later years of his life, Storm regrets that a common acquaintance of theirs did not live to see 'die zweite Periode meiner Novellistik'. To which Heyse replied, 'Ja, als du in Öl zu malen anfingst' ('when you began to paint in oils'). And this distinction between Storm's earlier and later work as that between water colour and oil painting describes with some accuracy the difference between the two styles. The earlier Novellen deal with sentimental situations from which the maximum of Stimmung is obtained; the later Novellen deal rather with problems—though still problems within the range of family affections—and are written with a much greater intensity of feeling. The difference between the earlier and the later Novellen is as Heyse's metaphor suggests a difference of colouring, a greater depth and richness is apparent in the later works, though the subject matter has not essentially changed, but remained what it always was: the affectional life of the individual within the family. Only that in the later works this affectional life is exposed to and jeopardized by much intenser dangers than those of mere sentiment.

The 'water colour' Novellen of atmosphere include such works as *Immensee, Späte Rosen, Im Sonnenschein, Auf der Universität, Auf dem Staatshof, In St. Jürgen, Eine Halligfahrt, Beim Vetter Christian, Ein stiller Musikant*. Some of these were written after 1870, but on the whole it may be said that the change from the earlier style takes place about that year. Storm himself remarks that he proposes to attempt a different type of Novelle which shall not depend upon Stimmung for its effect, and the first example of this new style is *Draussen im Heidedorf* (1871) —suggested to him like so many of his stories by an incident which came under his notice as a magistrate. It is one of the rare examples with Storm of love represented not primarily as a sentiment but as a devastating passion.

The Chronicle Novellen all fall within the years 1875–85. Opinions must necessarily differ as to their relative merits: but the consensus of opinion is in favour of *Aquis submersus* and *Renate* as the most striking and successful of this group. The theme of *Renate*—that of a young priest who becomes infatuated with a girl who lives under the suspicion of being a witch—has been treated, with considerable modifications, by Wilhelm Raabe in *Else von der Tanne* and by Hauptmann in *Der Ketzer von Soana*.

The last group of Novellen—the grouping under content does not correspond exactly to a chronological division—contains such works as *Viola Tricolor*, *Der Herr Etatsrat*, *Carsten Curator*, *Hans und Heinz Kirch*, *Ein Bekenntnis*, and *Der Schimmelreiter*. All of these are Problemnovellen, and the problem is in every case (with the exception of *Der Schimmelreiter*) connected with the relationship between members of the family: the position of the stepmother in respect of her stepdaughter and the former wife in *Viola tricolor*; the relations between father and son in *Der Herr Etatsrat*, *Carsten Curator*, *Hans und Heinz Kirch*; between husband and wife in *Ein Bekenntnis* and in *Viola tricolor*. In nearly every case Storm is building up upon a personal experience. In these later Novellen there is frequently a more pessimistic and gloomy strain than in the mood of resignation which informs the earlier ones. Towards the middle years of his life and in his later years

Storm underwent a number of painful experiences, in the death of his first wife, his exile for political reasons from his beloved Husum, in the distress caused by the drunken tendencies of one of his own sons: all these things intensified the elegiac sentiment of his earlier years.

His attitude to religion was a purely negative one. Like Keller and other writers of this period he had been influenced by the materialistic philosophy of the middle of the century: the theories of heredity and environment were accepted by him, wherein he seems to anticipate the ideas of the konsequente Naturalismus. In one of his most moving Novellen, *Carsten Curator*, one of the characters remarks: 'Do you think that the hour is indifferent, in which with the permission of the all-wise God a human being's life issues from nothingness?—I tell you every human being brings his life complete with him into the world; and all those who for centuries past have given as much as a drop to his blood have their share in it'. The same idea is expressed in the scene in *Aquis submersus*, in which the hero finds the prototype of the cruelty in the face of the owner of the castle in the portrait of an ancestress.

The basic emotional standpoint of Storm in the face of the universe is one of dread or misgiving. It informs many of his poems and finds a particularly succinct expression in the poem *Schlaflos*:

Aus Träumen in Ängsten bin ich erwacht,
Was singt doch die Lerche so tief in der Nacht?
 Der Tag ist gegangen, der Morgen ist fern,
 Aufs Kissen hernieder scheinen die Stern'.
Und immer hör ich den Lerchengesang;
O Stimme des Tages, mein Herz ist bang.

That is the underlying emotion of nearly all Storm's Novellen: a sense of the mutability of all existing things, and a feeling of fear in the face of the nothingness which confronts man at the end of life. For him to use his own words, 'Liebe ist nichts als die Angst des sterblichen Menschen vor dem Alleinsein'. Ultimately there is in the Novellen of Storm something depressing, distressing. He was himself never able to overcome a sense of the sorrow and distress of life, and it is with fear and misgiving in his heart that he envisages the world.

With regard to the technique and external form of Storm's Novellen, the Erinnerungsnovelle is the characteristic one. This may take the form of a man recounting an incident of his youth, or merely recalling it to memory in a series of pictures (as in *Immensee*), or, and this is a very favourite method with Storm, the narrator of the story may claim to have found an old manuscript (as in *Aquis submersus*): the appearance of 'a few very discoloured sheets of paper' is very frequent in these stories. The fiction of an old discoloured manuscript for the Chronicle Novellen is very useful to Storm in that it helps him to create a sense of the past by means of a slightly archaic style. Nearly all the Novellen of Storm are framework stories; they are told to an audience of worthy Bürger of Husum, to a little circle one may suppose consisting of the local magistrates, the doctor, the members of the learned professions generally—and the incidents and settings of the stories themselves are such as are consistent with this audience. The framework technique of *Der Schimmelreiter* is peculiarly elaborate. The first narrator finds in an old journal a story, in which story again a narrator appears. He finds his way into a Frisian house, in which an old man (that is to say, the third narrator) tells him the actual story of the Schimmelreiter. This is a *tour de force* in the matter of framework technique which is only equalled by C. F. Meyer in *Die Hochzeit des Mönchs*.

To summarize now the contribution of Storm to the Novelle. His modifications of the form consist first in a somewhat excessive use of Stimmung as the poetic content in the place of the clearly outlined event of the original Novelle. Speaking of his story, *Draussen im Heidedorf*, he says: 'I think that I have given proof therein, that I can write a Novelle without the atmosphere of a definite Stimmung: an atmosphere (Stimmung) which does not develop itself of its own accord for the reader out of the facts narrated, but is contributed to the story by the author *a priori*'. This Stimmung is predominantly one of elegiac melancholy, of resignation in the face of fate, and of misgiving in the face of the universe.

Already in Storm the danger of sentimentality is present; in writers with a less severe artistic conscience and sense of form, this lyrical Novellenform—as Paul Heyse calls it—becomes a mere indulgence in sentiment to the destruction of the form. Even so Storm's treatment of the form, at least in his early works, constitutes a softening, weakening and blurring of outline; though in the later works a greater austerity is apparent. In the later works too he opens up the Novelle to the discussion of psychological problems, a line which will be largely exploited by Paul Heyse and later writers, so that towards the end of the nineteenth century the Problemnovelle becomes a recognized type. The subjects of Storm's Novellen are taken exclusively from the life of the family and the family is placed in the framework of a firmly established, unquestionably accepted Bürgertum.

(f) GOTTFRIED KELLER

Storm, like Stifter and Gottfried Keller, was the poet of the Bürgertum of the second half of the nineteenth century, considered as a definite form of life and society—firmly established and assured of itself and as yet unshaken by the advent of the disintegrating forces of socialism. The intellectual-political-social world in which Storm and Keller live is that of the materialistic-optimistic liberalism which dominated German thought during the middle of the last century in spite of a pessimistic undercurrent: 'diesseitig' (neither Storm nor Keller are concerned with transcendental sanctions) and 'lebensbejahend'. Keller affirms the idea which his predecessor Jeremias Gotthelf attacks from the side of organized religion. It is not hereby suggested that Keller is irreligious: only his religion is a 'diesseitige', which, renouncing any belief in or anticipation of a life beyond that of this world, lays its stress upon the accomplishment of the duties which life imposes upon the individual.

It has been pointed out that for Storm the characteristic form is that of the Erinnerungsnovelle—the single Novelle placed in a framework of memory, whether that memory consist in the personal memory of the narrator, or more indirectly and impersonally in the discovery of a faded manuscript—whereby the past is evoked with an atmosphere of sentiment, of longing or resignation, and the Stimmung evoked is necessarily an elegiac, sentimental one. For Keller the characteristic form is that of

the cyclical framework Novelle, the grouping together of
a series of stories, which are connected by a similarity of
theme or motive or intention, and held together by a
framework, which is variously elaborated. This habit or
perhaps constitutional tendency to see things in groups,
amplifying and complementing one another, is in itself
a proof of the wider, more organic and systematic view
of life which is symptomatic of the epic standpoint.
Keller's lyrical poems do not play the same important
part in his literary output as the poems of Storm in his
creative work. Though the Swiss writer began as a lyric
poet, his whole tendency was away from the personal
subjective lyric to the more objective art of the narrator.
This transition in his art is a parallel to the transition in
his personality from the individual person to the public
citizen, and it is noticeable that a great many of Keller's
poems are written in celebration of national and municipal occasions. But already in his early poems the ten
dency to write cyclical groups is apparent. It becomes the
predominant form in his prose work. His early novel,
Der grüne Heinrich—afterwards entirely rewritten—has
in its form a certain likeness to the framework narrative.
Though it is in intention an autobiographical work, and
in its inner form an Erziehungsroman in the manner of
Wilhelm Meister, it will be seen on examination to be
rather a collection of episodic events held together by the
framework of a biography. This impression is further
heightened by the inclusion of various narratives which
do not really form part of the immediate experience of
the characters of the novel but are, as it were, let into the
main narrative: thus quite early in the work the story of
'Meretlein' which can easily be detached from the con-

text as an independent Novelle. It may be noted in passing that this inclusion of independent Novelle-like elements in the main course of the narrative is characteristic also of the *Don Quixote* of Cervantes. That Keller is essentially a writer of Novellen and not of novels is revealed by the manner in which all his episodic characters and events are elaborated and given an independent importance to which, as ingredients of a novel, they are not entitled.

Apart from his two novels, *Der grüne Heinrich* at the beginning of his career, and *Martin Salander*—his least successful production—at the close, all Keller's prose work is in the form of Novellen, and consists of four groups of stories: *Die Leute von Seldwyla*, a collection of ten Novellen which appeared in two separate volumes with an interval of several years between them; *Die Zürcher Novellen*, a collection of five Novellen; *Das Sinngedicht*, six Novellen; and the *Sieben Legenden*. With regard to these various collections, the framework varies considerably. *Die Leute von Seldwyla* and the *Sieben Legenden* are framework Novellen only implicitly; that is to say, there is no narrative framework to connect them outwardly; their interconnection consists in a unity which is imposed upon them by the similarity of subject matter in the various stories. In *Die Leute von Seldwyla* they are grouped round a certain entirely imaginary town and its inhabitants; in the *Sieben Legenden* the connection lies not only in the subject matter but in the consistent attitude of mind to all these miraculous stories of mediaeval saints which Keller presents. Certainly in the first volume of the Seldwyla stories and in the *Sieben Legenden* there is a very definite scheme in the arrangement of the stories, their grouping being so arranged that they serve to support and contrast each other, and so heighten the effect of the whole work. In the second volume of the Seldwyla stories the arrangement is more fortuitous. In *Die Züricher Novellen*, however, the framework is more explicit. The first three stories are framed in a narrative which has independent value. Originally the work was to be called *Herr Jacques* from the character to whom the stories are told. Herr Jacques is a young gentleman of Zurich, who is discontented with his place in the scheme of things and is anxious to be an original. His godfather undertakes to make clear to him that originality consists in being such a person as is worthy to be imitated. 'Only he is worthy to be imitated who carries out properly what he undertakes and always achieves something solid in its due place, even if it is not something unheard of and fundamentally original.' This he succeeds in doing, and in converting Herr Jacques from his youthful mistaken ideas, by narrating the stories of three Zurich worthies, all of whom were original in their way.

The three stories are entitled *Hadlaub, Der Narr auf Manegg*, and *Der Landvogt von Greifensee*—the action of the first two taking place in the Middle Ages, that of the third in the eighteenth century. With regard to this latter —one of Keller's most delightful works—it may be pointed out that it is itself a framework Novelle within a framework Novelle, for all of the principal characters who appear in it—seven in all—have their life histories related. *Die Züricher Novellen* are in so far an imperfect cyclical Rahmengeschichte, because the enclosing narrative comes to an end after the third story, and the two remaining stories are added without any reference to it.

Ursula is an historical Novelle, dealing with Switzerland at the time of the Reformation and the religious wars caused by the preaching of Zwingli. The fifth story is *Das Fähnlein der sieben Aufrechten*, which brings us back to the life of the small Bürger in Switzerland in the nineteenth century. However, the finest and most carefully worked out of all Keller's framework Novellen is *Das Sinngedicht*, and indeed the summit of this Novellenform in any language; for here the connection between framework and the Novellen contained in it is closer and more intimate than in any other work: the artistic perfection—the unity of idea which pervades the whole work—gives it a completeness and satisfying beauty, which is far removed from the clumsy makeshift work of Tieck in *Phantasus*. In no other such work—Boccaccio of course does not attempt anything of the kind—is the relationship between the stories told and the story which encloses them so organic. In most of the other cyclical frameworks the framework is merely there as a purely external means of connecting the individual stories, which occupy the centre of interest. In *Das Sinngedicht* the framework is itself a Novelle and indeed the *raison d'être* of the work, whilst the individual stories are there to support and elucidate the theme of the framework. And all the stories have a common motive: the problem of marriage. In his search for the right kind of wife, whom he eventually finds, the hero is assisted by the wisdom he gains from the stories told. The organic nature of the whole work is further heightened by the dialectical method employed in the story-telling: one story illustrates one point of view, whereupon the next story serves as a criticism thereof by representing another point of view. There are individual stories in the other collections which are as good as or better than any included in *Das Sinngedicht*, but no complete work of Keller has the same perfection of artistry as a whole—unless it be the *Sieben Legenden*, where the organic nature of the work is less obvious.

Keller's attitude to the theory of the Novelle was a purely practical one. *Apropos* of a letter of Otto Ludwig about the *Leute von Seldwyla*, Keller wrote: 'I was again struck by the worrying about the construction, this *a priori* speculation, which is legitimate with the drama but not with the Novelle and such things. With this school (of writers) there is a continual search for the secret method, the prescription and the alchemist's elixir, which after all simply consists in doing the best one can in an unprejudiced manner'. And he adds in excuse for this outburst: 'That may sound the rough and ready method of an uncultured fellow but is nevertheless true';[16] repeating in another letter the same rejection of *a priori* theories as to the nature of the Novelle: 'I am of the opinion that there are for novels and Novellen just as little *a priori* theories and rules as for the other genres.,..The idle talk of the scholiarchs is mere nonsense the moment they attempt to interfere in the creation of living works'.[17]

In spite of the fact that Keller cherished the plans of many of his Novellen for years before he actually worked them out (the inspiration of the majority of his works dates from the 'fifties, the actual execution does not take place until twenty years later), he is far less concerned about questions of form, consciously and theoretically, than Otto Ludwig. The form is with him not a deliberately thought-out principle, but an organic growth, asserting itself naturally and inevitably. His attitude, as is sug-

gested in the above quotation from his letter, is that of
the honest and conscientious craftsman, doing the best
that he can with his material, but taking delight in it, and
allowing himself without misgiving the right to elaborate
detail and to linger over ornament, in which he delights
as an individual, even though the severity of the form
may be loosened thereby. This gives to most of his works
a richness and fullness which is perhaps incompatible
with the severer form of the Novelle, and continually
withdraws the attention of the reader from the main outline to the contemplation, generally the delighted contemplation, of some individual detail, which is embroidered
and exploited until every possibility of curious, grotesque
or fanciful interest has been extracted from it. The linger-
ing over detail, however inimical it may be to the economy
of the composition as a whole, is one of the great charms
of all Keller's work. In this he resembles Storm, with the
difference that Storm expatiates upon details generally
for their sentimental value, whilst Keller expatiates upon
them for their purely vital value.

It has already been suggested that Keller is amongst
all these writers of Novellen the one who is most cen-
trally epic, holding the balance almost perfectly between
the two functions of narrating and describing but with
that slight tendency to lay the greater stress upon description, which is entirely consistent with the principles
of the literary movement of Poetic Realism, and consists
in a feeling for the actual value and interest of natural
things as such. Keller is one of those writers of opulent
imagination who are aware—to use his own words—
'von dem goldenen Überfluss der Welt', and the richness
and inventiveness of his imagination reveals itself in his

delight in curious detail. Actual material things are a source of pleasure to him, and he will describe a whole catalogue of oddities—such as the collection of Züs Bünzlin in *Die drei gerechten Kammacher*—or elaborate a fantastical character, or paint in great detail a piece of pageantry, not merely for its value in the development of the story, but because it is in itself a source of pleasure to him. All this detracts from the purity of the form as the theorists of the Novelle usually conceive it:—it represents in effect the antithesis of the view held by Friedrich Schlegel that 'sie das Lokale und das Kostüm gern mit Genauigkeit bestimmt, es dennoch gern in allgemeinen hält'; but it is here a question of Keller's preference for actual concrete life to the rigidity of an abstract form. On the other hand it may be said that the element of the 'event', the 'happening' which is the core of the Novelle in its original form, receives a far greater prominence than in some of the works which have been discussed, where it is sacrificed to Stimmung, or metaphysical significance or even to mere description—as in Stifter's stories. And with this renewed stress upon the happening as such comes also a firmer line in the construction of the story, so that it is generally easy in a Novelle of Keller to see the point at which the action reaches its climax and turns into a new and unexpected direction—the Wendepunkt, which Tieck demands; thus in *Romeo und Julia auf dem Dorfe*, the scene in which Sali strikes Vrenchen's father; in *Der Schmied seines Glückes*, the scene in which John Kabys betrays his benefactor by seducing his wife; in *Kleider machen Leute*, the scene in which the tailor decides to propose to Nettchen. In all the stories of Keller it is not a question of the mere 'event' being sacrificed to any other element;

but rather of its being enriched and loaded, perhaps even overloaded with a wealth of attendant circumstance which to anyone but a sheer purist for style must be added delight. A Novelle of Keller in comparison with one of Goethe—not to go back to the classical example of Boccaccio—is like a picture of Titian or Paolo Veronese compared with the more severely linear compositions of the early Florentine painters.

With regard to the subject matter of Keller's Novellen, in spite of some excursions into history and exotic settings, it is generally drawn, as Storm's subject matter was, from the life of the middle classes and peasantry of the district in which the poet lived. *Die Leute von Seldwyla* consists almost entirely of stories whose subject matter is the Bürger or peasant life of Switzerland. But *Pankraz der Schmoller*—again a story within a story— starting off from a Swiss *petit bourgeois* setting takes the reader for the bulk of the incident to India. (See in this story, as an instance of Keller's almost wilful delight in apparently unimportant detail, the account of the two children pouring milk upon their Kartoffelbrei and making subterranean passages for it to flow through—an incident which, trifling as it seems, somehow remains in the memory.) In *Frau Regel Amrain und ihr Jüngster*, there is the same *petit bourgeois milieu*; *Romeo und Julia auf dem Dorfe* is a peasant story; *Die drei gerechten Kammacher* returns to the world of small tradesmen and their apprentices. In the second collection of the Seldwyla stories, the action of all the Novellen—with the exception of *Dietegen*— takes place in a bürgerlich *milieu*, ranging from that of the travelling apprentice to the owners of prosperous factories. In the midst of this predominantly middle-class contemporary range of interests *Dietegen* goes back to the end of the fifteenth century and presents a story with tragic situations but with a conciliatory close in which the feuds between the rival Swiss states form the background.

In the *Züricher Novellen* there is a greater variety of subject matter in spite of the similarity of theme in most of the stories. *Hadlaub* deals with the life of the Minnesinger in the fourteenth century who was instrumental in preserving for future generations the Manessesche Handschrift, one of the few important manuscripts of mediaeval German lyrics; whilst *Der Narr auf Manegg* describes the downfall of the celebrated House of Manegg one hundred years later in the fate of its last descendant. *Der Landvogt von Greifensee* gives an unrivalled picture of the rococo society of Zurich in the eighteenth century—including a delightful sketch of the aged Bodmer—and centres round the real but fantastically developed character of Salomon Landolf and the adventures of the five charming young women with whom he was at various times in love. None of these stories, in spite of their setting in the past, is historical in the sense that it introduces historical events of importance: the historical element consisting rather in the use of Zeitcolorit. But in *Ursula* Keller gives an epic picture of the sixteenth century with battle pieces, religious persecutions, heretical movements, which show that he could certainly have managed historical subjects on the grand scale. At the same time, considered as a Novelle, *Ursula* seems to be of all his works the one least suited to its form, and to resemble rather a sketch for an historical novel. In *Das Fähnlein der sieben Aufrechten* Keller returns to a *petit bourgeois* setting, with Schützenfeste, quarrelsome Bürger and the naïve slightly ridiculous charm of the Biedermeier society.

In nearly all these stories—with the exception of *Pankraz* and *Frau Regel Amrain und ihr Jüngster* which are inspired by personal experience—Keller draws his subject matter from local sources—an incident recorded in a newspaper (*Romeo und Julia auf dem Dorfe*) or a piece of local gossip (*Kleider machen Leute*). Actual events form the germ of which his Novelle is an elaboration—that is to say, that significantly enough his sources are generally in life and not in literature. But in the *Sieben Legenden* he is doing what so many of the earlier Novellisten did (Goethe in *Der Prokurator*, for instance), retelling stories already treated in literature. The immediate source of these legends was a collection published in 1804 by a certain Theobul Kosegarten. But these mediaeval saints' stories are remodelled by Keller to such an extent that the spiritual content of them is not that of asceticism but of a joyous acceptance of life. They represent a retelling of religious stories in the spirit of Keller's own 'diesseitig' and 'lebensbejahend' religion. The most famous of them is the last—*Das Tanzlegendchen*; but the whole group represents Keller's art at its finest.

The last collection of Novellen, *Das Sinngedicht*, has a greater variety of subject matter than is present in the earlier works. None of the stories deals with the 'Kleinbürgertum' of Switzerland which would appear to be Keller's special province: the social level has been raised in all of those dealing with contemporary life—in *Die arme Baronin*; *Regine*; *Die Geisterseher*—to one approximating to that of Goethe's Novellen; and we move in a circle of leisured, cultivated people. With this shifting of the social scene comes also a more generalized treatment of *milieu*: and in this latest work of Keller there are none of those detailed and grotesque descriptions of reality which form the particular charm of the works dealing with the lower levels of society. Nor are the characters so highly individualized, whilst the element of oddity, of the 'original' type, disappears in the character drawing altogether. Two stories deal frankly with the exotic, *Don Correa* and *Die Berlocken*, both of them having literary sources. *Don Correa* is put together from the account of the lives of a Spanish admiral and a Spanish adventurer, both of them living in the sixteenth century. *Die Berlocken* is based upon an incident related in Grimm's *Correspondance Littéraire*. The connecting link between all these stories is not, as in the other works, a local one, but a unity of motive: all of them treating some aspect of the relations between man and woman in respect of marriage. In so far as Keller is a representative of Poetic Realism, it must be said that in *Das Sinngedicht* the realistic element is almost absorbed in the poetic, and that of all his works, with the exception of the *Sieben Legenden*, it is the most poetically imaginative; at the same time it does not in any way represent a return to Romanticism.

So much for the subject matter of Keller's Novellen. Their specific subject matter must now be described. It has been shown that in Storm's work the content was extraordinarily restricted, and that whatever aspects it might assume, it was in essence the affectional life of individuals within the family with which he was dealing, and that a vast number of his Novellen were, not to put too fine a point upon it, love stories. However restricted

Keller's subject matter may be—and with the exception
of his last two works, he deals almost exclusively with
the middle and lower middle classes of the Swiss people
—the intellectual and emotional content, the range of
interests which he covers is very much more comprehensive than that of Storm: not only the affectional life
of the individual (in *Das Sinngedicht* he is dealing not
merely with individual love affairs but with the whole
problem of marriage, with the relationship of the sexes
regarded as a principle—that is to say, the basis of the
work is not, as with Storm, a purely emotional, sentimental one but an intellectual one), but education (*Frau
Regel Amrain und ihr Jüngster*), history (*Ursula*), social
and religious questions (*Das verlorene Lachen*), political
tendencies (*Martin Salander*), art (*Der grüne Heinrich*).
Keller's art touches life at a far greater number of points
than Storm's or Stifter's or Otto Ludwig's.

If it be asked what is the essential quality of all Keller's
work the answer is that it is the expression of German
Bürgertum in the middle of the nineteenth century. So
too is Storm's but with a difference. For Storm 'das
Bürgertum' is the setting, the established order of things
which he loves and reproduces with an affectionate touch,
because he feels himself secure in it, because it is the state
of affairs which affords protection; but for Keller 'das
Bürgertum' is a given setting indeed, but one to which
he stands in a much more critical attitude; and though it
affords him protection, it also imposes responsibilities.
With Keller the social conscience is much more highly
developed than with Storm: Storm writes from within
'das Bürgertum' as the private individual, Keller as the
citizen. The characters of Storm's Novellen are all private

individuals, enclosed within their family life, which obscures for them their relationship to the state: from the characters of Keller's Novellen invisible strands go out which connect them with the wider life of the state.

This attitude, loving but at the same time critical of Bürgertum, accepting its protective setting but at the same time acknowledging the responsibilities of the individual towards it, this attitude accounts for the great importance which the idea of education plays in the works of Keller as a whole. In fact it may be said that in the majority of his works the paedagogic idea is present, and that the aspect in which the idea of the Novelle as a form is envisaged—namely the event striking into the life of the individual and modifying it—is practically always: what educational value has the event upon the character of the person whom it befalls? In nearly every story some character or characters is being educated, a test is applied to him—in this respect there is a similarity between Keller and George Meredith—and Keller, like a rather more benign but still *Old* Testament God, rewards or punishes according as his hero stands the test.—And this test will have successful results if the characters are in their essential being genuine, real, ' echt';—if they are shams their shamming is revealed and they are condemned by Keller to ignominy, poverty or ridicule. Thus the two brothers of the *Die arme Baronin*, Viggi Störteler in *Die missbrauchten Liebesbriefe*, John Kabys in *Der Schmied seines Glückes*; on the other hand Wilhelm in *Die missbrauchten Liebesbriefe*, Strapinski in *Kleider machen Leute*, in spite of their folly and weakness, are fundamentally sound and so are rewarded with wealth and a beautiful wife. This paedagogic element exists in all Keller's works—in *Der grüne Hein-*

rich and *Martin Salander* as well as in the Novellen; it appears in its plainest and least assimilated form in *Frau Regel Amrain und ihr Jüngster*, which is actually nothing more or less than a manual on the education of a good citizen. So much so that a few years ago long passages from it were printed in the newspapers to admonish people of their duty to vote. This story, together with the last of *Die Leute von Seldwyla* stories, *Das verlorene Lachen*, seems to be an example of the paedagogic, discussional element in the Novelle getting the upper hand at the expense of the form. In spite of their thought content, from the point of view of pure narrative both of these stories, like so many of the later Novellen of Tieck, are extremely wearisome.[18] Perhaps the further criticism may be permitted that in spite of his much vaunted and usually prevailing human kindliness and charity, there is sometimes a little savagery in Keller's treatment of his unsuccessful characters, and more than one instance of lapses from good taste.

In most of the Novellen of Keller there is a strong element of humour: both *Die drei gerechten Kammacher* and *Der Schmied seines Glückes* are essentially humorous Novellen—*Die Kammacher* a farce, *Der Schmied seines Glückes* a satirical comedy. Hardly any whole Novelle of Storm is purely humorous, though humorous characters and situations occur in various works. But whereas Storm's humour is always sentimental, Keller's humour never is, but astringent and frequently satirical. It ranges over a great wealth of expression: it can be crudely domestic, as in *Die drei gerechten Kammacher*, ironic in *Der Schmied seines Glückes*, graceful in *Der Landvogt von Greifensee*, subtle and playful as in *Das Tanzlegendchen*.

But there is hardly a Novelle, except the tragic ones, in which it does not appear. In which connection it may be pointed out that whereas the bulk of Storm's stories are unhappy in their endings, with Keller there are only two tragic stories, *Romeo und Julia auf dem Dorfe* and *Regine*. Poetic Realism of course does not exclude tragedy; but with its insistence upon the goodness of life, the 'diesseitig' value of real and material things, it tends to avoid the appearance of tragedy. And it is only to be expected that Keller who represents most fully and definitely the positive, 'lebensbejahend' aspect of this view of life should in his works give a picture of life which is rather optimistic than tragic. The feeling that pervades everything that Keller wrote is that life is good in all its manifestations, not the least in the beauty which exists in material things by the very fact of their existence. Where Stifter sees them all under the aspect of eternity and prizes them for their enduring qualities, their subjection to eternal laws, where Storm sees and prizes them for their transitoriness, finding an added beauty in them that they are all subject to decay, Keller sees and prizes them for their mere being and the wealth of poetry which is inherent in them as such.

In Gottfried Keller's works the German Novelle reaches a maximum, beyond which no development is possible, except in the development of some individual and one-sided tendency at the expense of totality and comprehensiveness. What distinguishes the Novellen of Keller from the classical prototypes of the Novelle is not so much that they are different in form, but that the severe outlines of the original form have been considerably filled out—the slim figure of the maiden has acquired the opulent contours of the matron. 'To load every rift with ore' was the aim of Keats in writing poetry, and that is the achievement of Keller as a writer of Novellen. The austere line of the original form has given place to a richly coloured and detailed painting. The subject matter of some of the stories might be equally well treated by Boccaccio: *Romeo und Julia auf dem Dorfe* for instance, or *Der Schmied seines Glückes*—one can easily imagine what mischievous delight Boccaccio would have taken in the telling of the latter—but what Boccaccio would have told in five or ten pages Keller tells in fifty or a hundred, and the additional pages are filled with that detailed and localized account of reality, which is one of the most precious elements in Keller's art—but one which the theorists of the Novelle regard as lying outside its scope. Once again the main interest of the Novelle rests upon the event itself and its effect upon the person whom it befalls; though the interest is increased by the description of the attendant circumstances, the event is not submerged by it as it is in Stifter. As with Goethe there is an ethical element in addition to the purely 'incidental' element: and this takes the form of paedagogic intention. In most German Novellen the centre of gravity is shifted from the incident to some more internal interest: in the best of Keller's Novellen, though this internal interest is present, the stress is fairly distributed between event, material surroundings and the inner interest, which can generally be described as education of personality.

Chapter VIII

THE NOVELLE AS A SUBSTITUTE FOR TRAGEDY

In the account of Otto Ludwig, mention was made of his unremitting but unavailing effort to master the form of the drama and to write a poetical tragedy which would bear comparison with those of Shakespeare. Theodor Storm, though without the ambition of Ludwig to be dramatist as well as Novellist, was concerned to vindicate for the Novelle by means of his own writings the power to arouse tragic emotion. With both poets the effort was unsuccessful; and their lack of success was due not only to reasons of personal temperament, which unfitted them for the creation of tragedy, but also to the general tendency of an age whose spiritual atmosphere was alien to tragedy: bürgerlich as opposed to heroic. It is, however, important to note that, in spite of the fundamentally optimistic attitude to life of the writers of Poetic Realism in general, Germany was passing all the time through a period of pessimism, which found expression in the extreme popularity of the philosophy of Schopenhauer from the middle of the century onward.

This pessimism was the natural result of political disappointment and disillusion. In spite of the increasing importance of the Bürgertum in public affairs and its growing self-confidence in its position as a solid element in the state, the failure of the essentially bürgerlich Revolution of 1848 was felt as a tremendous set-back to the political aspirations of the patriots of the 'forties.

Rudolf Haym, in a speech at Halle in 1857, sums up the prevalent feeling in the words: 'Wir standen und wir stehen in dem Gefühl einer grossen Enttäuschung'.[1]

Even in the writers of Poetic Realism a pessimistic as well as an optimistic strain makes itself heard, and if with Gottfried Keller the optimistic prevails, it is equally true to say that Theodor Storm's reaction to life was on the whole a pessimistic one. Indeed it may quite reasonably be argued that the surrender to the world of material things which characterizes the movement is in essence a *défaitisme* of the spirit whose aspirations to high endeavour had been thwarted. Certainly with Theodor Storm the loving attachment to material things is a form of protection set up against the insecurity of the universe. And as Romanticism has been described as 'ein Flüchten aus der Wirklichkeit', so Poetic Realism might be described as 'ein Flüchten in die Wirklichkeit'—out of the world of metaphysical insecurity. But the consciousness of disillusion and the uneasy sense of the tragic nature of the universe, in so far as they caused the generation of 1850 to withdraw into the relative security of a bürgerlich world, with its apparently so firmly established order and its reassuring solidity, do not beget that heroic attitude to life which is the basis of real tragedy; and the middle of the nineteenth century in Germany produced no great tragic writer with the exception of Friedrich Hebbel, whose origins lie further back in the Jung-Deutschland movement.

That even a specifically bürgerlich world was not able to exclude entirely the sense of the tragic aspects of life goes without saying, and is amply vouched for in the works of Poetic Realism by such a monumental testimony as Stifter's Novelle *Abdias,* and in a more elegiac strain by numerous stories of Theodor Storm. Its problem was to find a form of tragedy which was in keeping with its own particular Lebensform and attitude to life.

Schopenhauer in *Die Welt als Wille und Vorstellung* (Book 4, Para. 51) differentiates between three types of tragedy: that in which the catastrophe is brought about by fate, that in which it is brought about by a villain whose will is directed towards evil, and thirdly that in which the tragic situation arises from the force of circumstances, from the fact that certain characters are by their nature such that, without ill-will on their part and without qualities which make of them exceptional personalities, they must necessarily, when brought into contact, cause one another the greatest unhappiness.[2] The question whether this third type actually is capable of arousing the specifically tragic emotion may be left out of account for the moment. The point is, that it is by its very nature more in keeping with the world of Bürgertum than either of the other types; and it is significant that, whereas Schopenhauer could cite a play of Sophocles and plays of Shakespeare as examples of the first two types, he has to have recourse to a modern work, namely Goethe's *Clavigo,* to provide him with an example of his third type of tragedy—a work which has a bürgerlich setting and one of which the protagonists are Bürger. Both the former types—the tragedy of fate and of villainy—belong to the realm of heroic tragedy. The last fate-tragedy was Schiller's *Braut von Messina,* itself a resuscitation of an outworn form, for the later fate-tragedies of Werner, Müllner and Houwald merely employed a debased conception of fate as a theatrical trick; the last full-blooded villain in German dramatic literature was Franz Moor in Schiller's *Räuber*. The Novelle, as has been pointed out, is concerned with chance rather than with fate, though it has to show the fateful effect of chance in the form of the event upon the characters which it presents. Further it is noticeable that the villain as such finds no place in it.[3]

The eighteenth century saw the emergence of a new form of drama, 'das bürgerliche Drama', not identical with Schopenhauer's third type of tragedy but having many points of contact with it, and this form of drama, which had divested itself of the heroic, was the characteristic form for the Aufklärung which, like the period of Poetic Realism a hundred years later, was a period of materialistic and bürgerlich culture. Characteristic for the bürgerliche Trauerspiel is the tendency to substitute for the more astringent emotions evoked by heroic tragedy the sentimental emotions of pity and forgiveness; as in the conclusion of Lessing's *Miss Sara Sampson*, for instance; and for the figure of the hero struggling against fate, characters of everyday format enmeshed in the net of contemporary circumstance. In the course of time, as its technique becomes more masterly, it is also able to dispense with the villain.

After reaching one high point of achievement in Schiller's *Kabale und Liebe* (1785), the bürgerliche Trauerspiel found no first-rate exponent until it was revived by Friedrich Hebbel temporarily in the middle of the 'forties of the nineteenth century in one outstanding work, *Maria Magdalena*. (The bürgerlichen Trauerspiele of Karl Gutzkow which appeared during the same decade are deservedly forgotten as works of very inferior poetical merit.) Hebbel himself occupies an anomalous position. Though his works furnish some of the most outstanding examples of Schopenhauer's third type of tragedy, they are so overlaid with 'kulturhistorisch' significance, present characters on so monumental a scale, that they appear to belong to heroic tragedy; and it is Hebbel who definitely rejects the villain as being incompatible with tragedy at its best. At the same time Hebbel is anything but a poet of Bürgertum, and his bürgerliches Trauerspiel is only fortuitously one: an application of his 'kulturhistorisch' ideas to the bürgerlich world of his day instead of to the historic and grandiose past. With Hebbel, Schopenhauer's third type of tragedy and the bürgerliche Trauerspiel do not coincide but fall apart. (His Novellen, which belong mainly to an earlier period, are the least important part of his works, and reveal a complete lack of talent for the art of the story-teller. *Die Kuh* (1849) is a *reductio ad absurdum* of his theory of the necessity of strict causality. *Matteo* (1839) may be described as a masterpiece of ethical bad taste. The absence of freedom of movement which Hebbel's preconceived philosophical framework tended to produce in his dramas is equally apparent in his Novellen. Hebbel wrote of Kleist's Novellen, that they were 'rigid with life'; his own Novellen are rigid, not with life, but as is more usual, with the lack of it.)

After Hebbel, the bürgerliche Trauerspiel languished again in German literature, at least as far as first-rate works were concerned, until the 1890's, when it was revived anew by Gerhart Hauptmann. It is noticeable that whereas the Aufklärung—a specifically bürgerlich age —developed its own type of tragedy, an inferior one indeed, the parallel age of Bürgertum in the nineteenth century made no use of the type of tragedy which its predecessor had placed at its disposal. Precisely during the years in which Poetic Realism was at its height there was no tragedy. An explanation lies to hand. The Bürgertum of the eighteenth century was in a period of becoming, was militant in the conquest of its position in the state, and its drama was militant also, i.e. *Emilia Galotti* and *Kabale und Liebe*. The basic content of these tragedies, the conflict between the Bürgertum and the nobility, could not be utilized by the Bürgertum of the second half of the nineteenth century, which had, to a certain extent at least, acquired its position within the state. Nor was the time yet ripe for the content which Hebbel proposes in *Maria Magdalena*—a conflict engendered of self-criticism. As has been suggested the bürgerlich view of life was for the generation in the middle of the century in Germany a refuge; the advantages of its seeming solidity and protectiveness were more apparent than its shortcomings. It is not until the end of the period, with its approaching dissolution under the attacks of industrialism and internationalism, that self-criticism begins in the later works of Gottfried Keller—*Das verlorene Lachen* and *Martin Salander*.

The question whether the Novelle as a genre is capable of arousing the tragic emotion, answered in modern times in the negative by Bernhard Bruch,[4] in the affirmative by Hermann Pongs,[5] is a question which should not be asked and cannot be answered until the preliminary question has been decided: in what does the specific quality of the Tragic consist? Attention has been drawn earlier in the chapter to the three types of tragedy postulated by

Schopenhauer, of which the third, the tragedy of ordinary circumstance, appears to belong more specifically to modern times. It was laid down by Aristotle that the emotions which tragedy must evoke are pity and fear; and later writers, as for instance, Corneille, have regarded admiration as a possible ingredient as well. One thing is certain, that the emotion which the earlier writers of tragedy aroused was, in spite of the softer element of pity which finds a legitimate place in it, on the whole a sterner, more tonic one. It is Lessing, the typical Aufklärer, whose whole argument with regard to tragedy, in his correspondence with Mendelssohn and Nicolai as well as in the *Hamburgische Dramaturgie*, tends to make pity the specifically tragic emotion.[6] Yet though pity may be evoked by the spectacle of the hero struggling against destiny, it is rather an exaltation of spirit akin to admiration which his unavailing struggle evokes; and the idea of forgiveness can necessarily find no place either in the tragedy of fate or in the tragedy of villainy. However these, the more sentimental emotions, are the ones which not only Schopenhauer's third type of tragedy but also the bürgerliche Trauerspiel itself arouses. The attitude of mind which makes them possible may be described as 'understanding'—*tout comprendre, c'est tout pardonner*. It is precisely this attitude of mind which the writer of Novellen aims consciously or unconsciously at producing.

Schopenhauer, though a confirmed enemy of the bürgerliche Trauerspiel as a genre, tends, in his whole philosophy and in particular in his interpretation of tragedy, to support the validity of his third type of tragedy by the stress which he lays upon suffering rather than upon conflict; and this general attitude of his makes him the spokesman of the whole generation in the middle of the century, a generation suffering under the disillusionment of great ideals unrealized and defeated, and accounts for the extreme popularity of his philosophy from the 'forties onward.

It has been shown why the bürgerliche Trauerspiel, which would appear to be the most suitable form in which Poetic Realism could express its sense of the tragic aspects of life, could not be utilized by the bürgerlich generation of the middle of the century. But these tragic aspects could not be entirely repressed, as the efforts of Otto Ludwig to write tragedies and the attempts of Theodor Storm to develop the tragic possibilities of the Novelle testify. And it was precisely in the Novelle, in spite of the prevailing optimism in the works of Stifter and Keller, that the generation found a vessel for the expression of its particular sense of the 'Gebrechlichkeit der Welt', to use a phrase of Kleist's, stressing rather the suffering inherent in the fate of human beings, in their relations to one another, than the conflict between man and fate, and evoking rather the sentimental reactions of pity, forgiveness and above all 'understanding', than the specifically tragic exaltation of spirit. The Novelle is the sentimental substitute for tragic drama during the period of Poetic Realism.

This aspect of the Novelle is most apparent in the works of Theodor Storm who, more than any other writer of the period, is concerned with subjects which are in his opinion tragic. It is noticeable that with the exception of *Der Schimmelreiter*, his last Novelle, in which the hero is presented in conflict with nature, all the Novellen with unhappy endings deal with characters whose misfortunes are due to failure to understand each other (*Hans und Heinz Kirch*), and who suffer under the force of adverse circumstances without setting up an adequate resistance to them (*Der Herr Etatsrat*). Similarly, in the two Novellen of Gottfried Keller with unhappy endings, *Romeo und Julia auf dem Dorfe* and *Regine*, the protagonists, unable to cope with the force of circumstance, seek refuge in suicide. And it may be observed that when a tragic dramatist arises in Germany at the end of the century in the person of Gerhart Hauptmann, he makes suicide the *dénouement* for characters who are lacking in the power of resistance to a hostile fate (*Vor Sonnenaufgang* and *Einsame Menschen*). The aim of the writer of Novellen such as Storm, to arouse the emotions of pity and forgiveness as the expression of an attitude of mind which involves 'understanding' of the characters presented, leads necessarily to a closer investigation of the psychology of those characters, and so prepares the way for the psychological Novelle of the end of the century, which in its insistence upon detailed traits of character, blurs the sharp outline of the form, shifting the stress from the outstanding single event to the description of the person or persons whom it befalls.

Apart from Theodor Storm, three other writers may be here mentioned, who in the second half of the century made use of the form of the Novelle for subject matter of tragic content, all of them however robuster in their sentiment than Storm: Friedrich Halm, Theodor Fontane and Wilhelm Raabe.

Friedrich Halm, who attained considerable popularity as a dramatist during his life-time, was the author of three Novellen of first-rate quality, which did not become generally known until after his death in 1870, though one of them, *Die Marzipanliese*, had already appeared in 1856 in Gutzkow's journal, *Unterhaltungen am häuslichen Herd*. Halm is clearly influenced very strongly by Kleist in his style, though the compact prose of Kleist is loosened, in his subject matter and in the uncompromising carrying through of the central idea. In *Die Freundinnen* (1860) which has certain affinities in subject matter with *Die Marquise von O.* and relates a similar instance of 'confusion of feelings', the tragic situation is solved in a conciliatory manner, characteristically for the trend of tragedy at the time, by understanding and forgiveness.[7] *Die Marzipanliese* relates the retribution which overtakes a criminal in the pursuance of his efforts to secure a fortune. Even more Kleistian in its presentment of a character who is dominated by a single idea is the Novelle *Das Haus an der Veronabrücke* (written between 1862 and 1864). The hero Ruggiero is, in the unshakeable force of his will at least, a pendant to Michael Kohlhaas, and the Novelle would no doubt have long since taken its place among the masterpieces of the nineteenth century were it not that the action of the hero offends the moral sense so greatly as to destroy the aesthetic pleasure in the artistry with which it is described. (An elderly husband attempts to force his wife into adultery in order to obtain an heir.) For this reason Paul Heyse excludes it from his Novellenschatz.[8]

Like Halm, Theodor Fontane wrote three Novellen,[9] *Grete Minde* (1880), *Ellernklipp* (1881), and *Unterm Birnbaum* (1885), all three of them dealing with tragic subject matter. In the sombre atmosphere which surrounds them all they stand apart from the bulk of his

novels which, though they are often unhappy in their con-
clusions, move in a world of social relationships in which
sinister undercurrents are not permitted to rise to the
surface. Only the incident of the Chinaman in *Effi Breist*
approximates in feeling to the prevailing Stimmung of
the Novellen. *Unterm Birnbaum* is perhaps essentially
only a Kriminalgeschichte: a crime concealed, suspected,
brought finally to light and expiated, but the interest lies
mainly in the actions and psychology of the criminal,
whose peace of mind is disturbed more by fear of detec-
tion than by remorse for his deed. In *Ellernklipp* a father
murders his son in order that he may marry the girl with
whom his son is in love, but ultimately commits suicide
on the spot where the murder had been committed. As
with the principal character in *Unterm Birnbaum*, however, the suicide of Balzer in *Ellernklipp* is not an ethical
act of expiation, but rather the result of nerve strain. The
finest of the three Novellen is undoubtedly *Grete Minde*,
based upon a chronicle of the town of Tangermünde,
which relates the action of a girl in the sixteenth century,
who set the town on fire because her paternal heritage
was withheld from her by the town council. The Novelle
has a certain balladesque character, with reminiscences
of old folk-song motifs. It is clear that Fontane worked
backwards from the final situation as given in the chronicle
and was mainly interested in motivating it in the psychology and earlier history of the heroine.

A writer of deeper emotional significance is Wilhelm
Raabe, whose fame as a writer of novels is mainly attached to works which do not represent his art at its
maturest and best. Such works as *Die Chronik der Sper-
lingsgasse* (1856) and *Der Hungerpastor* (1864), whilst

already revealing the salient qualities of his mind, have about them too much of the sentimental predilections of the age in which they were written to enable them to claim the unqualified appreciation which his later works deserve. The attitude of mind which he consistently reveals is, in spite of a fundamentally pessimistic strain, far more heroic in temper than that of Storm; and though he is painfully aware of the misery and suffering of human existence, his works glorify the spirit in man which is able to pass beyond it. During his long life—he was born in 1832 and died in 1911—he wrote, in addition to a large number of full-length novels, a series of Novellen of outstanding excellence.

Although the subject matter of some of these Novellen is taken from contemporary life—*Wer kann es wenden?* (1862) for instance, which perhaps from a formal point of view can hardly be described as a Novelle—in his best works Raabe draws his incidents and characters from the historical past of Germany, using the historical element with a sureness of touch and an exact sense of the relationship between historical event and setting and the fate of the individual whose fortunes are involved, which distinguishes his stories on the one hand from the Chronicle Novellen of Storm, in which the fate of the private individual is merely projected into the past, and on the other hand from the Kulturgeschichtliche Novellen of Riehl, where the experiences of the individual are merely an illustration of the given cultural background. Like Storm he adopts a slightly archaizing style.

Among the best of his Novellen may be mentioned *Else von der Tanne* (1869), a story whose action is set in the years of desolation following the Thirty Years' War.

Its theme is that of the innocent girl suspected of witch-craft—a similar subject is treated in Storm's *Renate*—and destroyed by the savage cruelty of the superstitious mob. The impression which it creates is unusually pessimistic for Raabe, who does not incline in his works as a whole to leave his characters shattered by the calamities which befall them. Nor is this the final impression in *Der Junker von Denow* (1862), in which the hero atones for his par-ticipation in a mutiny, which besmirches his knightly honour, by self-imposed death. Greatest of all his Novel-len, with at least an approximation to genuine tragic effect, is *Des Reiches Krone* (1870), a story of Nuremberg in the fifteenth century, showing the utmost depths of human suffering irradiated by the triumphant greatness of soul of hero and heroine alike. The final scene in which the imperial crown is brought back to Nuremberg and the heroine Mechthild recognizes her lover, who has spent his strength in winning it and now returns a leper, is unsurpassed in its high-hearted beauty.

Des Reiches Krone, in which fate is conquered by human courage and love, Stifter's *Abdias*, the history of a dogged but unavailing struggle against a malevolent fate, and Storm's *Der Schimmelreiter*, the story of a struggle be-tween man's will and the blind forces of nature, are the three works in which the pathos of the Novelle approaches most nearly to the emotion aroused by heroic tragedy.

Chapter IX

THE PSYCHOLOGICAL NOVELLE

(a) PAUL HEYSE

Compared with Keller and Storm, Paul Heyse, who was their friend as well as their contemporary, is the aesthete of the Novelle as well as its mass-producer. In the course of sixty years devoted to the writing of Novellen—from 1850 until 1914—Heyse published about twenty-four volumes of Novellen alone, apart from an equal mass of dramas, lyrics and translations. But for those who wish to obtain an idea of Heyse's achievements in this genre the selected edition in three volumes is to be recommended in preference to the twenty-four volumes.[1]

The subject matter of these Novellen varies very much: there are Italienische Novellen, Meraner Novellen, Troubadour Novellen, Dorfnovellen and a majority dealing with the society of his day. The prevailing types, however, are those dealing with Italy or the Mediterranean generally, which is tantamount to saying, for Heyse, dealing with the 'land of beauty'; and the Novellen which treat psychological problems in modern society. Heyse was amongst other things a student of romance culture and literature in a dilettante fashion, and his Troubadour Novellen are monuments of his learning rather than of poetical imagination.

Aesthete and mass-producer—the two apparently contradictory terms and ideas—elucidate Heyse's position as a writer of Novellen and suggest at once the weakness and unsatisfactory nature of that position. During his life-time, at least during the later years of the last century, he was named side by side with Keller, Storm and C. F. Meyer. The poets corresponded one with another on subjects of literature as writers of equal standing. Modern criticism has sorted them out a little and given Heyse a less important place than the others. In effect he is very little read nowadays. Ermatinger writes of him: 'His Novellen are lacking in ideas and ultimately all dead, for the basic concepts of conventional morality, which are intended to give them life, are not ideas at all'.[2] This severe judgment must be accepted with this reservation, that the critic is speaking here of Ideendichtung as such. Though Heyse's writings cannot claim to be Ideendichtung they contain many positive qualities which entitle them to respect and even admiration. Nevertheless the fact remains that they present a far more superficial view of life than the works of Keller, Storm or Ludwig, or indeed of any of the writers so far considered.

A letter from Keller to Theodor Storm *apropos* of a nervous breakdown of Heyse's is illuminating. Keller writes: '...joking aside, I almost believe that the fact that Heyse has been writing for nearly thirty years, without having for a single year enjoyed distraction and variety by means of official duties, teaching or some other form of workaday activity, is now revenging itself'.[3] Keller was for many years municipal secretary to the town of Zurich; Storm was all his life a magistrate, Mörike a country parson and schoolmaster, Stifter a civil servant. All of these writers were anchored through their civil occupations in the Bürgertum and were conscious of responsibilities to it. Paul Heyse was a man of independent means, greatly favoured by nature and circumstance, able to devote himself entirely to the cultivation of literature; and though he certainly was profoundly aware of his responsibilities to his art, so much so indeed that it may be said that the whole mass of his literary production—Novellen, dramas and lyrics—was an offering made by a devout votary on the altar of Beauty,[4] yet, in respect of life he was, compared with Keller, Storm and Mörike, irresponsible. That is to say, he was not rooted in certain social forms of life in the same way as the others were, but was able to float arbitrarily on its surface. Stifter, Keller and Storm wêre representatives of a definite Bürgertum which existed in Germany in the middle of the nineteenth century, representatives of it because their whole existence was conditioned by it. Heyse stands outside of that Bürgertum and is the representative of no social form, because he is tied to none by circumstances, but is at liberty to move where he will. He is the representative of the individual floating on the surface of society and able to sever his connection with it whenever he will, since that connection is not an essential one.

But Heyse came to be during his life-time the specialist and authority on the Novelle; and though the present generation may find less solid value in his works than in those of his greater contemporaries, yet he did some service to the genre as such in his insistence upon the observation of the form, and in his investigation of all possibilities of the genre. He enunciated the most popularly accepted theory of the Novelle—in his 'Falkentheorie'; he made a very admirable and useful collection of representative German Novellen which he published together with Hermann Kurz from 1871 onwards—a second collection with Ludwig Laistner was published between 1884 and 1888. To this collection—*Deutscher Novellenschatz*—he prefixed an essay on the Novelle, and each individual Novelle he supplied with a short critical introduction. His critical writings on the subject as well as his actual practice are concerned with the working out of the essential form of the Novelle; and in his *Jugenderinnerungen und Bekenntnisse* he gives interesting accounts of his artistic procedure. In the chapter 'Aus der Werkstatt' one can read with what conscientious care he approaches a subject, amplifies it, remodels it, motivates or suppresses until the subject is made to yield its maximum of effectiveness. One can see that hardly Otto Ludwig himself has considered the technique more carefully or brought it to a higher point of perfection as far as its effectiveness is concerned. No doubt this insistence upon the excellence of form, considered in its more external aspect of technique, is a very useful and important function on the part of a poet, and may prove invaluable in arresting a tendency in literature towards careless, slipshod composition. As a further example of this in German literature the severe formality of Platen's poetry may be instanced, setting itself up as a sort of protest against the later Romantic lyric poets whose sense of form had been entirely destroyed by their imitation of the Volkslied. Yet with Heyse, at any rate, it is purely an external matter, and the word 'effectiveness' stands with him in contrast to the word 'profundity'; his meticulous and praiseworthy skill in using his subject matter to the best possible advantage can achieve almost anything except inform that subject matter with an idea-significance, which by his very nature he is unable to give it.

As it is significant for Storm that his characteristic form is the Erinnerungsnovelle, so it is significant for Heyse that his characteristic form is what may be called the 'Bekanntschaftsnovelle'—the term is something in the nature of unfavourable criticism. Hans Bracher in his work on the *Rahmenerzählung und Verwandtes bei Keller, Meyer, Storm* gives the following schema for Heyse's methods: 'He meets someone at the *table d'hôte*, in an hotel, on a journey who attracts his attention by some peculiarity. Heyse observes him silently and finds something enigmatical about him, makes his acquaintance, whereupon the person in question relates the story of his or her life'. And he sums up the method in the phrase: 'An hotel is the ideal place for the technique of the Bekanntschaftsnovelle. Heyse can't manage without it'.[5] Heyse's attitude to the stories he tells is clearly much more irresponsible than that of Storm or Keller, much more arbitrarily individual. (Later on in the works of Thomas Mann the position of the poet who has no responsibilities to bürgerlich society becomes in itself the problem for which he strives to find a solution.) In the framework stories of Storm and Keller, the connection between story-teller and the lives of the people whose stories are told is much more intimate and ethically responsible. With Heyse the connection is substantially mere curiosity. With all the skill which Heyse unfolds in the story itself, there is a lack of ethical motive for the telling of the story and the reader is frequently surprised to find that the principal character reveals the most secret affairs of his or her life to a person utterly unknown, whom he or she happens to meet in an hotel.

Heyse's first published Novelle, *L'Arrabbiata* (1852),

has for its setting the Bay of Sorrento, and one may say that this type of natural beauty remains characteristic not only for his landscape but for his ideal of beauty altogether. *L'Arrabbiata* was for years cited as the most perfect specimen of the Novelle in European literature—an exaggerated estimate of it, certainly, though as far as the technique is concerned it reveals all the excellence and the essential qualities which Heyse in his later theoretical writings demands: it is a single incident isolated from the background, and having the strong-marked silhouette which impresses it upon the memory. Lauretta, a young fisher maiden of Sorrento, is known as L'Arrabbiata because she will tolerate no love-making from the young men but repulses their advances with violence. Tonino, a young ferryman who is in love with her, rows her across to Capri as part of his normal duties; on the way back in the evening he attempts to embrace her. She bites his hand savagely, and during the respite thus obtained jumps overboard. Tonino, overcome with remorse, fishes her out and rows her back to Sorrento without any further incident or even exchange of conversation with her. In the evening Lauretta comes of her own free will to Tonino's hut and binds up his hand and, so we are led to infer, his heart also.

It is in effect a very charming little idyll, without any very great depth or significance to it, such as there is consisting in the drawing of the fierce, untamed Lauretta, whose heart determines both in repulsion and surrender her course of action. And this type of woman reappears again and again in Heyse's stories—indeed his Novellen are nearly all about women.

Heyse has written several volumes of Italienische

Novellen, and in all of them Italy is conceived of under the aspect of the 'land of art and beauty'—with Heyse it is always the oleograph Italy. There he is at home. The landscape contains shining sea, cypresses, marble villas, olive trees, dark-eyed maidens, the complete romantic *mise en scène.* Among Heyse's Novellen dealing with Italian subjects the following may be mentioned as being particularly good: *Das Mädchen von Treppi* (1858) (Heyse describes in his *Jugenderinnerungen* the changes which the original anecdote underwent before it could be adapted to the Novellen form), *Die Stickerin von Treviso* (1868) and *Nerina* (1875), which deals with the sufferings of the Italian poet Leopardi. It will be observed that in all four Novellen the title refers to a heroine, who is the centre of interest.

But these Italian Novellen represent only one type; there are a great number, indeed the majority, which deal with the society of Heyse's own time. In these, as indeed in the Italian Novellen, the interest is nearly always in the psychology of some given person, and a great parade is made of the psychological problem as such. As examples of this type two of the better-known works, *Zwei Gefangene* (1876) and *Himmlische und irdische Liebe* (1885), may be cited. It will astonish modern readers to know that in his own day Heyse was regarded as an extremely immoral writer, who upheld in his Novellen a code of morality which was subversive of the accepted one. Thus in 1888 a work appeared, *Paul Heyses Novellen und Romane*, which was in effect 'ein Widerspruch gegen die unsittlichen Dichtungen Heyses'.[6] The author of this work in another place writes as follows:

Only a poet like Heyse can make the impossible possible.

With him people divulge the secrets of their hearts to total strangers: so called decent young girls discuss indecent subjects; to marry a widow is immoral and to love the wife of another is moral; faithfulness is a vice, death is for healthy people, who normally prefer to remain alive, a consummation devoutly to be wished; the ten commandments are not binding upon geniuses, poets, artists and exceptionally gifted women; adultery is a natural right and marriage an immoral relationship. That is Heyse's philosophy of life.[7]

All this is very much the expression of its particular period. It was written in 1888. But taken in connection with the judgment of Ermatinger already quoted, it is indicative of the change in the attitude to Heyse which has taken place since his life-time. Quite apart from the technical element of effectiveness which in itself secures a certain amount of popularity, it is clear that Heyse was popular in his day because he was in the bad sense 'modern'—up-to-date. He brought the latest daring attacks and rebellions against the accepted conventions of society. But in his attitude there was nothing profoundly ethical: he was not a moralist, like Nietzsche, shaking at the ethical foundations of his generation; he was merely a frondeur tilting at the social conventions of his generation. Akin to him is all that specious Problem Literature of the 'nineties and the beginning of this century, which found indeed its most popular expression in the drama of France and Germany and England and is now forgotten, because, like Heyse, it dealt with problems which were not fundamental ones at all, but only the outcome of the special conditions of the time.

Heyse's Novellen make on the whole pleasant reading. In addition to those already mentioned, the following would seem to reveal his art at its best: *Andrea Delfin* (1859), a moving story of Venice in the eighteenth century but with the ending *manqué*; *Der verlorene Sohn* (1869), a valiant attempt to achieve a really tragic situation; *Geoffroy und Garcinde* (1871), a Troubadour Novelle; *Der letzte Centaur* (1870), a characteristic presentation in fantastic and ironic form of the conflict between modern civilization and ancient naturalness. It is significant that most of the Novellen that can be read with pleasure to-day are those which deal with more exotic subject matter than the social conditions of Heyse's own time. Heyse tells often a good story and is technically free from faults. His form, like his style, like his tone, is polished, easy, 'weltmännisch'. He writes an excellent German prose, but that, like everything about him, is lacking in those characteristic qualities which distinguish the greatest writers.

If it be asked what Heyse contributed to the development of the German Novelle, it must be admitted that his contribution in so far as it brings something new is rather to be deplored than welcomed. His positive merit lies in his reminder of the form, regarded as technique; the value of a careful examination and working out of the possibilities of the genre Novelle as such with a view to obtaining the maximum of effectiveness. But with regard to the content he sets the Novelle off upon a false track in laying the stress upon supposed individual psychological problems, which have ceased to be problems to-day. In all his numerous Novellen he contributes hardly anything which is really original and fruitful. *L'Arrabbiata* remains even to-day his most famous Novelle; but to place it, as a former generation did, on the same level of excel-

lence as *Der arme Spielmann* or *Die Judenbuche* or *Romeo
und Julia auf dem Dorfe* is to betray a complete lack of
sense of values in literature.[8]

(b) CONRAD FERDINAND MEYER

If Heyse may be described as the aesthete and mass-producer of the Novelle, the Swiss poet Conrad Ferdinand
Meyer is the aesthete and virtuoso. Meyer, like Heyse,
lacks that rootedness in the bürgerlich life of his time—
though in a different way. He is an observer of life rather
than a partaker in it. This attitude to life in both poets
gives to their work something of the exotic, something
which is remarkable by its variance from the normal type
—in the scientific sense the quality of a freak product.
Both poets, standing outside the Bürgertum, within the
limits of which Keller, Storm and Stifter found inspiration
and security, are representatives of that aesthetic in
dividualism of the end of the nineteenth century which
was the outcome of the liberal conception of the individual
in his relation to society, and led to the dissolution of the
Bürgertum of which it was itself the outcome; just as in
the realm of economic life the principle of liberalism led
to the dissolution of the Bürgertum in the emergence of
socialism.

In Meyer's Novellen the dissimilarity to the prevalent
type, the uniqueness, is more apparent than in the Novellen of Heyse, for the very good reason that Meyer possesses as a poet a personality much more marked and
original than that of Heyse. One thing may be observed
with regard to Meyer. He tends in so far to return to the
classical type of Novelle, in contrast to the type which had

become characteristic for the writers of Poetic Realism, in that he shifts the social plane of his characters up into the bürgerlich-aristocratic world instead of keeping to the 'kleinbürgerlich' world which was the special province of Keller. The same thing may be observed of Paul Heyse, the characters of whose Novellen except in his occasional excursions into stories of peasant life, are inhabitants of the world of education and culture. It is permissible to find in the two types of Novelle—the Romance and the Germanic—a difference which is inherent in the spirit of the Mediterranean and of the Northern peoples; and to see precisely in Keller and Meyer, the two writers of the neutral territory of Switzerland, the representatives of the two cultures: the Germanic bürgerlich and the Romance aristocratic culture. Living in the same town as Meyer, Keller is directed towards German ideals in literature. Meyer, in spite of the fact that he writes in German (his correspondence is mostly in French), is directed towards Romance ideals in literature.

A further contrast may be observed between Keller and Meyer: Keller can make use of everyday mediocre subject matter because of his strength; Meyer must use incidents which contain the big historical gesture because of his weakness. Keller, secure in his rootedness in Bürgertum, need not assert himself with an impressive gesture; Meyer, floating in his Ästhetentum, must conceal his weakness and insecurity behind the heroic pose, the flamboyant setting. The two writers are exact antitheses: Keller is 'lebensbejahend'; Meyer is 'lebensfürchtend'. Keller writes out of his wholehearted acceptance of life in every form, whether it reveals itself to him as history or breaks upon him as contemporary event; Meyer writes out of his fear of actual life, his inability and conscious inability to deal with it, and lives only vicariously in the characters of grand format which he sets upon his stage. Meyer writes: 'The mediocre saddens me because it coincides with something analogous in myself; therefore I desire the grandiose so intensely'. Keller neither feared 'the mediocre', nor was he aware of it within himself, and if he had been he would have been unconcerned about it. Meyer takes refuge in the past because he is afraid of reality, i.e. the present. As he himself says: 'the past gives me a feeling of peculiar calm and greatness'. In one important respect therefore his works differ from the classical Novellen much more than those of Keller do: his subject matter is never taken from contemporary life, is never gossip raised to the level of literature—as Keller's subject matter often is, and as that of the original type of Novelle usually was. It is always taken from the historical past, and places important historical characters upon the stage.

All this is so closely connected with the personality of Conrad Ferdinand Meyer as a human being, that it becomes necessary briefly to say something of his personal history. The son of very cultivated parents, he was an example of that lack of vitality which often accompanies an over-refinement: a similar case is that of the Novellist, Eduard von Keyserling. From his boyhood Meyer revealed a timidity in the face of life which was unquestionably pathological, and developed in course of time to such an extent that he spent some time in a mental home. The whole of his poetic activity as a writer of Novellen lies between the years 1870 and 1890, after which year he succumbed again to mental disorder. Timidity in the face of life is the key to his poetic activity, as it is with Grill-parzer; as it is in a certain sense with Platen. Both Meyer and Grillparzer seek refuge from life in the vicarious life of their art, but in a different way. Grillparzer disguises his weakness under the form of some superior quality; Meyer leaves it as weakness but sets up an heroic façade in front of it.

Like Platen, Meyer found his way to his own particular expression through contact with the art of Italy; but whereas Venice acted as the open sesame upon Platen's imagination and determined the form of his poetry, with Meyer it was the art of Rome. With both poets art over-shadows life both as a source of inspiration—as the stimulus to write—and as the source of their subject mat-ter. Both of them give a rarefied form of life—a styliza-tion of it, in the sense that the life they represent is not seen at first hand but already moulded by art, pre-eminently by the plastic arts. Thus Meyer's Novellen are full of reminiscences of paintings or sculptures, and he frequently has recourse to the description of an imaginary picture in order to present a psychological situation, to symbolize an event.

Meyer wrote in all eleven Novellen—if *Jürg Jenatsch* be included as a Novelle, though it may perhaps more correctly be classed as a novel. The subject matter of all of them is taken from the historic past—they are historical in a sense in which Storm's Chroniknovellen are not his-torical, in so far as they deal actually with characters who are known to history, or with situations which are illuminating for Kulturgeschichte. Further the subject matter is predominantly taken from the period of the Renaissance, if the term be stretched so as to include that whole period in European history in which the individual is beginning to assert himself and rebel against the constraint imposed by church or tradition or state. Of the eleven Novellen the one which deals with the earliest historical period is *Die Richterin* (1885), in which the scene is laid partly in Rome, partly in the Rhaetian Alps at the time of Charlemagne, who himself appears as the *deus ex machina*. The latest period which Meyer presents is the eighteenth century in *Der Schuss von der Kanzel* (1878), the weakest of his stories, in which he presents an 'original' who is somewhat akin to Salomon Landolt in Keller's *Landvogt von Greifensee*. In between these two extreme dates lie *Der Heilige* (1880), which deals with the conflict between our English King Henry II and Thomas à Becket; four Novellen treat of the Italian Renaissance in the strictest sense: *Plautus im Nonnenkloster* (1882), of which the narrator is the Italian humanist Poggio; *Die Hochzeit des Mönchs* (1884); *Die Versuchung des Pescara* (1887); and *Angela Borgia* (1891). *Das Amulett* (1873) has as background the French wars of religion in the sixteenth century; *Jürg Jenatsch* (1876) the history of the Grisons early in the seventeenth century; whilst *Gustav Adolfs Page* (1882) has its action in Germany during the Thirty Years' War; and *Das Leiden eines Knaben* (1883) takes place at the court of Louis XIV. With the exception of *Der Schuss von der Kanzel* there is not a single Novelle in which one of the more famous characters of history does not appear; and there is probably no single writer who has, in so restricted a range, placed so many famous people before his readers: Charlemagne; Henry II and Becket; Dante, Can Grande della Scala; Ezzelino di Romano; Cosmo de' Medici, Poggio;

Lucrezia Borgia; Vittoria Colonna; Coligny and Montaigne; Gustav Adolf and Queen Christina of Sweden; Louis XIV, Madame de Maintenon—all of them characters of unusual vitality and originality and active participation in the life of their time. And immediately the doubt arises whether any poet who was not a Shakespeare could possibly have breathed life into all these gigantic figures, so various in their ways, yet all of them so bursting with energy, with vital force. It is true that many of them appear only episodically: Dante merely as the teller of the story of the faithless monk; Can Grande della Scala as the listener to it; Louis XIV and Madame de Maintenon as the listeners to a story which their court physician tells them to beguile an autumn evening. Yet one feels that there is a certain arrogance on the part of a poet who undertakes to present so large a number of the world's greatest personalities in work of so small a compass.

Two things come up for discussion here in the choice of Meyer's characters. First the difference between the dramatist and the Novellen writer. It is quite true that only a superhuman poet like Shakespeare could have dramatized such varied but vital supermen; but a writer with much less creative power can use them as characters in a Novelle. The reason is that the dramatist must conceive them from within, must live them and let their actions be the outcome and expression of their inner life; but the Novellist, who is concerned in the first place with the event and not with the action, can record their gestures, their appearance, their characteristic attitude and so give an image of them seen from outside rather than from within. And if the reader ask himself in reading these Novellen whether Meyer has really penetrated into

the characters of Dante and Can Grande and Louis XIV
—the answer is 'No'. They are not really there as living
characters at all but as theatre 'supers', going through
all the gestures associated with the characters they represent, but not living inwardly. Secondly, in spite of all this
parade of supermen and superwomen, of heroes and Kraft-
naturen, the characters whom Meyer really presents to
us from within are all weaklings and beings whose life
is moving in uncertainty and doubt and the shadow of
disaster: the unstable monk in *Die Hochzeit des Mönchs*;
the feeble-minded youth in *Das Leiden eines Knaben*; the
conscience-tortured Stemma in *Die Richterin*; the general
suffering from a mortal disease in *Die Versuchung des
Pescara*; Henry II and Thomas à Becket both seen from
a semi-pathological point of view, both wounded in their
most vulnerable feelings, in *Der Heilige*. The grand gesture, the historical setting, the heroic attitude is façade
with Meyer; the threatened insecure building behind it
is the reality, the real Meyer. And this gives to all
Meyer's work that sense of conflicting elements, which
prevents it from making the effect of an organic unity.
It is fundamentally weakness masquerading as strength:
uncertainty and insecurity disguised by the bold gesture.
Form and subject matter are nearly always in conflict,
except perhaps in the one Novelle, *Das Leiden eines
Knaben*.

The duality in Meyer's personality comes out in many
ways; even in spite of his weakness and timid withdrawal
from life there is an element of strength in him. It is by
sheer strength of will that he forces his way out of the
darkness of mental depression into the light of day in
which he can achieve something: and every single work

of his is an achievement, something wrested from the forces that threaten to submerge him. And he proposes to himself always the most difficult problems of form, as though to test his will power, his ability to the utmost: the subtle conflict between king and prelate is related by a simple-minded crossbowman. Meyer could hardly have made it more difficult for himself than by mirroring the psychological workings of the mind of Becket in the consciousness of the Swiss soldier who tells the story; and the technique of *Die Hochzeit des Mönchs*, with Dante himself as the story-teller, is more complicated than that of any other framework story.

The characteristic form for Meyer is that of the framework Novelle—just as for Storm it is the Erinnerungsnovelle; for Keller the cyclical framework story; for Heyse the Bekanntschaftsnovelle. Meyer himself writes: 'The tendency to use the framework is quite instinctive on my part. I like to keep the object at a distance from myself or more correctly as far as possible away from my eye'.[9] The type of framework Novelle which Meyer uses may be defined more closely as that of the virtuoso framework, for he tends by the choice of the person who tells the story, or the situation in which it is told, to make his task as difficult as possible, so that the effect is rather that of difficulties triumphantly overcome, of a *tour de force*, the skill of which amazes though it may not necessarily delight. As an instance of this virtuosity of technique the framework Novelle *Die Hochzeit des Mönchs* may be considered in detail. The scene is the Court of Can Grande della Scala at Verona. The Duke and his courtiers are gathered round the fire when Dante, the exile, enters and asks for hospitality, which is granted him. The company

is engaged in relating instances of sudden changes of
vocation with good or evil results, and Dante is bidden
to contribute a story. He agrees, saying that he will develop his story from an epitaph which he read on a tomb-
stone years before in Padua. Translated from the Latin it
runs: 'Here lies the monk Astorre with his wife Antiope:
Ezzelin had them buried'. Now the form of the Novelle
is that of a narrative set in the past and seen as something
completed. If therefore Dante had related his story in
such a way that he said: 'I know what happened; as a
matter of historical fact, it was thus and thus'; then the
result would have been the normal type of framework
Novelle. But Meyer hits upon a more ingenious method
than this: all Dante knows is the fact expressed by the
epitaph; he makes up the story as he goes along, so that
what we are listening to is not a piece of the past completed and laid aside; but a piece of the present going on
before our eyes and not yet completed. But that is not
enough for Meyer: he adds to the ingenuity of the form
still further; the characters in the story which Dante tells
are fitted on the characters of the persons present to
whom he is telling the story. He takes his listeners and
makes them the actors in his drama, adapting the characters of the personages of his story to what he considers
to be the characters of the persons before him. The word
drama is here used deliberately, because this Novelle of
Meyer's stands on the very frontiers between narrative
and dramatic poetry, confusing and interchanging them
in a way which is both paradoxical and perverse and out-
doing in ingenuity anything that the Romantics did in
this line. Epic poetry deals with the past; the drama
creates a fictitious present. The characters in *Die Hochzeit*

des Mönchs exist both in the past and the present. The virtuosity of this method is astonishing. When the butler enters the circle of courtiers (in the framework) Dante immediately uses him as the majordomo in the story he is telling, his peculiarities of speech and gesture being transferred to his equivalent in the Novelle. Further, Dante acknowledges and at the same time annuls the presence of the court jester, in the framework, by obliterating him with a gesture in the Novelle, '"ich streiche die Narren Ezzelins" unterbrach sich Dante mit einer griffelhaltigen Gebärde, als schriebe er seine Fabel, statt sie zu sprechen, wie er tat'. Again: in the court circle are sitting two ladies; the wife of Can Grande, a woman of commanding presence, and—as is suggested though not openly stated—the mistress of Can Grande, a woman of more facile charm. Suggested too, but only suggested, is the jealousy of the wife for the mistress. In the Novelle the monk hero forsakes his affianced bride, whom Dante endows with the personality of Can Grande's wife, for a woman who is modelled on the personality of Can Grande's mistress; and is murdered by the rival whom she has supplanted. But Meyer's ingenuity goes no further than this, though it may well be asked what would have become of the form if he had made use of the trick, so common in the drama, of making the characters of the play step out of its framework and become living persons; if at the point in the story at which Diana stabs Antiope, the wife of Can Grande had also stabbed her rival.

This Novelle of Meyer's is not cited here as an example of perfection in the Novellenform, but merely as an example of extreme virtuosity and ingenuity in the manipulation of technique, in what appears to be the rather perverse pleasure of Meyer in setting himself technical conundrums and solving them. Technical skill can go no further than this; but the result partakes too much of the nature of a *tour de force* for it to be entirely satisfactory as a work of art. If Meyer's command of technique in this Novelle be compared with an equal mastery in Goethe's Novelle, the difference between an arbitrary and a legitimate use of technique will be apparent. In Meyer's Novelle technique has become in modern slang a 'stunt' —always a sign of decadence in art, since it exists for its own sake and not as something subservient to the significance of the work. Herein it may be said that Meyer approximates to the cult of sheer artistry, of *l'art pour l'art*, which was the ideal of the last years of the century.

But Meyer's sense of form was in reality far less genuine and sure than the ordinary historian of literature asserts. No doubt there is a certain surface brilliance about it as in the technique employed in the narrative here and in *Der Heilige*—and this brilliant overcoming of technical difficulties, this bravura effect, blinds the reader to the fact that the inner form is often very faulty and that which ought to be a single unity is in reality a confusion of two separate themes. In this very Novelle, *Die Hochzeit des Mönchs*, two themes are imperfectly welded—two themes which are not necessarily connected at all: the theme of the monk who forsakes his vows, and the theme of the faithless bridegroom. The renegade monk is not at all necessary to the second half of the story: the bridegroom who abandons his bride for another on the eve of the wedding. Similarly in *Der Heilige*, the real theme, the conflict between King and Prelate, is entirely falsified by the episode of Becket's daughter

Grace whom the King abducts, thereby causing her death. In *Die Richterin*, the real theme, that of a woman whose present life is disturbed by the memory of a past crime, is obscured, during a great part of the Novelle, by the theme of brother and sister love. In all three of these works the inner form of the story is not impeccable but indeed very faulty. In fact, in his form as well as in his subject matter, there is with Meyer a good deal of façade, concealing the inherent weakness and dualism.

As there is in Keller's Novellen a loading of the form with detail—an overloading perhaps—but still an enrichment by reason of the living quality of the detail; so in Meyer's works there is a similar overloading of his form with historical detail, which does not in any way contribute to the convincingness of the theme, but merely clogs with the weight of mere learning. This is particularly noticeable in *Das Leiden eines Knaben*, in which Meyer bolsters up his main narrative with continual references to the historical and literary conditions of the time. Thus the reader is informed that Madame de Maintenon, who is merely the listener to the story, is a granddaughter of Agrippa d'Aubigné; he is reminded of Madame de Sévigné, of Molière's last performance in *Le Malade Imaginaire*; that le Duc de Saint Simon is writing *Mémoires*, and that Condé won battles for Louis XIV. This is merely another instance of that quality in Meyer which leads him to overdo everything and produces an excess of ingenuity, an excess of strength, an excess of learning, an excessive mannerism of style. Keller wrote once, defending the sober quality of his own style: 'Es liegt mein Stil in meinem persönlichen Wesen: ich fürchte immer manieriert und anspruchsvoll zu werden, wenn ich den

Mund voll nehmen und passioniert werden wollte'. Meyer was a man and a poet without passion, an observer of, not a participator in life. When he has to deal with passion in his works, he does not find the natural expression for it, but uses a mannered, forced style, which aims at producing the effect of plasticity, but in reality merely chills the feeling of the reader.

It is usual to speak of Meyer's Novellen as being specifically historical Novellen[10]—and this is superficially true. But essentially Meyer was concerned not so much with the historical event and setting as with the ethical problem which was incorporated in the event of each Novelle. His Novellen are in the first instance Problemnovellen—just as those of Paul Heyse were—with the possible exception of *Das Leiden eines Knaben*. He himself wished to be recognized as a Problemdichter, to be appreciated as the describer of conflicts of the soul: he wrote in a letter: 'Je n'écris absolument que pour réaliser quelque idée'. 'Certaines profondeurs de l'âme où j'aimerais descendre.' He resented praise of his work which stressed his power of resuscitating the past, because this was to him of secondary importance as compared with the problem of conscience which was the real theme of his stories. The proof of this inherent method of his—the proceeding from the problem to the characters and events and setting by which it was to be rendered 'anschaulich'— can be gathered from the fact that he made various attempts to 'place' the problem incorporated in his Novelle *Die Richterin*, and tried Sardinia and Sicily for settings before he finally decided upon the Rhaetian Alps at the time of Charlemagne. The essential content of all Meyer's Novellen is the ethical problem, a problem of conscience.

With regard to the last of his Novellen, *Angela Borgia*, he writes: 'Cette nouvelle est à proprement dire l'histoire de la conscience'. And if it be asked for what reason he places these problems in historical settings, the answer is given in his own words:

Je me sers de la nouvelle historique purement et simplement pour y loger mes expériences et mes sentiments personnels, la préférant au Zeitroman, parce qu'elle masque mieux et qu'elle distance davantage le lecteur. Ainsi sous une forme très objective et éminemment artistique, je suis au dedans tout individuel et subjectif. Dans tous les personnages du Pescare, même dans ce vilain Moroni, il y a du C.F.M.[11]

The statement calls to mind Friedrich Schlegel's description of the Novelle, that it is particularly suited to render a subjective mood indirectly and as it were symbolically because of its natural tendency to objectivity. Meyer's Novellen form a singularly striking example of this, one in which at first sight the subjective and objective elements are an exact antithesis, and weakness, insecurity and doubt are concealed beneath the heroic attitude and the sculptural gesture.

The real Conrad Ferdinand Meyer has only lately been discovered.[12] Earlier biographers and critics of his work drew attention rather to the heroic façade than to the insecure dwellings it fronted and concealed. It seems a truer estimate of him to recognize that this too, with its strong, self-reliant, active and vital characters, is a wish-fulfilment of the real Meyer, who suffered under all the spiritual problems of a declining age.

Meyer's contribution to the development of the German Novelle was too original, too personally individual to have any real influence upon the genre as such. More-

over the German Novelle as a genre seemed to have
exhausted most of its possibilities with Keller; every possible aspect of it had apparently been exploited and
Keller's Novellen represent the summit of the development. Conrad Ferdinand Meyer's Novellen at the close
of that development, like the stories of Kleist at the
beginning, are too individual to be assimilated to any
traditional form. Every writer of Novellen no doubt contributes certain individual features and enlarges the possibilities of the genre thereby; but not every kind of individual characteristic can be assimilated or is such that a later
writer can profit by it. Kleist and Meyer are individual
writers, whose specific qualities cannot easily be assimilated to the tradition of the genre, and their contribution
compared with that of Keller, for instance, may be described as morbidly individual. Another writer of Novellen
whose works are open to the same criticism is E. T. A.
Hoffmann. All three writers have a certain originality
which marks them out from other writers of Novellen and
impresses them upon the memory and the imagination.
Though their works considered singly may or may not
conform to Heyse's theory and supply the 'Falcon', yet
as a whole they have a more strongly marked silhouette,
make a more vivid impression than that which is received
from the works of other writers who have been discussed.
Though they are less central and lie more on the periphery
than the works of Keller, for instance, they attract more
attention and seem to possess a greater positive quality
than his. The reason is that, compared with the balance
and harmony, the equal distribution and completeness of
Keller's work, they obtrude some characteristic which is
developed at the expense of the harmonious whole.

The Novelle is a bürgerlich genre. It reached the summit of its development, realized its essential form as a German genre in the works of writers like Stifter, Storm and above all Keller, writers standing within the confines of that literary movement known as Poetic Realism, which was the most characteristic expression of German Bürgertum of the middle of the nineteenth century. The critic von Lukács in his book of essays, *Die Seele und die Formen*, writes: 'In the middle of the last century there were still in Germany, especially on the periphery, towns in which the old Bürgertum still remained strong and living, the Bürgertum which is the greatest contrast to that of to-day. Of this Bürgertum these writers were begotten, they are its genuine, great representatives....Their works are the historical monument of Bürgertum'.[13] Heyse and Meyer are no longer representatives of that Bürgertum, but individualists living outside of it. Heyse's individualism moves only on the surface of life, belongs to the world of fortuitous and irresponsible contacts—the world of hotels and railway carriages; and already in his works the cosmopolitanism of the twentieth century announces itself. Meyer's individualism is of that morbidly psychological nature which isolates the subject from the society which surrounds him. Both of them—Heyse in his cosmopolitanism, and Meyer in his susceptibility to the spiritual problems of his age—were representatives of the disintegrating forces from without and within, which were undermining the Bürgertum with its established mode and accepted code of life.

(c) TOWARDS THE CLOSE OF THE
NINETEENTH CENTURY

The two tendencies which were undermining the Novelle as a bürgerlich form were the gradual disintegration of the framework of bürgerlich society which was taking place during the last quarter of the nineteenth century, and the growing pre-occupation in literature with the psychology of the individual. The two tendencies are connected one with another as cause and effect. The historical events of 1870 had pernicious effects upon the intellectual life of Germany, in so far as they directed the interests of the nation at large upon external aims such as world-empire, Germany's legitimate place among the nations, the possession of material wealth and luxury. (The Gründerzeit catastrophe in the early 'seventies casts a lurid light upon the race for wealth.) All this led to the gradual invasion of the self-contained bürgerlich form of life by international elements which, together with the growth of industrialism and the accompanying development of socialism, loosened the solidarity of its fabric. The replacement of a quieter way of life by a more ruthless affluence is described in Raabe's novel *Pfisters Mühle* (1894). Heinrich Mann was unsparingly satirical of the new bourgeoisie at the turn of the century in some of his early novels; he was also an author of Novellen. Separated from the social framework within which his existence had developed hitherto—a framework embodying a definite view of life with its own moral code based on ideals of truth, genuineness, competence and ability in the conduct of life, courage in the face of difficulties and resignation in the face of misfortune—the individual as such became an object of heightened interest in his uniqueness. The general and perhaps inevitable tendency for literature to employ the method of descriptive analysis in dealing with the psychology of the individual assigned less and less importance to the 'event' as the concrete core of the Novelle; and the more subtle the analysis of psychology became, the more volatilized the element of event became also. It may, however, be reasonably argued that, in so far as 'understanding' of the characters had come to be the ethos of the Novelle,[14] it was only logical that increasingly subtle methods should be employed to obtain the completest understanding possible. In this respect the genre contained within itself the germs of its own dissolution. Far-reaching in its consequences was the abandonment of the established ethical code which was common to all the writers of Poetic Realism in favour of a relativistic one, in accordance with which each 'case' was judged in respect of its individual circumstances; a change of ethical standpoint which can be observed already in the novels of Fontane, where similar instances of marital infidelity meet with different treatment at the hands of society (*L'Adultera* and *Effi Briest*). The end of the nineteenth century and the beginning of the twentieth century see the dissolution of the Bürgertum as an established mode and code of social life, and with it the end of the Novelle as a specifically bürgerlich genre. The subject matter of the Novelle deals henceforth either with questions of individual psychology detached from any standardized background of accepted bürgerlich ethics, or with the problem of the relation of the individual to a Bürgertum already in decay.

Before, however, writers representing this phase in the transition of the Novelle are discussed, two representatives of an earlier phase must be considered, who, though they do not stand within the circle of the Bürgertum which is the enclosing atmosphere of Poetic Realism, have at least definite affinities with the writers of that movement, like whom they possess also a very definitely accepted social background. These writers are the Austrians Marie von Ebner-Eschenbach and Ferdinand von Saar, though with the latter in a lesser and diminishing degree; and the equivalent for the Bürgertum of the Poetic Realists is for them the Austrian aristocratic world as it still existed at the end of the last century.

'The higher nobility of Austria', writes Walzel, in his essay on Ebner-Eschenbach, 'forms a world to itself. It appears to be detached from the conditions under which the life of other human beings plays itself out. A wall separates it from the rest of humanity and protects it at the same time. One might speak of a life of beautiful appearance were it not built up very solidly upon great material wealth. It is the life of the grand seigneur and his family and also of an appendage of relatives not always provided with means.'[15]

It is in this world, a more specialized one certainly than the world of German Bürgertum, but one which, analogous to the latter, has its own established social mode, that the Novellen and tales of Marie von Ebner-Eschenbach are set. Whether in the 'Palais' in Vienna or in the castle in the country, she approaches the lives of her aristocratic friends or of her peasant subordinates as a member of the higher Austrian nobility and applies in her estimate of their characters and fates the ethical and social code which is binding upon herself as a member of that caste. Not that she accepts unreservedly the view of life which is held as a standard by her caste—a number of her works can be regarded as a criticism, though a good-humoured and tolerant criticism of its weaknesses —but her view of life is fundamentally determined by her position within the Lebensform of the Austrian nobility.

Meeting with considerable discouragement in her earliest attempts at writing, since a Comtesse who was an authoress was in herself a violatión of the social code of her world, she persevered with little success until the publication of her first volume of *Erzählungen* (1875), which was followed in 1881 by *Neue Erzählungen, Dorf- und Schlossgeschichten* (1883) and *Neue Dorf- und Schlossgeschichten* (1886). By the time she had reached the age of seventy she was recognized as one of the most eminent of Austrian writers, and her eightieth birthday afforded an opportunity for further acknowledgments of her fame and popularity.

She contributes nothing new to the form of the Novelle; what novelty there is in her work lies rather in the subject matter, in the revelation of a social class with its ideals, prejudices, weaknesses and its point of view with regard to its own members and its dependents, which had not hitherto been so competently and reliably described in literature. Her ethical standpoint, the differences inherent in the two social classes being conceded, is substantially that of the writers of Poetic Realism, and she has some affinities with Gottfried Keller, though the paedagogic element is not so pronounced in her. She is a realist in the sense in which her German contemporaries were realistic, but she knows that crude realism is not the business of the artist, though she was at one time claimed by the Naturalists as a pioneer of their movement. And it is as an artist that she handles her subjects, but with an artistry too self-effacing to call attention to itself.[16]

She is more concerned with the inner life of her characters than with their external appearance, but in accordance with the nature of the Novelle she reveals her
characters rather by means of their actions than by a
description of their feelings. And her ability in every form
of narrative is above question. She wrote Novellen in
dialogue form (*Ohne Liebe*), in letter form (*Der Neben-
buhler*), achieving even the *tour de force* of a Novelle
in postcards (*Die Poesie des Unbewussten*). In *Komtesse
Muschi*, again in letter form, the typical young sporting
countess, with no thoughts except for her dogs and horses,
reveals herself fully and unconsciously. In *Krambambuli*
her hero is a dog, whom she places before a tragic alternative of conflicting loyalties. In *Die Freiherren von Gem-
perlein* in humorous form, in *Nach dem Tode* with a more
tragic emphasis, the intimate connection of the land-owner
with his land, his profound affection as well as his consciousness of his responsibilities, is the ethical basis. Her
subject matter is in general taken from contemporary life,
though in one or two stories (*Jakob Szela* and *Der Kreis-
physikus*) she turns back to the period of Polish political
disturbances for a more historical background.

Though her work does not substantially differ from
that of the writers of Poetic Realism as a whole and is
without any very striking originality, it entitles her, by
its simplicity and truth, its observation and understanding
of human nature, and the complete absence of sensational
and meretricious elements, to a place among the 'Little
Masters' of the nineteenth century. As a cultural document of a world which has now disappeared it has an
additional value.

If Marie von Ebner-Eschenbach has affinities with

Gottfried Keller, Ferdinand von Saar reveals in temperament and predilections similarities with Theodor Storm. As with Storm the prevailing mood of his works is one of elegiac melancholy. He confesses a preference for the past, but a past of which the final outposts are still visible in the present; for people, their real life and activities belonging to earlier days, who are unable to adapt themselves to present conditions; for artisans and merchants, who have fallen a victim to industrialism; for aristocrats, who still cherish the memory of former greatness.[17] But he lacks the rigid ethical standard which Storm in common with all the writers of Poetic Realism possessed, and his treatment of his characters is more indulgent, more forgiving. (A similar softness, which is perhaps characteristic of Viennese writers, is apparent in Grillparzer also, though it is absent in Stifter and Ebner-Eschenbach.) And though his view of life may be considered like that of the last named to be determined by the ethical and social mode of the Austrian nobility, with him more particularly that of the Austrian officer class, he steps outside of that circle in practice in relinquishing the military profession to become an independent literary man—which Keller, Storm and Stifter never were. The transition from a socially self-contained world, with the obligations and responsibilities which it imposes, to the freedom of individualism—a transition which, as has been pointed out, is the general tendency in German literature during the last quarter of the century—finds a characteristic exponent in him, and it is significant that the Viennese writers at the end of the century hailed him as their master.

His Novellen, which continued over a period of nearly forty years (the first, *Innocens*, was published in 1866), appeared in various collections under the titles *Novellen aus Oesterreich* (1877), *Drei neue Novellen* (1882), *Schicksale* (1888), *Frauenbilder* (1891). All these together with *Schloss Kostenitz*—fifteen Novellen in all—were republished in two volumes in 1897 under the original title *Novellen aus Oesterreich*. In addition to these collections *Herbstreigen* appeared in 1896, *Nachklange* in 1899, *Camera Obscura* in 1900 and, finally, *Tragik des Lebens*, a year before the author's death in 1906.

Saar's Novellen like those of Storm deal for the greater part with the theme of love (though not within the circle of the family), with a preference for situations in which it appears as an unreasoning attraction to which the characters yield without setting up any real resistance even when they realize that they are being drawn towards disaster. Frequently the theme is that of a woman's love for an unworthy or insignificant man—thus *Die Geigerin*, *Schloss Reichsegg*, *Geschichte eines Wiener Kindes* and, to a certain extent, *Schloss Kostenitz*, though here the heroine, the most ethereal of Saar's female characters, yields only in imagination and perishes in the moral conflict, which her inwardly acknowledged guilt sets up. Like Heyse, Saar tends to make the personality of a woman the centre of interest—in addition to the Novellen mentioned: *Marianne*, *Die Troglodytin*. Where the interest centres round a man he is usually one who has been defeated by circumstance (*Vae Victis*, *Tambi*, *Leutnant Burda*, *Seligman Hirsch*) and though not necessarily a weakling, of so sensitive an emotional nature, that he is unable to bear up against an unusually cruel blow of fortune, and seeks refuge in death, Leutnant Burda indeed with a desperate and extravagant display of courage.

The ethical attitude of Saar towards his characters hardly involves a moral judgment upon their conduct, but a mere acceptance of it in the spirit of pity. This tendency to apply no ethical standard to the characters but to treat them as perfectly neutral 'cases', with regard to whom it is not even necessary to understand sympathetically and forgive, but merely to observe with a supposed scientific detachment, is one of the connecting links between Saar and the writers of the Naturalistic movement at the end of the century. Their output in Novellen was indeed small and without distinction and necessarily so, for the importance assigned by them to the detailed description of *milieu* destroyed the possibility of a clear-cut narrative with a central incident so far outstanding as to command the attention by its strangeness. The so-called Novellen published by Arno Holz und Johannes Schlaf under the title *Papa Hamlet* in 1889 are not Novellen, whatever else they may be. But Gerhart Hauptmann's early work *Bahnwärter Thiel* (1887) has more formal qualities and exhibits the same characteristics as some of the Novellen of Saar: a detached transcription of reality in which the only ethical element is a sense of pity, though it is true that the transcription of reality is more meticulous, less artistically elaborated, than is usual with Saar. Hauptmann's other naturalistic story, *Der Apostel*, is merely a sketch for the novel *Der Narr in Christo, Emanuel Quint*.[18]

Saar's form, like that of Storm, is almost invariably the framework story—the framework being very variously treated. In some few Novellen the narrator of the story is a third person, but in the majority it is Saar himself. In three of the earliest Novellen he appears as the Austrian lieutenant, who comes across the subject matter of the stories he relates in the course of his professional duties; in the later Novellen he appears like Heyse as the independent literary man, though his relation to the characters of the enclosed story is rarely so fortuitous as it is in the 'Bekanntschaftsnovellen' of Heyse. Saar's Novellen are fundamentally psychological Novellen, and in some of them—*Der Excellenzherr*, for instance—the event is of so slight a nature that the subject matter offers nothing distinctive enough to be regarded as a 'Falcon'.[19]

Like Ebner-Eschenbach and Saar, Eduard von Keyserling, the descendant of an old Courland family, belongs essentially to an aristocratic world, though one already in decay, and the mode of life of that world determines his attitude to men and events and his handling of them in his novels and Novellen. In a prose style of great delicacy and distinction and in a prevailing mood of weary resignation he presents erotic conflicts, the protagonists of which give the impression of being sub-normal in vigour and vitality and as it were surprised to find themselves overtaken by violent emotions, with which they are unable to cope (*Wellen, Am Südhang*). With an infinite subtlety and by means of the most delicate brushwork he builds up the psychology of his characters and traces the slightest reactions of their emotional life. But this detailed psychological motivation, like the minute description of *milieu* in the Naturalistic writers, is inimical to the Novelle and prevents the firm outline, which is essential to the genre, from emerging, indeed implies an abandonment of the attempt to produce it. When, in addition to the disintegrating effects of psychological description, the methods of psycho-analysis and the scientific dissection of personality in other forms are brought to bear upon the genre, its downfall is completed. To compare a work like Schnitzler's *Fräulein Else* or Leonhard Frank's *Die Ursache*[20]—their skill of psychological analysis being nowise denied—with a classical Novelle is to deplore the degradation of a noble and dignified art form, existing in its own right, to the rank of a menial of science.

Chapter X

NOVELLE AND SHORT STORY

A question which poses itself again and again with the consideration of twentieth-century writers' shorter prose fiction is this: should a particular work, such as Hofmannsthal's *Reitergeschichte* or Kafka's *Ein Hungerkünstler*, be considered as a Novelle or a short story? The characteristic masterpieces of the nineteenth-century Novelle—Kleist's *Michael Kohlhaas*, Gotthelf's *Die schwarze Spinne*, Keller's *Romeo und Julia auf dem Dorfe* or Meyer's *Die Versuchung des Pescara*, to name just a few—are tales of between 20,000 and 40,000 words in length, and their characterization and plot structure have a complexity that is not permissible in a short story, which is frequently between 2000 and 4000 words long; the two works by Hofmannsthal and Kafka which have just been mentioned fall into this last category, judged by their length. At the time when the short story was developing in nineteenth-century America and elsewhere, from Edgar Allan Poe onwards, the Novelle was already established as the dominant form of shorter narrative fiction in Germany, and the mid-nineteenth-century writers there took little or no interest in the briefer form; the 'Kalendergeschichten' of J. P. Hebel and Gotthelf might be mentioned in this connection, or Hebbel's *Die Kuh*. It was towards the end of the nineteenth century that the short story came to full fruition in Europe, as with the masterly and richly varied creative writings of Maupassant and Tchehov, and it was at this period that German writers first took the genre seriously and recognized the challenge to the artist of a narrative that is restricted to ten or twenty pages in length. Sociologically, the growth in popularity of the short story coincided with the widening of the reading public beyond the professional middle classes to include the mass public that was increasingly to be catered for. The short story was limited in length because of the requirements of the popular magazines, and of the wider public's demand for complete works of fiction which could be read at one sitting by people whose leisure was much more limited than that of the public for whom C. F. Meyer was writing. With Naturalism in Germany there came a new approach to the short story in the form of the 'Skizze'. The prose pieces in Arno Holz's and Johannes Schlaf's *Papa Hamlet* (1889) and in Schlaf's *In Dingsda* (1892) show naturalistic close observation focused upon one brief episode, one small picture; naturalism has merged into impressionism, and didactic realism has shown itself capable of coming to terms with poetry. Atmosphere, miniature painting, and lyricism are stressed at the cost of clarity and liveliness of plot. The short story, as it has developed in the first half of the twentieth century, can be characterized as falling into two types. On the one hand there is the poetic short story, often akin to the sketch, evocative and indirect in its comments on character, tending to use imagery and symbolism self-consciously. Two English writers on the short story may be quoted here. Sean O'Faolain has said: '. . . the short story is an emphatically personal exposition. What one searches for and what one enjoys in a short story is a special distillation of personality, a unique sensibility which has recognized and selected at once a subject that, above all other subjects, is of value to the writer's temperament and to him alone....'[1] For H. E. Bates: 'The short story...has an insistent and eternal fluidity that slips through the hands', and it possesses 'something of the indefinite and infinitely variable nature of a cloud'.[2] Distinct from the prose-poem or single emotional-psychological mosaic-piece, there is the narrative of comparable length which aims primarily at being a concentrated sequence of events, an objective delineation of plot. But of course such subdivisions frequently merge, and, whether regarded as short stories or Novellen, Hofmannsthal's *Bassompierre* and *Reitergeschichte* certainly combine plot and poetry.

If it is at all true that the Novelle has declined in twentieth-century Germany, one reason for any loss of the prestige it enjoyed earlier lies in the increasing popularity of the short story. The two internationally most distinguished writers of German fiction during the first half of the present century, Thomas Mann and Kafka, wrote short stories as well as Novellen, quite apart from their novels; and since 1945 in particular the short story, following international, especially American and English, models, has become firmly established as a literary genre in its own right. Klaus Doderer, who has written a history of the German short story, has said: 'The short story has its chance in the twentieth century, just as the Novelle had in the nineteenth'.[3] Hermann Pongs has expressed his dislike for the term 'Kurz-geschichte', but reluctantly accepts it since it has become established German usage.[4] But if the term 'Kurz-geschichte' has only recently been acknowledged as a respectable literary term, it was used as a German word as early as 1904,[3] and the short story as such has been in existence in Germany somewhat longer. As Doderer has pointed out, the word 'Novelle' was extensively used in German up to about 1920 to indicate both the traditionally shaped Novelle of nineteenth-century proportions—that is, the Novelle as it is understood in the earlier chapters of this book—and also the newer type of short narrative, the short story. The early collections of Thomas Mann's shorter fiction were entitled 'Novellen', and contained brief sketches of approximately 3000 words and works as complex in structure as the Novellen of C. F. Meyer. Later editions, in the 1950's, of the same prose works, have been entitled 'Erzählungen'. Earlier in the present century some German writers wished to retain the term 'Novelle' for stories of 3000–4000 words on the grounds that they were reviving the form as originally practised by Boccaccio, but this has been less usual since 1945.

It is difficult, probably impossible, to formulate *a priori* definitions of the Novelle and of the short story which can separate them satisfactorily. The purely empirical way of measurement by length seems to be the only obvious way of distinguishing between them, but this too is only a rough and ready method; while Kleist's *Das Erdbeben in Chili* would be regarded by most English readers as a short story, it takes a time-honoured place in the history of the German Novelle. A theoretical definition of the Novelle, such as those attempted from the time of Goethe and Tieck onwards, will hardly cover all types of Novelle, as has been indicated earlier in this book; on the other hand many good English or American

'short stories' fulfil admirably the traditional requirements of the nineteenth-century German Novelle.
Similarly, most definitions of the short story can also be
applied to the Novelle. Benno von Wiese[5] quotes
Bernhard von Arx as wishing to limit the definition of the
Novelle to a 'tale of medium length', though von Wiese
feels that this is going too far. But he too is reluctant to
subscribe to any *a priori* theory of the Novelle as a form,
and points out that the value of a literary work is independent of any question as to the 'purity' of its outer
form: 'However much the theorists may resist such
transgressions of the frontiers, no narrative writer of
distinction ever allows a binding law to be prescribed to
him here'. Writing in 1960, another critic, Manfred
Schunicht,[6] goes so far as to maintain that the writers of
histories of the German Novelle have been faced with the
almost insoluble task of writing about an epic form, 'concerning the principles of which there is up to the present
day complete obscurity'. 'The literary value of a Novelle
of Kleist, Keller or Thomas Mann does not depend on
whether a turning-point or a falcon can be found in it'.
One can certainly agree with the caution of his prognosis
that 'the further development of the German Novelle is
unpredictable. The theorist cannot prophesy what latent
possibilities of development this form may still conceal'.
In this century more than in the last, short story may
merge into Novelle, Novelle into novel. An author may
occasionally prefer to refer to himself as a 'Schriftsteller'
and to his shorter works of fiction as 'Erzählungen'; he
leaves it perhaps to his readers to decide whether they
shall call him a 'Dichter' who writes 'Novellen'. But
some examples of middle-length fiction are so far distant

in substance and structure from any nineteenth-century conception of the Novelle that one is reluctant to apply the term to them. The survey of the Novelle in the first half of the twentieth century, which follows in the next, concluding chapter, has been drawn up with this fluidity of the term Novelle, as it is often used today, in mind.

Chapter XI

THE NOVELLE IN THE TWENTIETH CENTURY

During the nineteenth century the Novelle was the dominating form of shorter prose fiction in German literature, associated with the existence of a middle-class society which on the whole felt convinced of its own stability and security. Even during the period when its prestige as a consciously practised literary form was being urged vigorously, there were sceptical voices to be heard denying the possibility of a definition of the Novelle that could be both precise and comprehensive, and some of the great masters of the form, like Keller, had little use for theories about the Novelle or even for the word itself. As a historical landmark the war of 1914–18 clearly marked the outward end of the nineteenth-century form of society in which the Novelle had flourished, though already at the turn of the century authors were conscious that this particular middle-class world was in a precarious condition. The precise description of externalities that was emphasized by the Naturalists had the effect of clogging up the narrative sequence of the Novelle, and the intensive preoccupation with psychological states and with the subconscious mind which was ushered in as a consequence of the work of Sigmund Freud in Vienna at this time had a similar effect of reducing the element of action in the Novelle form. Viennese psychology has had a wide effect on the whole of European thought, of course, and the new approach to character and action in the novel, in the work of Proust and Joyce, for instance, is part of the difference in texture, mood and style that separates many writers of Novellen in the present century from those of the earlier period.

The introduction of a professional psychiatric attitude to character and events in the Novelle is revealed with obviousness, though without the highest quality of literary distinction, in the many Novellen of the Viennese Artur Schnitzler. These tales have no unified social background; and although their characters belong for the most part to the leisured and well-to-do middle class, as did so many of Freud's patients, they are unaware of any responsible relationship to it and live as individuals, concerned entirely with the gratification of their own needs for pleasure and erotic experience. They provide evidence enough that the middle class, to which they nominally belong, is in an advanced stage of decay. It is difficult to feel much sympathy with the trivial, worthless and egoistic men and women who populate the world of Schnitzler's Novellen; but they and their environment are described with a softness and grace which is peculiar to Viennese writers, and characterizes also the works of Grillparzer and Saar, though in a less intense form, whilst the prevailing mood is sentimental, frivolous and at the same time faintly melancholy.

Schnitzler's activities as a writer of Novellen began in 1892 with *Sterben*, already a piece of bravura writing describing the last year of a consumptive in which the dying hero makes a demand upon his mistress similar to that made by Herodes in Hebbel's tragedy, from the fulfilment of which she escapes, however, by more natural means than those which Mariamne employs. This was followed in the course of the next five years by *Die Toten schweigen*, *Der Ehrentag* and *Die Frau des Weisen*. *Leutnant Gustl* (1900), which brought Schnitzler into conflict with the military caste, is interesting as an early experiment in the technique of the interior monologue. The same form of narrative is employed by him later in *Fräulein Else* (1924). Amongst Schnitzler's Novellen pride of place belongs to *Der blinde Jeronimo und sein Bruder* (1900), a story of great beauty which fulfils almost all of the traditional formal requirements of the genre, and, describing the devotion of one brother to another and the undermining and re-establishment of confidence between them, moves in a different atmosphere from that of erotic adventure. *Dämmerseelen* (1907) and *Masken und Wunder* (1912) contain several stories dealing with mysterious and inexplicable happenings, treated with coolness and detachment. The Novellen, *Frau Beate und ihr Sohn*, *Casanovas Heimfahrt* and *Dr. Gräsler, Badearzt*, which were written between 1913 and 1918, have as a basic theme the reluctance to admit the approach of age (in the 'Gesammelte Schriften' they are published together under the title *Die Alternden*), and this theme underlies also *Frau Berta Garlan* written already in 1900. Of these stories *Frau Beate und ihr Sohn*, which utilizes to some extent the methods of psychoanalysis, is the most revolting in subject matter, *Dr. Gräsler, Badearzt* the most trivial. Later Novellen are, in addition to *Fräulein Else* (combining stream of consciousness and psychoanalytical methods), *Spiel im Morgengrauen* and *Traumnovelle* (psychoanalytical), in all of which the characteristic qualities of Schnitzler are apparent. His last Novelle bears the title *Flucht in die Finsternis* (1932).

The difference in mood occasioned by writers' growing awareness of the implications for them of depth-psychology is shown in *Ein Brief*, the 'Lord Chandos Letter', first published by another Viennese, Hugo von Hofmannsthal, in 1902. In this introspective essay a young gentleman of Elizabethan England describes the growing sense of alienation from the normal social life of his class which has befallen him, and how moods of apathy and of nausea with life are offset by a newly discovered sharpness of sensory perception and by an acute desire to make words and language into a precise and delicate vehicle to express the disturbing state of sensitivity which has come upon him. The Lord Chandos letter is an important landmark in German Neo-Romanticism, with its new awareness of the aesthetic implications of the psychologists' investigations into hitherto little-known aspects of the human mind.

Briefly my case is this: I have completely lost the capacity to think or speak about anything in a connected manner.

At first it gradually became impossible for me to discuss a higher or more general subject and, in so doing, to let my mouth voice those words which after all everybody uses frequently and without hesitation. I experienced an inexplicable uneasiness even in merely pronouncing the words 'mind', 'soul' or 'body'. I found that it was inwardly impossible for me to make any judgment about court matters, parliamentary affairs, or anything else you might choose. And this was not because of any possible kind of circumspection on my part, for you know my frankness and how it can merge into frivolity: but the abstract words, which the tongue naturally has to utter in order to bring out any judgment, crumbled away in my mouth like mouldering fungi.

Hofmannsthal's contributions to shorter narrative fiction are a slight proportion of his work as a whole, though as a critic he was repeatedly and sensitively appreciative of the German Novelle of the nineteenth century. In a letter of 13 July 1896 he believed that he was on the point of finding, imprecisely and intuitively, the key to the Novelle form which, if discovered, should make it possible 'to recognize a piece of imaginative prose as form through and through, like a lyrical poem'. On another occasion he wrote: 'Nobody is by definition less of a psychologist than the Novellist. He sees characters as the general element and the situation as the particular'.[1] His two short tales *Das Erlebnis des Marschalls von Bassompierre* (1900) and *Reitergeschichte* (1899) represent the author's wrestling for the transformation of prose fiction into poetry, for the replacement of individual psychology by imagery and symbolism. *Bassompierre* is based closely on Goethe's story in the *Unterhaltungen deutscher Ausgewanderten*, and in its concentrated brevity marks a deliberate turning back to the older Italian novella tradition. The proximity of erotic passion and death by plague is given poetic significance through imagery and style rather than through rational causation. A similar juxtaposition of sensuality and violent death is central to the more original *Reitergeschichte*, which narrates the exploits of a squadron of Austrian cavalry in northern Italy in 1848. The supernatural is introduced, when Wachtmeister Lerch leaves a deserted village and is confronted by his own double; this and other motifs lead up to the final *pointe*, the cold-blooded shooting of Lerch by his commanding officer for an act of minor insubordination. Hofmannsthal combines in this tale detailed observation and precise, concentrated narrative with a dream-like atmosphere; the deliberate lack of overt motivation in the final brutality of Lerch's shooting is perhaps an invitation to the reader to seek its interpretation in unconscious phenomena which are revealed indirectly in imagery and atmosphere.

The early Novellen of Thomas Mann are sometimes regarded as the final flowering of the nineteenth-century Novelle of upper middle-class society and as characteristic examples of the dissolution of this genre and of the inner decay of the society that is portrayed there. His first published tale *Gefallen* (1894) relates the bitter feelings of a young man who discovers that the actress whom he has loved is a courtesan. *Der kleine Herr Friedemann* (1898) reflects naturalistic views on heredity and environment as comprising a man's fate; because of the carelessness of a drunk nursemaid, an infant falls from a table, grows up to be a cripple, and seeks through absorption in aesthetic experiences consolation for his feeling of being excluded from normal life. Thomas Mann already expresses here the intellectual problem of the clash between Naturalism and Neo-Romanticism as literary movements and as ways of looking at life. He is sensitively aware of the apparent inevitability of scientific materialism and accepts the implications of the socialists' condemnation of the upper middle-class manner of living; at the same time he is personally fascinated by the appeal of an aestheticism that links erotic elements with a drug-like intoxication which leaves the individual a passive victim of irrational forces. The distinction of Thomas Mann's earlier writing lies to a considerable extent in the masterly irony and sense of distance which he achieves; it is this which enables him to depict the complex aesthetic attitude of this period in German, and European, literary history with the cool detachment of the model scientific observer. Other so-called Novellen originally collected in the same volume as *Der kleine Herr Friedemann* are short stories, or else sketches in the sense of Holz's and Schlaf's approach: *Das Wunderkind* builds up a picture of a child piano virtuoso and his audience through a series of psychological impressions; *Enttäuschung* anticipates *Der Tod in Venedig* when it permits a young man, absorbing the beauties of St Mark's, Venice, to be accosted by a stranger whose world-weary pessimism has only one more disappointment to face: 'death, this last disillusionment'.

Tristan (1902) states with sharp irony and unsparing lucidity the problems indicated in earlier work. The aesthetic poseur Detlev Spinell is the antithesis of the self-confident, vulgar businessman Klöterjahn, and both are shown in unsympathetic light, both are caricatures of upper-class society of the time. Klöterjahn is the successful materialist, the conformist to the requirements of his social group; but if Spinell has dissociated himself in disgust from this form of bourgeois living, the sterile egocentricity of his cult of the artist is a poor alternative. Spinell's attentions to Klöterjahn's wife form a parody of Wagner's opera; when Spinell awakens in Klöterjahn's wife through the music of *Tristan* new and disturbing emotions, he is unwittingly precipitating her death from tuberculosis. The pivotal point of the Novelle lies in the scene where he directs her feelings to such a 'love-death' experience. Sickness sensitizes the mind and its appreciation of artistic beauty; the extravert, Klöterjahn, is healthily free of these complications, but Mann shows him here as using his freedom in order to live like an animal.

Tonio Kröger (1903) has long been Mann's most popular Novelle, for it states the theme of the antithesis between the majority of carefree, practical people and the psychologically insecure man of artistic temperament with lyrical warmth and personally felt fervour. Tonio is the scion of a patrician North German family, and the environment of his early years is the Lübeck of Mann's childhood, which the author chronicled most fully in the family-novel *Buddenbrooks* (1901). After breaking away from this essentially bourgeois background, Tonio at the age of thirty is a successful writer, with Munich, the nineteenth-century artistic capital of Germany, as his adoptive home. The tension between middle-class society and the isolated artist is linked with the contrast between North and South Germany. Indeed, the important emotional experiences of Tonio's life derive from his schooldays in his home town: his admiration for Hans Hansen, the handsome, uncomplicated boy, and, a year or two later, for blue-eyed, freckled, blonde-plaited Ingeborg Holm. Hans and Ingeborg represent ideals which he cannot attain; they are beings who have no difficulty in taking their social background as they find it and who are carried through life by their spontaneous vitality. If Tonio becomes a creative writer, it is because he has been rejected by those whom he loves and has 'died' to real life. The conversation in Munich with Lisaweta Iwanowna enables him to realize more clearly the gulf between normal, spontaneous feeling and the sterile sense of inferiority from which he suffers.

Feelings, warm, heart-felt feelings are always banal and unusable, and the only qualities that are artistically creative are the irritabilities and cold ecstasies of our degenerate, artistic nervous system.... The creative artist is finished as soon as he becomes a human being and begins to have feelings.

Tonio's return visit to the north is a farewell to his childhood, a final recognition that there can be for him no revivification of the emotions that once bound him to Hans and Inge. The artist may indeed be taken for a criminal, and the theme of crime as an alternative mode of self-expression for the man of artistic temperament is developed in Mann's last work, the comic novel *Die Bekenntnisse des Hochstaplers Felix Krull* (1954). *Tonio Kröger* has remained a favourite among its author's works because it approaches the central problem of most of his work in a direct, non-parodistic manner, and because its echoes of Theodor Storm's moods and its careful, lyrical use of *Leitmotive* add to its warmth of texture.

Der Tod in Venedig (1911) is the culminating work of the earlier period of Mann's development and the last Novelle he was to write with a creative artist as its central figure. It is more polished and sophisticated than *Tonio Kröger*, and like all his work up to that time reflects his preoccupation with the irrationalism of Schopenhauer, Wagner and Nietzsche. Mann regards Gustav Aschenbach, the self-important middle-aged writer who has become a nationally representative figure, with much less sympathy than he does Tonio Kröger. Tonio hoped to bridge the gulf between art and normal social life by means of love, but Gustav Aschenbach's achievement is the result of cold, calculating will-power alone. The precarious balance of his life as an author is only preserved by anxious, constantly vigilant self-discipline on his part. The first section of the narrative is largely descriptive of Aschenbach's psychological constitution, and it is not until he arrives in Venice that the tension of the work becomes highly compelling. Italy has a disintegrating and demoralizing effect upon Aschenbach's carefully calculated self-control. Long-repressed instinctive forces take on sudden and unexpected forms in Aschenbach's consciousness; his attempts at rejuvenating himself by means of cosmetics recall the pathetic folly of the central character of Goethe's *Der Mann von funfzig Jahren*. Aschenbach refuses the warnings of common sense that he should hasten away from the cholera-infested town, and finds his death in a deck-chair on the beach while absorbed in his homosexual longings for the Polish boy Tadzio. The art of the tale lies in the gradual inevitability with which the hero, through an initial mood of temporary fatigue, becomes false to the principles that have previously dominated his life. This sense of inexorable fatefulness is cleverly conveyed by the use of minor figures who are both naturalistically convincing and symbolical: the man with the rucksack in Munich, the Venetian gondolier, the hairdresser, the guitar-playing street-singer, or the coolly warning Englishman. Aschenbach's composure is further undermined by his own nightmarish dreams, and he excuses his obsession with the boy by reference to classical precedents. Nietzsche's conception of a Dionysian Greece flickers before his dying mind's eye as he fancies that Tadzio is beckoning him towards the 'promising and the monstrous'. All this is achieved by means of highly skilled planning on the author's part, and the fate of Aschenbach is presented in so purely intellectual a manner as to preclude the possibility of any warmly emotional reaction to it on the part of the reader and indeed to suggest that none is aimed at or desired.

The First World War and the establishment of the Weimar Republic caused a fundamental change in Mann's outlook. After years of disturbing self-examination, he rejected the aesthetic irrationalism closely associated with Schopenhauer and Nietzsche, and consciously identified himself with thought of a social-democratic and rationalistic trend. Henceforth his work was to deal not with the problem of the artist and society, but with the wider task of the nature of man's life in society. His major energies were devoted to his novels *Der Zauberberg, Joseph und seine Brüder* and *Doktor Faustus*, and the Novelle occupied a more subordinate position now than it had done before 1914. It is significant that three such tales assume middle-class family life and the social-democratic state to be of positive value. *Herr und Hund* (1918) is of least significance artistically, being a long-winded, trivial account of the relationship between a pet dog and its master. *Unordnung und frühes Leid* (1926) reflects the family life of a professor of history during the inflation period of the early 1920's. The centre of the outward action is the afternoon party given by his adolescent children to their friends, an occasion which reveals how the younger generation can take for granted a social instability which causes their father irritation and anxiety. Cornelius is only on the edge of this party, the observer whose mind is preoccupied with thoughts about the melancholy nature of justice and the historian's need for objectivity. The grief of his infant daughter Lorchen breaks through his façade of non-committal observer and shows him too as emotionally vulnerable. *Mario und der Zauberer* (1929) is Mann's first political Novelle, reflecting in part the issues of *Der Zauberberg*, and in its opposition to Fascism anticipating the political commitment of *Doktor Faustus*. In the course of a family holiday in Italy, the first visit since Mussolini's seizure of power, the narrator feels alienated from the petty nationalistic pride that he sees around him at the seaside. Within the framework of this holiday atmosphere Cipolla's performance with its mixture of unpleasant cunning and hypnotic gifts is a solemn warning by the author of the difficulties which reasoned democracy may encounter when attacked by a man of unscrupulous daemonic power. More than once in his work Italy has been assigned the role of a demoralizing agent. Tonio Kröger rejects the idea of going to Italy in order to revisit the scenes of his childhood, but Gustav Aschenbach's holiday in Venice proves utterly disastrous. Mann evidently had little sympathy for the glorification of the sunny south which began in German literature with Goethe's Italian journey of 1786 and has since found many echoes in nineteenth- and twentieth-century German writers.

In Mann's later novels myth and parody frequently find themselves in uneasy juxtaposition. Something of this atmosphere is reflected in the few shorter tales that were written during or after the Second World War. *Die vertauschten Köpfe* (1944) takes Indian legend as its material, but recounts a horrific and confusing series of incidents in a mood of amused contempt; the tension between intellect and instinct, the frequent theme in the author's earlier tales, is again emphasized. *Die Betrogene* (1953) reveals Mann in his bitterest mood; the love of the fifty-year-old Rosalie von Tümmler, widow of a general, for a young American ends in her sudden death of cancer of the womb. Passionate yearnings, romantic appreciation of nature and an unthinking adulation of 'the heart' are here seen as illusions that have originated in clinical abnormality. The spirit of parody hovers over Mann's conception of the character of Moses in *Das Gesetz* (1944), an Exodus pendant to the Genesis tetralogy *Joseph und seine Brüder*. But for all the slyness which is read into the biblical leader's character, the humanist Mann acknowledges the formulation of the Ten Commandments on the solitary heights of Mount Sinai as an achievement of world significance. Mind and instinct are once more in conflict, the prophet of the invisible Jehovah and the worshippers of the golden calf. The tables of the law represent here the foundation of western civilization, and are the Word which reasserts itself as man's moral conscience from generation to generation.

Mann's outstanding contributions to the Novelle form were made during his earlier period. For a sense of the full texture of his literary achievement, the novels must be given pride of place; but a consideration of his shorter narrative works, both late and early, reveals much of the variety and range of his imagination and offers a fair reflection of the development of an author whose writing dominated German literature for over fifty years.

Arnold Zweig's *Novellen um Claudia* (1912) is entitled a novel ('Roman'), and is interesting as a formal experiment. It can be considered as a cycle of Novellen within a framework, or as a novel in which the character development of Claudia and Walter, from their engagement to an evening three months after their marriage, is traced in a series of episodes of Novelle length. The inset stories are, however, less substantial than the framework of the young couple's relationship to each other, to Claudia's mother and their friends. Arnold Zweig, while depicting the tensions and psychological complexities of his characters, finds a series of happy endings which make this work more comfortable and less challenging than that of Thomas Mann; the *Novellen um Claudia* has been one of its author's most popular works. It was not until after the First World War that Arnold Zweig became directly concerned with social and political problems, as in his best-known novel *Der Streit um den Sergeanten Grischa* (1927). The realism of this novel is also present in other short stories and Novellen which Arnold Zweig has written during the last forty years, and which may well have been of influence on some younger authors; two volumes of his *Ausgewählte Novellen* were published in Berlin in 1952. Comparable in form to Zweig's *Novellen um Claudia* is the 'Roman in elf Erzählungen', *Die Schuldlosen* (1950), by Hermann Broch. The impetus to the use of this form, Broch relates, was derived from a reconsideration of five independently conceived tales which his publisher wished to bring out in book form. The author revised them and added much new material consisting of further Novellen and some lyrical inter-mezzi. He says in his epilogue to the work that 'Novellen in themselves do not give totality of life, but totality of situation'. The result is a somewhat dis-jointed whole. Its main character, Andreas, is a wealthy man who during the inflation period of 1923 can afford to be indifferent to the social situation of Germany, thanks to his flair for playing the Stock Exchange. His personal irresponsibility causes the death of an innocent young woman, but ten years later he takes his own life, in circumstances which are modelled on the story of Don Juan. Hans Erich Nossack has shown an interest in the type of formal experiment that Zweig and Broch were essaying in his 'Roman einer schlaflosen Nacht' (*Spirale*, 1956). Alfred Döblin's last novel, *Hamlet oder Die lange Nacht nimmt ein Ende* (1957), shows a young Englishman's homecoming after the Second World War, severely hurt in body and mind; he identifies himself with Hamlet, and makes obsessive efforts to probe conflicts long dormant in his parents' lives. Döblin too uses as structural device a framework enclosing a series of inset Novellen which throw light obliquely upon the hero's quest.

Hermann Hesse (born in 1877) has shared with Thomas Mann the distinction of being awarded the Nobel prize for literature. His main work too has been in the field of imaginative prose, ranging from short stories to long novels, though Hesse is also a sensitive lyrical poet. If Mann's earliest stories reveal a preoccupation with the world of scientific positivism as well as with that of aesthetic Neo-Romanticism, Hesse's beginnings hark back to earlier literary models, the pre-industrial middle-class sphere of Keller's Novellen and the emotional atmosphere of early nineteenth-century Romanticism. The first two collections of tales, *Diesseits* (1907) and *Nachbarn* (1908), reveal a style which combines simplicity, gentle melancholy and unpretentious humour with an accomplished fluency. The background of these Novellen, as also of the subsequent collections *Umwege* (1912) and

Schön ist die Jugend (1916), is that of much of Hesse's own childhood in the small town of Calw in Württemberg, the 'Gerbersau' of these tales. Hesse's approach to this environment is not without irony, but there is little of the sharpness of Thomas Mann's writing. In *Die Verlobung* the narrator regards the hero with a mixture of patronage and sympathy reminiscent of Keller's mood at times. Like so many of Keller's Novellen, Hesse's stories turn upon the question of the 'Tüchtigkeit' of the hero, the particular problem being the realization of his proper vocation: a narrower conception of the problem with which Keller's heroes are faced of finding their true function in life. Alfred Ladidel (*Ladidel*, 1912) is a young man whose vanity comports ill with his lack of ability and his childish avoidance of serious problems. Tempted by an unscrupulous young woman to rob his employer, he soon has regrets and makes full confession, but finds that he can no longer remain a lawyer's clerk. He has much more aptitude as a hairdresser, and finds contentment and a congenial bride in a milieu which he had previously regarded with some condescension. *Kinderseele* (1918) again treats the theme of the guilt of a thief, this time of a boy. In *Ladidel* and *Robert Aghion* (1913) the hero is successful; in *Walter Kömpff* (1908) he fails and ends disastrously, though here the issue is complicated and also deepened by the existence of spiritual problems as well. The narrator and central character of *Die Marmorsäge* proves inadequate to the task which it becomes his duty to undertake. Having aroused the love of a young woman who has been compelled by her father to accept the attentions of a man to whom she is indifferent, he fails to see the implications of his behaviour and is thereby in part responsible for her suicide. These earlier works frequently have a melancholy tone, and the collapse of their small-town world with the coming of the First World War caused considerable changes in Hesse's writing. He made Switzerland his adoptive home, and sought in the study of Jung's psychology and of oriental religions a deepening of his own outlook. This is shown first in the novel *Demian* (1919) and in the Novelle of the same year *Klein und Wagner*. The conflict between convention and adventure is seen in the character of a bank-clerk who disappears to avoid the routine of work and family responsibilities, desperately seeking to lose his old personality and to discover the romance that he craves for. In Italy the repressed instincts of his subconscious mind come above the surface; he takes his own life after being on the verge of murdering a woman who has been his mistress. *Klein und Wagner* (the names represent different facets of the one personality) is Hesse's most complex Novelle in its plot structure and, like others of his writings in the 1920's, reveals a starker, more un-compromising approach to characterization than is found in the earlier tales. The collection of shorter prose, *Fabulierbuch* (1935) includes short stories in an Italian setting, among which *Aus der Kindheit des heiligen Franz von Assisi* portrays an episode from the boyhood of St Francis, for whom Hesse felt considerable affinity. This volume also contains the Novelle *Im Presselschen Gartenhaus*, which narrates sensitively the student friendship of Mörike for the more vital, but less stable Wilhelm Waiblinger, and their pity and practical help towards the insane poet Hölderlin. *Traumfährte* (1945) is a volume containing fairy-tales in the Romantic manner, while *Späte Prosa* (1951) consists of short pieces of autobiography, especially of reminiscences of the pre-1914 years, cast loosely in fictional form.

If Hesse's tales sometimes lack dramatic tension and vitality, they attract through the atmosphere of melancholy, either gently self-mocking or searingly poignant, which they evoke, and through their lyrical charm. Somewhat similar qualities are to be found in the prose of Robert Walser, whose own life embodied situations and themes that might have found their place in Hesse's stories, which Walser admired. Happiest when he was walking or writing, Walser had jobs with various banks and insurance companies in Switzerland and Germany, but he preferred to give up work once he had earned enough money to enable him to live in frugal independence for a while. From 1906 to 1913 he lived with his brother Karl, a painter, in Berlin, and during this fruitful period appeared the three novels which first made his name. During the war years he issued some volumes of prose sketches, and it is in delicate, ironic short stories developing from the brief sketch that much of his most charming work can be found (*Kleist in Thun, Die kleine Berlinerin,* or *Die Tante*). Walser's work is impressionistic in method, and the paucity of action and characterization is a drawback in his longer works. *Der Spaziergang* (1917), of Novelle length, is a sustained interior monologue in which with bird-like lightness of fantasy the narrator reveals his thoughts as he takes one of his walks, lunches with a patroness, argues with an income-tax official, and makes his way back from the town as evening approaches.

Most of Max Dauthendey's shorter prose works are impressionistic and lyrical short stories rather than Novellen in the nineteenth-century tradition. The twelve tales of *Lingam* (1909) are love stories with an Asiatic background, and *Die acht Gesichter am Biwasee* (1911) are set in a legendary Japan.

As Walser admired Hesse, so Kafka admired Walser. From the formal point of view Franz Kafka's work developed from the sketch, and the collection of little mosaics *Betrachtung*, published in 1913, are polished, light impressions based on observation of life in and around his home-town, Prague. But even in the few lines of *Die Bäume* Kafka leaves the unmistakable imprint of his personality and his preoccupation with problems of reality and appearance:

For we are like tree-trunks in the snow. Apparently they stand smoothly poised, and with a little shove you ought to be able to push them out of the way. No, you cannot do that, for they are firmly fixed to the ground. But look, even that is only apparently so.

The impressionistic sketch, in Kafka's case supported by a realism based on urban lower middle-class life in Prague, becomes a vehicle for more than fantasy and gentle melancholy, it soon takes on a many-faceted symbolism with psychological and metaphysical implications. Another starting-point towards Kafka's work is the parable, where a concisely stated fictional narrative is used to exemplify moral or metaphysical problems; fairy-tale becomes 'anti-fairy-tale', dream becomes nightmare. The terseness and restless tensions of Kleist's prose find their counterpart in the work of a German-speaking Jew who, living as a member of a minority within a predominantly Czech-speaking community, used language of puritanical simplicity to express a complexity of thought and feeling with an imaginative originality that has been unique, though widely influential.

Kafka's first sustained narrative that has been preserved is a Novelle rather than a novel or short story: *Die Beschreibung eines Kampfes*, written during 1904–5. From the formal point of view it appears as a parody of the traditional technique of the 'Rahmenerzählung'. At midnight on a winter's evening the narrator prepares to leave a party, when a stranger joins him and insists on accompanying him on a walk through the silent city. The stranger tells him his story, which in its turn contains the story of the Fat Man who wishes to re-create the outside world to suit himself: 'But now—I beg you—mountain, flower, grass, bushes and river, give me a little space so that I can breathe'. Soon the Fat Man tells his story, how he chases a stranger to find out why he prays. The Man Who Prays tells the Fat Man that he too is contending with the instability of outer reality:

And I hope to learn from you what things are really like, things which sink around me like a fall of snow, though before other people even a little Schnaps glass stands on the table as securely as a monument.

After telling his story, the Man Who Prays is blown away by clouds, the Fat Man disappears in a waterfall, and the stranger and the narrator continue their walk. The last spoken words in the narrative are 'Oh God!' As the narrative pierces through one inset story to another, the hope seems to be implied that the true heart of reality may be revealed beneath the layers of appearance; but the central experience is not the revelation that might be expected, it is a memory of early childhood, of a boy overhearing his mother as she talks to a neighbour sitting in the garden below. For the Man Who Prays this is a specially notable incident, incomprehensible and full of mystery to him; for his interlocutor the Fat Man, on the other hand, it is 'such an ordinary incident'. This earliest tale of Kafka, not published in its entirety until after his death, indicates the revolutionary approach of a man who uses the device of the framework-technique to break down normality in the narrative form and to explode conventional confidence in the security of rounded characters and a three-dimensional outside world.

But it was with a short story that Kafka first felt sure that he had reached his own, mature method of self-expression. *Das Urteil* (1912), the judgement passed by a bedridden father on a conscientious, but guilt-haunted son, who obediently commits suicide, blends the hitherto disparate aspects of Kafka's writing—fantasy, realism, speculation and psychological analysis—into a new unity. This tale is the first of a number of masterpieces in the short story form, such as *Ein Landarzt, Ein Hunger-künstler, Ein Bericht für eine Akademie* and *Josefine, die Sängerin.* Here fantasy becomes reality, reality becomes fantasy within an artistically poised narrative that exists in its own world, without reference to the conventions of previous prose-writers. These tales are not Novellen, unless the term is extended to cover all short fiction; they are short stories, and outstanding examples of this form in German literature.

Of Kafka's mature works that he completed and published during his life-time, two closely approach the Novelle form: *Die Verwandlung* and *In der Strafkolonie.* *Die Verwandlung* was written immediately after *Das*

Urteil, an indication that the author wished to apply his new vision of storytelling to the middle-length narrative form as well as to the short story. He immediately throws the reader, with the dry terseness of a chronicler, by means of an 'unerhörte Begebenheit' into a world of psychotic delusion which his narrative art preserves as a reality in its own right: 'When Gregor Samsa woke one morning from restless dreams, he found himself transformed in his bed into a monstrous insect'. As an insect, Gregor's habits and movements within the room that soon becomes his cage are described with meticulous precision. The life of the family within the confines of an urban flat, the hostile father and the conventional mother, the violin-playing daughter, the lodgers who have to be taken in now that Gregor is no longer capable of earning a living as a commercial traveller, the charwoman who is to be dismissed once she has got rid of Gregor's corpse, the relief and new enjoyment of life which the family antici-pate now that Gregor is out of the way; the insensitive materialism of this family is delineated with impassioned calculation. The reader has to contend with two layers of 'reality': the reactions of the family, and Gregor's con-sciousness that he is undeniably an insect ('What has happened to me? he thought. It was no dream.'). Christine, in Gotthelf's Novelle, is transformed into a death-bringing black spider; Gregor, as an insect, is harmless and well intentioned, but equally shunned. Perhaps one would prefer to interpret Gregor's state as the delusion of a sick mind; in revolt against uncongenial and exhausting work which lets the family batten on him, and at the same time guilty that he is rebelling against duty, he takes refuge in mental illness. But

Gregor not only sees himself as an insect; his family, the lodgers and the charwoman do so too. The tale has a clearly marked turning-point, the crisis caused when Gregor creeps out of his room to hear his sister playing the violin to company: 'Was he an animal, as music moved him so? He felt as if the way were being shown him to the unknown, longed-for food'. The humiliation of his animal shape is perhaps the necessary rejection of materialistic values before the attainment of spiritual reality. But the revulsion with which he is despised and rejected, especially by his sister, brings about the final collapse of his will to live, and in the morning the charwoman establishes the fact of his death by prodding his corpse with her broom.

Kafka regarded *In der Strafkolonie* as most characteristically expressive of the new narrative method he had adopted with *Das Urteil*. This tale was written in October 1914, and to some extent it reflects the author's dislike of war and his horrified anticipation of meaningless suffering which, it seemed to him, would be involved. If *Die Verwandlung* describes bourgeois family life in terms of cold distaste, *In der Strafkolonie* is by implication a condemnation of a civilization where through the lethargy of the majority of the population, an antiquated and brutal form of execution by slow torture is still allowed to be operated by a fanatically enthusiastic officer in a penal settlement for infractions of an absurd military code: 'The injustice of the procedure and the inhumanity of the execution were beyond doubt'. On hearing the visitor's disapproval of the system, the officer releases the condemned man and lets himself be killed by the machine instead. Apparently a humane liberalism has triumphed

over the last remnants of a barbaric tradition; but the
visitor's hostility to the soldier and the condemned man,
as his boat is putting off from the shore, may perhaps
imply that modern rationalism has no consolation or
meaning to offer the mass of ordinary people. *In der
Strafkolonie* is Kafka's most frightening tale, constructed
with a painful inexorability until the last two or three
pages, which form a puzzling coda. The story where
Kafka expounds most directly his agonized search for
purpose in life and for spiritual vision is possibly *Forschungen eines Hundes*, written during the last years of his
life and published posthumously. Here human aspirations
are translated into terms of fable; the autobiographical
reflections of a solitary dog in his search for 'food from
above' centre upon the two important experiences of his
life, his vision of the dancing dogs in his youth and of the
hunting dog in his old age. Kafka's imaginative prose,
whether one considers the sketches, the short stories, the
three novel-fragments or the works of Novelle-length
which have been discussed here, forms the most incisive
break in German prose with nineteenth-century narrative
methods, as with the pre-1914 world altogether. In a
tale like *Die Verwandlung* the Novelle finds fulfilment
and dissolution, at least if it is regarded as belonging
typically to the nineteenth century. But if the Novelle
form should be regarded now as 'finished', as capable of
no more original nor more tortuous shapes than those
devised by Kafka, with persistent vitality it has nevertheless continued to exist; just as the English novel, once
said to have been 'ended' by James Joyce's *Ulysses*, continues to thrive and its authors do not often feel compelled
to follow the path that led on to *Finnegans Wake*. But

there remains the thought, perhaps an uncomfortable one, that European prose has never been the same since Kafka and Joyce.

Stefan Zweig (1881–1942) belonged to a social background very similar to that of Schnitzler and Hofmannsthal; he too came from a prosperous Jewish family and grew up in intellectual circles in Vienna at the turn of the century. Many of his Novellen are loaded with that psychological reflection which was one of his main characteristics; aware of the complexity of his own personality, Zweig mirrored his own tensions in his work, and his concern with erotic problems is influenced to some extent by the work of Freud, about whom he wrote a biographical appreciation. Zweig was aware that the Danubian monarchy was in a period of neo-romantic twilight, but he himself was constantly on guard against allowing himself to drift into a state of indifferent hedonism or parodistic coolness. His first interest was in a subtle analysis of humanity, particularly of humanity against a Viennese background; but this was accompanied by a warmth of heart and an urge to teach moral lessons. This emotional sincerity, however, could be a danger to the objective balance and form of his works, although it brought a note of human sympathy which is frequently lacking in the cleverly sophisticated Novellen of those pre-1914 writers who were intensely inquisitive about psychological problems, but less interested in people as human beings. *Phantastische Nacht* illustrates the development of a man about town from the egocentric, bored life of an unattached member of fashionable society to the conviction, reached overnight, that an uncalculating interest in the emotions and aspirations of other people, in all classes of society, will yield a richer happiness. In this Novelle the main story is related in the first person as a written memoir, while a brief editorial introduction informs the reader that the events described took place in 1913 and that the narrator was subsequently killed in the first months of the war. *Brief einer Unbekannten* somewhat similarly recounts the life of a woman whose illegitimate child has just died, in the form of a long letter addressed to the father of the child, a successful writer and insouciant man of the world for whom this relationship was so fleeting as to be almost forgotten. *Vierundzwanzig Stunden aus dem Leben einer Frau*, another framework story, is an episode in the life of an English woman whose approach to a wild young man at Monte Carlo is intended in the first place to save him from the folly of his gambling. The conflict between the philanthropic urge to help and the consequences of involvement in complex and confusing psychological situations is further adumbrated in one of Zweig's best-known Novellen, *Der Amokläufer*. Here the setting is the Far East (Zweig had visited India before the First World War, but had never felt any liking for a civilization which was so different from anything he knew); a German doctor on board a ship returning from Australia and Singapore to Europe narrates to the author the events which have led to his departure from the East in a state of nervous exhaustion. 'Enigmatic psychological things have a really disturbing power over me', the narrator says. In his conjuration of exotic environment and its effect on character Zweig recalls here the manner of Somerset Maugham. Like Maugham, Zweig is always capable of telling a good story, with colourful, rounded characters and a freely inventive sense of plot, though he may lack the finest originality.

Zweig's Novellen are for the most part about erotic themes, set in the 'world of yesterday'. Some of his most effective work in the Novelle form is, however, concerned with purely humane issues. *Buchmendl*, like the brief short story *Episode am Genfer See*, is about a harmless individual who comes to grief because of the meaningless interference of the First World War with his life. *Die unsichtbare Sammlung*, a cameo of life in Germany during the inflation period, portrays the pathos of a blind old man whose happiness is based on delusion. Perhaps Zweig's finest tale is the *Schachnovelle*, written a year before the author took his own life in South America out of despair at the havoc that was befalling Europe. Dr B., having been arrested by the Nazis after Hitler's march into Austria, has occupied his solitary confinement by learning the more complicated manœuvres of chess from the only book that he had in his hands at the time. After his release he becomes a refugee, and while on a boat from New York to Buenos Aires he is tempted to intervene in a game in which a hard, dogmatic professional chess expert is involved, but the renewed preoccupation with this game causes him to betray his nervous unbalance. Zweig's characters are often on the edge of mental instability; but in the *Schachnovelle* the hero's condition is treated with particular sympathy since his ill-health is a consequence of his political persecution. The linking of inset story and framework is especially well done.

Two volumes of Zweig's Novellen were published before 1914, and a further three collections appeared in the 1920's. Robert Musil's vast novel *Der Mann ohne*

Eigenschaften (1930–43) looks back on Viennese life shortly before the collapse of the Danubian monarchy, while Heimito von Doderer's intricate novels *Die Strudlhofstiege* (1951) and *Die Dämonen* (1956) span that era and the Austria of the 1920's. Neither of these two Austrian novelists, however, has made a major contribution to the Novelle. Of Musil's three short studies in erotic situations, *Drei Frauen* (1924), the best is *Die Portugiesin*, which portrays the desperate jealousy of a South Tyrolese knight who has neglected his refined Portuguese wife for the sake of local political feuds and, a sick man, succeeds only after setting himself a physical task of herculean difficulty in convincing himself that his suspicions of his wife have been unfounded. Doderer's *Das letzte Abenteuer* (1953) has a lyrical atmosphere of medieval fairy-tale that is hardly characteristic of the author's two large-scale realistic panoramas of Austrian society.

Franz Werfel devoted his main energies in his later life to the novel. His early Novelle *Nicht der Mörder, der Ermordete ist schuldig* (1920) is, however, in many ways a characteristic document of Expressionism. This tale has faults which are encountered in the novels too, in particular a prolixity and a tendency to labour the author's points. The theme, hinted at in the title which Werfel says was taken from an Albanian proverb, is the conflict between father and son: 'Whether the father is hard or soft, is in its ultimate sense almost a matter of indifference: he is *hated* and *loved*, not because he is evil and good, but because he is a father'. A son narrates his upbringing in an Austrian cadet-school, and how his father, a martinet in army uniform, domineered over him in childhood and youth. As a junior officer, the son seeks escape in an opium den and by joining a conspiracy of anarchists who plot to kill the Czar when the latter proposes to visit Vienna. Nothing comes of this, as the Czar's visit is cancelled, but the young man's subversive associations are discovered; after being confronted by his father's violent insults, he comes close to murdering him, but overcomes the temptation and eventually emigrates, on 1 August 1914, thankful to escape from the old world to America. Interwoven with this is an episode in which the son of a fairground attendant is in fact arraigned for killing his own father. The drier, more restrained realism of the later 1920's, the 'Neue Sachlichkeit', is evident in Werfel's studies of people struggling to maintain the last vestiges of bourgeois values, or bourgeois illusions, in face of poverty and death (*Der Tod des Kleinbürgers*, 1927) or of poverty and shame (*Kleine Verhältnisse*, written in 1927 and published in 1930).

Jakob Wassermann (1873–1934) was a personal friend of Hofmannsthal, Thomas Mann, Schnitzler and other writers of that generation. A number of his longer works suffer from careless formal construction and slipshod style, and it is probably a few of his Novellen that will cause Wassermann to continue to be widely remembered. *Der goldene Spiegel* (1911) consists of brief narratives held together by a fairly elaborate framework, in the manner of Keller's *Das Sinngedicht*. The four books entitled *Der Wendekreis* (1920–1924) contain novels and Novellen, whose unifying feature is the concern for the solstice of man's life, which the author associates with the age of fifty; the most important of the Novellen are contained in the first volume, *Der unbekannte Gast* (1920). Of these, *Adam Urbas* is an economically told treatment of the father-son conflict from the point of view of the older generation, set in a peasant-farming milieu. Wassermann's best known Novelle, *Das Gold von Caxamalca*, first appeared with two other tales, collected under the title of *Der Geist des Pilgers* (1923). This impressive and exciting tale, which is based on parts of W. H. Prescott's *History of the Conquest of Peru*, describes the wanton and stupid destruction of the peaceable Incan community by Spanish soldiers. There is reflected here a melancholy longing for a world where the ideal of the brotherhood of man might find realization.

The Novelle tended to break away from its nineteenth-century traditions in the hands of such writers as Thomas Mann, Kafka or Stefan Zweig; the emphasis on subtle psychological phenomena perhaps accounted for the affinities such writers had both with Naturalism and Neo-Romanticism. Writers like these were analyzing early twentieth-century Central Europe in terms of its being a decaying civilization, and most of them were hoping, or after 1918 came to hope, for the eventual transformation of society along democratic or socialist lines; Stefan Zweig and Werfel, in particular, were close to the Expressionist movement, which on the whole laid its main emphasis on drama rather than on fiction. At the same time, both before the First World War and afterwards, there were many authors who maintained a traditionalist point of view, which is illustrated by their avoidance of subject matter taken directly from contemporary urban, industrial life, by their distrust of the new psycho-analytical approach to human behaviour, by their cultivation of the Novelle form in accordance with its

earlier lines of development, and by the practice of a
smoother and less adventurous prose style.

Paul Ernst began as a Naturalist, but soon turned away
from this movement as from Neo-Romanticism, and in
the first decade of the present century became theorist
and practitioner of 'Neo-Classicism'. He advocated
greater attention to form, which was to be achieved in
part by the avoidance of milieu descriptions and impressionistic detail, and in part by the careful manipulation of
plot. Problems of general human significance, he maintained, were revealed more clearly in the older social
classes of aristocracy, craftsmen and peasants than in the
more recently developed urban bourgeoisie and proletariat.[2] His was a hierarchical ideal of society where the
mass of the people should accept that they were inferior
to the leader-personalities; but literature should appeal
not only to a limited intellectual élite, it should be
capable of uniting the nation. Ernst's neo-classical
approach to the Novelle was to seek to revive its original
form as the novella of Boccaccio; it was to be short, concise, expressing in simple language issues of general
moral and social significance which were to be conveyed
through a quick-moving plot. Ernst's major contribution
to literature lies in these tales, of which he wrote several
volumes; in the collected works the material, which
extends back to the pre-1914 period, is ordered according to its subject matter. The *Komödianten- und Spitzbubengeschichten* (1927) are comic stories mostly with an
Italian background; *Geschichten zwischen Traum und Tag*
(1930) introduce supernatural elements, sometimes with
a Far Eastern exoticism; *Geschichten von deutscher Art*
(1928) introduce nationalistic themes, and others, as in

the *Romantische Geschichten* (1930),· have a Romance, medieval setting. Ernst is a skilful narrator with an amazing fecundity of plot-construction, though his self-imposed conciseness and simplicity of language led him to depict the tragic themes, that appealed to him so often, with a baldness that can give an impression of unsympathetic hardness. Two of his best-known stories, *Das Porzellangeschirr* and *Das Eisenbahnwägelchen*, illustrate his conception of the relationship of fate to character and the close link between fate and individual moral responsibility. But these many tales of Paul Ernst are not Novellen in the sense in which the term is applied to the stories of Hoffmann, Gotthelf, Keller, Stifter, Storm or Meyer; they are, in fact, significant as a contribution to the development of the short story as a literary form in Germany. This is the case too with the *Anekdoten* of Wilhelm Schäfer, the first collection of which appeared in 1908, and a last collection in 1949, three years before his death; the *Anekdoten* are better known than the traditional-type Novellen which Schäfer wrote. These short stories often treat significant, touching or amusing episodes from historic moments or from the lives of well-known figures in the German past. While Ernst turned to Italian *novelle* for his formal models, Schäfer sought to revive the manner of J. P. Hebel and the 'Kalendergeschichte'.

An idealization of the aristocracy and of upper-class manners generally sometimes went with the cult of a neo-classical Novelle tradition. Emil Strauss' most distinguished Novelle, *Der Schleier* (1920), concerns a woman's discovery of her husband's infidelity and the gentle, but effective manner in which she regains his loyalty; the setting is the home and lands of a well-to-do country gentleman. Rudolf G. Binding cultivated an aristocratic ideal in the heroes and heroines of his Novellen. *Unsterblichkeit* (1921) takes as central figure a haughty young daughter of a Belgian estate-owner who, in spite of her indignation at the German air force's requisitioning tracts of the family land, falls in love with a German fighter-pilot. The earlier *Der Opfergang* (1912) relates most effectively a situation which recurs frequently in Binding's work, a man divided between his affection for a good wife and his passion for another woman, who in this case is also shown as noble-hearted in her way; the background is that of the palmy days of the Hamburg patriciate.

Part of the early twentieth-century reaction against urban modernism in Germany was the revived emphasis on the country life. The regional tendencies of the earlier Poetic Realists were developed into 'Heimatdichtung'; a peasant-farming life was placed in the forefront of the work of many novelists and writers of Novellen, where it was sometimes seen with detailed realism, while at other times it became imbued with mythological symbolic significance. But there is not one of these authors who has the range and vitality displayed by Gotthelf in this field nearly a hundred years earlier. Ludwig Thoma, a Bavarian regionalist, achieved great popularity with his *Lausbubengeschichten* (1904) and other humorous short stories of peasant life. Hermann Sudermann's first novel *Frau Sorge* (1887) is centred upon a peasant-farming family in his East Prussian home district, though a couple of years later he was to make a name for himself in the *avant-garde* of Naturalist dramatists. His main contribution to the Novelle consists of the four *Litauische Geschichten* (1917), of which the outstanding one is *Die*

Reise nach Tilsit; a Baltic fisherman becomes so ensnared by the sensual charms of a young woman, a maid in his household, that he plans to murder his loyal, submissive wife. At the moment of crisis he repents of his evil intentions, and the intervention of chance, or fate, gives him the opportunity to save his wife at the sacrifice of his own life.

During the Nazi period rural regionalism in German literature was exploited for political purposes and, when allied with racial prejudice and inflated nationalism, it became notorious as 'Blut und Boden'. Hans Friedrich Blunck was closely associated with National Socialism; his Novelle *Bruder und Schwester* is a sentimental and superficial treatment of the incest theme, though *Die Wiederwitte*, the tale of a solitary countryman who falls victim to irrational forces in nature, makes a more forceful impression. Hans Grimm, notorious as a persistent champion of Hitler even after 1945, wrote a series of tales about life in South Africa, where he spent his childhood. These *Südafrikanische Novellen* (1933) were published from 1916 onwards. *Dina* depicts a man's situation between his white wife and his native servant-girl, and the tale ends with an episode of brutal harshness. *Mordenaars Graf*, portraying a father's loss of his son in a climbing accident, is more sympathetic. Hans Franck, whose most popular Novelle is *Die Südsee-Insel*, has traits in common with Wilhelm Schäfer, and Josef Ponten resembled Grimm in his nationalistic enthusiasm for Germans beyond the German frontier. Heinrich Zillich, close to Hans Grimm in some ways, wrote about the German-speaking minorities in Rumania (*Die gefangene Eiche*). Paul Alverdes also combined nationalism with a fondness for peasant-farming milieux.

Ernst Wiechert (1887–1950) was born in East Prussia, went to school in Königsberg and subsequently became a schoolmaster. For him the First World War was a decisive experience, confirming him in his pessimistic conception of life as a process of unavoidable suffering and in his distrust of authoritarian officialdom and militarism, which he subsequently came to regard as primarily responsible for the breakdown of stable society and for the unhappiness of those individuals who were seriously concerned for humane values. His heroes are solitary, sensitive individualists who are happiest in a life of idyllic closeness to nature; their dislike of industrial life and of the complexities of modern urban civilization is part of their anarchic idealism. Their feelings rebel against the materialism and cynicism they find around them, but their will to reform the world is disheartened by the harshness of the world's reaction to them. Their minds are continuously haunted by metaphysical queries; doubts about the place of evil in the world of a good Creator are held in check by the occasional experience of happenings of a moral and mystical beauty. Wiechert's heroes undergo emotional stresses similar to those felt by Rousseau and his German followers in the late eighteenth century; *la voix du cœur* is their guide to moral problems.

A revival of the spirit of primitive Christianity, which is seen as divorced from dogma and theology, is the message of Novellen like *Der Hauptmann von Kapernaum* (1929) and *Der Kinderkreuzzug* (1928). In the former an officer, anxious to atone for his participation in the First World War, changes places with a miner who is being held prisoner for his Communist activities, and meets death in his stead; the parallel with the crucifixion of

Christ is drawn. *Der Kinderkreuzzug* shows the pilgrimage made by a dozen half-starving children who leave their homes in the city (it is towards the end of the 1914–18 war) in search of the promised land of plenty in the country. The pathetic children and the hard-hearted grandfather are presented with too easy an appeal to the reader's emotional responses; and yet the author succeeds in his main point, to make these events convincingly responsible for the conversion of a young man returned from the army from bitterness to moral idealism. Wiechert's weakness lies in his too facile exploitation of feeling; his characters are essentially men of sentiment, to whom reasoned thought and humour mean correspondingly little. But this weakness is also his strength, for he undoubtedly achieves grandeur at times with an uncompromising and dignified simplicity of statement. In his novels the emotional basis can lead to a loss of coherence, while the traditional Novelle form acts as an artistic constraint on his urge to preach.

Together with his preoccupation with religious and moral problems, Wiechert displays a sensuous awareness of natural beauty, and his evocation of landscape links him to a certain extent with writers of the 'Heimatdichtung' school and with the earlier Poetic Realists. The East Prussian countryside is, however, not omnipresent with Wiechert, as is Schleswig-Holstein with Storm. *Geschichte eines Knaben* (1930) contrasts the happiness of a boy's memories of early years in the Dutch East Indies with his sense of alienation when circumstances in the First World War compel his father to return to East Prussia. Wiechert criticizes the narrow pettiness of the *petite bourgeoisie* in its lack of appreciation for the quiet independence of the boy Percy, whose only friend is the scion of the local aristocracy; separation from an older woman who has aroused his first erotic love and the knowledge that his own health is fatally undermined ultimately drive the boy to self-destruction. *Hirten-novelle* (1935) idealizes the life of a peasant community in a remote part of East Prussia. An orphan boy finds his vocation in the humble task of looking after the villagers' cattle and sheep, until the idyll is broken by the incursion of Russian troops in 1914, and the youth David loses his life in the defence of one of his sheep. The background of the forest is referred to characteristically on one occasion as 'ein grünes, gestaltloses Meer' ('a green, formless sea'). Like Percy in the *Geschichte eines Knaben*, David's youthful innocence is threatened by the fondness of an older woman; Wiechert fails here, as elsewhere, to depict erotic relationships with convincing realism. *Der brennende Dornbusch* brings out strongly the biblical characteristics which are interwoven into many of Wiechert's stories. Andreas, a quiet, patriarchal farm-servant, is opposed to war, and having been compelled much against his will to participate in the First World War, has a restless conscience until he has sought out and become reconciled with the father of a Belgian youth whose death he has caused. Wiechert's principles brought him into conflict with the Nazis. He wrote about these experiences and about his reactions to the Second World War not in Novellen, but in autobiographical writings and in his last novel, *Missa sine Nomine* (1950).

Something of the lyrical melancholy of Wiechert can be found in the writing of Bernt von Heiseler, whose Novelle *Apollonia* (1940) describes the remorse of a

Bavarian country girl whose ex-fiancé seeks death in the First World War after she has turned from him; there are reminiscences of Gotthelf's *Elsi, die seltsame Magd* here. *Der Dritte* (1952), by Hanna Stephan, narrates an incident during the flight westwards of refugees from East Prussia during January 1945.

Ricarda Huch was a practitioner of the Novelle in its traditional form. If Paul Ernst's sense of classicist discipline led him to compress the Novelle into a short story, a comparable attention to stylistic and formal precision caused Ricarda Huch to seek to combine the approaches of Keller and Meyer to the Novelle. While her major energies were devoted to the novel, to history and to criticism, three of her Novellen may be mentioned here. *Fra Celeste* (1899) is an anti-clerical tale satirizing the contrast between the popular preaching of an Italian monk and his clandestine love-life. *Der letzte Sommer* (1910) is Ricarda Huch's best-known tale, a skilfully constructed Novelle in letter form centring upon a revolutionary's mission to kill an important Russian political figure and his contacts with his victim's family. In *Weisse Nächte* (1943) the elderly authoress looked back from the Second to the First World War; a plot against the Czar in 1915 is foiled. The avoidance of disaster during a circus performance is not without echoes of Goethe's *Novelle*. In this tale Ricarda Huch manipulates her plot with a clever exploitation of the unexpected, while a nostalgia for the Old Russia permeates the whole with melancholy.

Ricarda Huch's sense of the grandeur of history and the cool weightiness of her manner are found also in the work of Gertrud von le Fort, who has been perhaps the outstanding practitioner of the traditional Novelle form in Germany between 1945 and 1960. In her Novellen the struggle between the intellect and the heart is usually a conflict between man and woman. The masculine forces of violence and power-seeking are shown as morally wrong, while a woman's humble faith in religious belief is seen as ultimately stronger than the complexities of a probing intellect or the brashness of brute force. Classicism, Renaissance and Catholicism are interwoven harmoniously in the first volume of her novel *Das Schweisstuch der Veronika* (*Der römische Brunnen*, 1928), where the authoress' conception of the tension between the sexes is made concrete against the background of Rome as seen by a young woman from a German professional family in the nineteenth-century tradition. The theme of the unguarded, vulnerable quality of goodness is shown in Gertrud von le Fort's first Novelle, *Die Letzte am Schafott* (1931). A similar theme, the young nun who loses faith in herself and her religion but ultimately regains belief and courage, is treated in *Die Abberufung der Jungfrau von Barby* (1940). In *Das Gericht des Meeres* (1943) woman as mother and centre of the family possesses an emotional strength which is lacking in the young nuns of the two earlier Novellen.

Gertrud von le Fort's most characteristic Novellen are of the post-1945 period. *Die Consolata, Die Tochter Farinatas* and *Plus Ultra* (1950) are again historical Novellen set in a Romance, Catholic atmosphere; they imply that womanly powers of love and forgiveness are especially necessary after the chaos and destruction of the war and immediate post-war years. The two tales of *Gelöschte Kerzen* (1953) and the longer Novelle *Am Tor des Himmels* (1954) are perhaps the most powerful of this writer's shorter fiction. *Die Verfemte* and *Am Tor des Himmels* effectively use a contemporary framework to contain an inset story from the seventeenth century. The former is set on a North German estate (Gertrud von le Fort owned property in Mecklenburg until 1945) and points to the inadequacy of the Prussian military code to satisfy a good woman's sense of humane behaviour. *Am Tor des Himmels*, written with the threat of nuclear weapons in mind, narrates the story of Galileo from the viewpoint of a young man who loses faith in the Church because it has refused to allow the free pursuit of astronomical knowledge. It was perhaps envisaged as a reply to Brecht's drama *Leben des Galilei*. *Die Unschuldigen*, dedicated to 'the memory of the dead children of the world war', is one of Gertrud von le Fort's starkest tales. A boy finds his death in attempting to dissuade his widowed mother from marrying a man with an unenviable record from 1939–45. The struggle between worldly and spiritual forces is once more reflected in the relationship between man and wife in *Die Frau des Pilatus* (1955); Pontius Pilate permits the crucifixion of Christ, but this act arouses his wife to a sense of responsibility that haunts her until she finds a martyr's death as one of the early Christians. *Der Turm der Beständigkeit* (1957), set in eighteenth-century France, has intricacies of plot which are almost conventional in the manner of minor eighteenth-century drama. Gertrud von le Fort has not experimented with the Novelle as a form, and the range of her themes is limited; but she can write with some power.

Werner Bergengruen writes in a traditionalist prose style and ignores the critical, experimental approach to

fiction initiated in the earlier years of the century by
Thomas Mann, Hofmannsthal or Kafka. He has been a
prolific writer, having produced over four decades a
flow of original tales without undue repetition of plot or
theme. Like Gertrud von le Fort, he links the pre-1914
world with his post-1945 experiences, and is a convert to
Roman Catholicism. He seldom places his stories in a
contemporary German setting; when he does not choose
historical subjects, he evokes the atmosphere of his own
youth by the Baltic (he was born in Riga in 1892). The
world he describes is 'die heile Welt', as he entitles one
of his volumes of verse. If disaster breaks into this world,
it is placed into a perspective given by the author's
optimistically conceived faith. His attitude to humanity
shows pity for man's weakness, which is seen as something comprehensible and worthy of forgiveness, or else
as an amusing foible which no benevolent reader (or
deity) need take seriously. His tales depend primarily
upon their plots for effect, not on atmosphere, characterization or metaphysical content; this last is implied
rather than outspoken. He can sketch with rapidity an
unusual place in a remote time, and is a virtuoso in the
sheer variety of events that he narrates. An essay *Genie
und Talent* (1949) develops a theory which expresses his
opposition to the cult of the artist as 'genius', as an
individual who may be different and therefore privileged.
He prefers to look back to the pre-Romantic conception
of the writer as a craftsman of intelligence and to ignore
the Romantics' praise of the superior outsider or
Nietzsche's cult of dynamic irrationalism.

Bergengruen began writing tales in the 1920's. His
first well-known Novelle was *Die Feuerprobe* (1933), a

story of adultery set in sixteenth-century Riga. By its title and its setting in medieval Italy *Die drei Falken* (1937) invites comparison with Heyse's conception of the Novelle as a conscious art form. The falcons, the only possessions of value left by a falcon-master at his death, come to symbolize the finer qualities in man's nature: a soaring imagination, an independence from humdrum everyday common sense and from love of money, and a generosity of spirit that rises above worldly considerations. The tone of the story is light and humorous, and this makes its more serious moments all the more effective. *Die letzte Reise* is another instance of the author's pursuit of classical restraint in the Novelle. The death of Winckelmann in 1768 in Trieste at the hands of a man whom he thought to be his friend is related to the art-critic's preoccupation with ancient Greece; it may have conscious echoes of Thomas Mann's *Der Tod in Venedig*. Another treatment of the theme of Winckelmann's murder is in the Novelle *Die Gemme* (1926), by Victor Meyer-Eckhardt. *Hornunger Heimweh* (1942) is one of Bergengruen's few works with a more or less modern German setting. A young man, needlessly fearful that he has caused another man's death, emigrates to America; the action loses force, however, by its division into two sections which are separated from each other by a long interval of time. *Der spanische Rosenstock* (1942) has been very popular; it is a slight romance, a pleasantly told, if somewhat conventional love story. *Das Beichtsiegel* (1946) narrates the difficulties of conscience faced by a priest who learns in the confessional certain facts and intentions which seem to demand his personal intervention.

In tales such as these Bergengruen is a polished

exponent of the traditional nineteenth-century Novelle form. At other times he writes short stories, modelled on the early Italian novelle (as in *Sternenstand*, 1947) or deriving from the anecdotes of the *Kalendergeschichten*. *Der Tod von Reval* (1939) is a characteristic and masterly example of Bergengruen's use of 'kuriose Geschichten' of the *Kalendergeschichte* type; although the unifying theme of the volume is death, the tales blend the macabre and the humorous with neat handling of plot. *Der letzte Rittmeister* (1952) consists of short stories mostly in a light vein with a Czarist Russian background. In *Die Flamme im Säulenholz* (1955) Novellen and short stories are not kept apart, for the one form merges into the other; *Das Florettband*, set in Riga in the 1860's, is charming in its whimsical irony and slight melancholy, while the title-story *Die Flamme im Säulenholz*, centred upon a plague-legend, recalls a motif from Gotthelf's *Die schwarze Spinne*. The tales of *Zorn, Zeit und Ewigkeit* (1959) are linked by their treatment of supernatural themes and by the subordination of the daemonic to the providential. Bergengruen may not have the exploratory depth and emotional tenseness that some writers possess, but his ready fluency and cool poise are a considerable achievement.

Edzard Schaper, like Bergengruen, has regretted developments in Russia since 1918. *Stern über die Grenze* (1949) treats a Christmas Eve episode on the Esthonian–Russian frontier. *Der grosse, offenbare Tag* (1949) has as its framework the arrival of East Karelian refugees from Finland to Sweden in 1944. In all too black-and-white terms, or rather white-and-red terms, the story is told of the persecution of a small church community by a young atheist member of the Communist establishment. The central episode of the swollen river and the drifting ice-blocks is graphically told. *Die Arche, die Schiffbruch erlitt* (1935) is a charming, sad tale of the shipment of a circus of animals across the Baltic.

Major formative influences upon Stefan Andres's writing were his childhood as a miller's son in a small Mosel village and the impression made upon him by the Catholic Church. His first novel *Bruder Luzifer* (1932) is autobiographical in its narrative of a young man who enters a monastery and later rebels against its discipline and leaves. Something of this early attitude is seen in the two Novellen *El Greco malt den Grossinquisitor* (1936) and *Vom heiligen Pfäfflein Domenico* (1936); in the former tale El Greco intends to paint the hated Grand Inquisitor as a cruel man, but wonders, when the work is finished, if he has not succeeded only in depicting the sadness behind his sitter's eyes. For Andres the conflict between the intellect and the senses expresses itself frequently in the tension felt by the person who is conscious of his failure to adhere to his religious principles (*Der Weg durch den Zwinger* and *Wirtshaus zur weiten Welt*, 1943). The five *Moselländische Novellen* (1937) may be regarded as examples of 'Heimatdichtung'; of these *Die Vermummten* is the best known. Andres's most substantial work lies in the field of the novel, particularly in his trilogy *Die Sintflut* (1949–59), a moral satire directed against the Nazi movement. His outstanding Novelle, *Wir sind Utopia* (1942), shows the tension between religious scruples and the bitterness of a war situation. During the latter stages of the Spanish Civil War a republican lieutenant takes prisoner a man who was twenty years earlier a monk. The ex-monk finds himself incarcerated in the same cell where he had formerly slept as a novice, for the building was previously a Carmelite monastery. Lying on his bed he stares up at the ceiling where there had always been a damp, rusty patch which he had formerly thought of as a map of Utopia, an ideal community where there should be no deep-rooted evil and where people would live peacefully and in quiet prosperity. Apart from the outward action, the central conflict is in the prisoner's mind; he intends to kill the republican lieutenant, but when the latter summons him to hear his confession, the ex-monk lays down his knife, inwardly relieved that the deed will not now be performed.

One of the characteristics of German literature since 1945 has been its renewed concern for topical, contemporary themes, after outspoken and free discussion had been impossible during the twelve years of Hitler's rule. Two older authors, both medical practitioners and well known for their writing before 1933, wrote impressions of German life amid the chaos and ruins during the hot, dry summer of 1947 in the form of the Novelle. In both cases, however, formal conciseness of plot is hardly respected. Hans Carossa's *Ein Tag im Spätsommer 1947* (1951) certainly has unity of time and centres upon two main characters, an old couple whose interests and activities are reflected during one day in their lives. Dr Kassian, a retired schoolmaster, spends some time in the town (Munich), where he meets various friends and acquaintances and hears of the plight of refugees from Eastern Europe. At night, after he and his wife and their maid have retired, somebody breaks into their home; but

the burglar, a novice at crime, has injured his knee on
some barbed wire, and when the Kassians treat him
kindly he is moved to repentance. The narrative is split
into two sections, and there are a number of subsidiary
episodes which are relevant to a picture of the mood of
Germany at this time, but not to sustained narrative
writing. Carossa called this work an 'Erzählung', but
Gottfried Benn's *Der Ptolemäer* (written 1947, published
1949) was sub-titled 'Berliner Novelle 1947'. It seems
deliberately to avoid the basic requirement of a novel,
Novelle or short story, that is, to tell a story, and to
be debunking the Novelle tradition. Its three sections,
'Lotosland', 'Der Glasbläser' and 'Der Ptolemäer',
correspond to three periods in time; the end of the
hard winter of 1946–47, the July sandstorms and heat
in the ruined city, and the autumn, when the narrator,
a Berlin hairdresser, thinks of retiring to live in solitude
by a lake but decides to stay on in Berlin after all, for that
is where he belongs. Against a backcloth of discomfort,
suffering and despair the narrator soliloquizes about art,
religion, science and the plight of humanity. He sees no
hope for the future, no moral goodness in individuals, no
consolation in the past, unless it is perhaps in aesthetic
creation or contemplation. On the other hand Carossa's
old couple, possibly invented as a deliberate answer to
Benn's protagonist, believe that humane behaviour is
worthwhile, however desolate outward conditions may
be. Benn's *Der Radardenker* (written 1949, published posthumously 1958) is similar to *Der Ptolemäer* in structure,
though it is more concentrated. Perhaps a more hopeful
note is intended with its closing thought that 'man is
not an end, not the lord of creation, but a beginning'.

Two Novellen by Albrecht Goes are concerned with moral problems that confronted Germans in the Second World War and, while placing them in a realistic setting, emphasize a humanitarian sense of responsibility towards these events. *Unruhige Nacht* (1949) reflects experiences during the war in Russia from the point of view of a Protestant army chaplain who has to attend the execution of a deserter. In *Das Brandopfer* (1954) Goes treats the subject of Germans' responsibility for the mass extermination of Jews during the war; this Novelle may well be the most effective and direct imaginative handling of this theme. The framework, where in settled, post-war conditions a young librarian learns from his landlady about the wartime events that impressed her so deeply, is somewhat wordy, but the central narrative, where a butcher's wife relates her growing sympathy and sense of responsibility for the handful of Jews in the town who have to come to her for their meat-ration, is moving and impressive. These two tales of Goes combine dignified simplicity with a direct, unpatronizing attitude to ordinary peoples' lives; emotional experience is conveyed with a minimum of literary artifice.

Jan Lobel aus Warschau (1948), by Luise Rinser, is also a memorial to the suffering of Jews under Hitler's régime. Women working in a nursery garden in Upper Bavaria during the last months of the war come into contact with a Polish Jew who is in flight from the authorities; they conceal him safely until the SS have gone and the allied occupation assures him freedom. But with the return of the local menfolk Jan realizes that he can only be a homeless wanderer; later he is killed while attempting to stow away in a ship taking immigrants from Trieste to Palestine. Colloquial dialogue alternates here with cool, crisp narrative style. In others of Luise Rinser's Novellen the central figures are young women with quiet will-power and fierce temperament. *Elisabeth* (1946) is about a governess' experiences with a family on a remote, neglected country estate. *Daniela* (1946, and not to be confused with the authoress' novel of the same title) describes life in a women's prison and the relationship between two women there.

The 'Gesamtwerk' of Friedo Lampe was not published until ten years after his death in 1945, but most of this author's work had been written before the outbreak of the Second World War. He was an heir to the impressionistic tradition, and his beautifully polished and sensitive prose recalls the manner of Robert Walser, while his kaleidoscopic presentation of multiple facets of life may have been influenced to some extent by Virginia Woolf. *Spanische Suite* or *Am Leuchtturm* (from *Von Tür zu Tür*, 1946) are short stories where the unity lies primarily in the occasion and place—an orchestral concert, or an afternoon at a North Sea island holiday resort—and where a variety of characters, whose experiences intertwine only in part, if at all, are sketched briefly but incisively through snatches of their consciousness. Lampe's two more substantial works of fiction, *Am Rande der Nacht* (1934) and *Septembergewitter* (1937) employ a similar technique, though on a more extended scale. Their unity does not lie only in one central passage or one single happening, for many fates are followed, both realistically and poetically, which all contribute to the creation of atmosphere. The 'slice of life' is in the one case an evening in a seaport town (presumably Bremen), in the other an afternoon in a small country-town in North Germany. Even if the association of ideas and impressions may at first sight appear to be fortuitous, both tales have a careful formal structure. The turning-point of *Am Rande der Nacht* is the wrestling match, while *Septembergewitter* more elusively centres upon a poet's impression of Leda and the swan and the coincident thunderstorm. These are not Novellen in a nineteenth-century sense, for the impressionist approach is that of a contemporary of James Joyce and Virginia Woolf. If they are thought of as novels, they are novels in miniature. Since 1945 the term 'Kurzroman' has occasionally been used, by Arno Schmidt, for example, in the case of his own impressionistic tales (*Leviathan*, 1949, *Aus dem Leben eines Fauns*, 1953).

Anna Seghers has collected together a selection of her Novellen and short stories, written between 1929 and 1952, into the two volumes of *Der Bienenstock* (1956), and provided them with a loose framework: not the noble company of Boccaccio's *Decamerone* nor of Goethe's *Unterhaltungen deutscher Ausgewanderten*, but Communist party members who meet in a house in southern France and finally recount how they took 'the first step' that led to their political conversion. *Überbringung des neuen Programms an das Südkomitee* (1949) tells of the transition to Communism in China, while other stories have a Central American setting derived from the authoress' years in Mexico; *Der Ausflug der toten Mädchen* (1943) has an element of fantasy that is unusual amid the sober realism of many of the tales. *Die Saboteure* (1946) is about sabotage in a German armaments' factory during the war, while *Die Rückkehr* (1949) preaches the foolishness of emigration from East to West Germany and the relief of the wanderer on returning home to the Democratic Republic. The earliest of these stories is concerned with Carpathian peasants after the First World War (*Bauern von Hruschowo*, 1929), and some of Anna Seghers's most recent tales take up themes reflecting rural life in Eastern Germany; 'Traktoristen', 'Bodenreform', 'Neubauern' and 'Bauernberater' feature largely in these hortatory narratives. Another East German prose writer, Willi Bredel, has published his collected tales under the title of *Auf den Heerstrassen der Zeit* (1957). Six of these Novellen, set in the period of the French Revolution and the Napoleonic Wars, were written between 1939 and 1940 while the author was a refugee in Paris and then in Moscow. Another longer tale, *Die Vitalienbrüder*, written in Moscow in 1940, interprets the fifteenth-century pirate Klaus Störtebeker as an enemy of the Baltic patriciate and friend of the workers and craftsmen. Bredel's narratives about Communists and Nazis in Germany before and during the Second World War are mostly short stories, though *Der Spitzel* (1934) is a substantial study of a man torn between two ideologies. *Das schweigende Dorf* (1948) is a grimly impressive Novelle about a Pomeranian village and its collective guilt in suppressing brutal murders that took place there during the last days of the war. The short stories of Bertolt Brecht (*Kalendergeschichten*, 1949) are too slight to be called Novellen; they have an unpredictable irony and wit, as in the *obiter dicta* of 'Herr Keuner', which one misses in the work of Anna Seghers and Bredel. The latter are more consistently conscientious in following the teaching of 'socialist realism', as defined by A. Zhdanov:[3]

> The truthfulness and historical exactitude of the artistic image must be linked with the task of ideological transformation, of the education of the working people in a spirit of socialism. This method in fiction and literary criticism is what **we call** the method of socialist realism.

Gerd Gaiser devotes his main energies to the novel and short story, but he has also on occasion used the Novelle form for the expression of personal wartime experiences. However, he moulds his topical material into poetic shape by skilful, stylized use of interior monologue and impressionism until it has transcended rapportage and become poetry. By his careful writing and his exploring of tense emotional situations he combines the telling of a good story with a poetic vision of deeply felt psychological problems. *Gianna aus dem Schatten* (from the volume *Einmal und Oft*, 1957) shows a German revisiting an Italian village which he had known some years before when he had been there during the war. The theme of guilt and revenge are developed with abrupt excitement from the apparently harmless premisses of a post-war summer holiday. *Aniela* (also in the collection *Einmal und Oft*) portrays a German soldier's love-affair with a local girl during the German occupation of Poland, and shows his sense of inadequacy and bewilderment in a situation which is too complicated for him to understand; does she love him, or is she decoying him for the purposes of the underground resistance movement?

Heinrich Böll is at his best in the short story, where he blends form and content most skilfully, and he is also more widely known outside Germany than any other German writer of his generation on account of his novels of contemporary German life. He has written a number of 'Erzählungen' which are of Novelle length, though they are constructed more on the lines of short novels than are the more closely knit Novellen of Gaiser. *Der Zug war pünktlich* (1949) gives the mood of soldiers travelling from leave in the Ruhr area back through Poland to the senseless horror of the Eastern front. *Das Brot der frühen Jahre* (1955) depicts a young man's first experience of falling deeply in love; interpolated in the events of a few hours in one Monday during the 1950's are flashbacks to the bitter memories of the hero's deprivations and hunger in his early adolescence between 1945 and 1948. This tale is the most powerful of Böll's narratives of Novelle length, forceful and realistic and yet poetically imaginative as well. *Im Tale der donnernden Hufe* (1957) shows the fantasy world of a couple of boys, its development as an escape and rebellion against the vulgar prosperity of their environment, and the impact of erotic experience. Böll's sense of humour, which can be either sharply satirical, surrealistically fantastic or humane and gentle in its understanding of the problems of the man in the street, is illustrated in the tales *Nicht nur zur Weihnachtszeit* (1952) and *Doktor Murkes gesammeltes Schweigen* (1958).

The short story has undoubtedly come into its own in German literature since 1945, and in Western Germany and Austria in particular the stimulus of American and British models has been considerable. The middle-length tale has likewise had its adherents among English writers, even though there is no generally accepted term for it; H. E. Bates for instance employs the word 'novella', and there may be a good case for adopting this spelling of the word rather than in continuing to refer to the term 'Novelle', which is hardly ever used in English except by students of German literature and does not let itself be anglicized easily. Bergengruen, Luise Rinser, Gaiser and Böll have been mentioned in connection with the Novelle, though they are equally adept at the short story, while other writers have neglected the Novelle in favour of the novel of 80,000 words or more, or the short story of less than 10,000 words. Elisabeth Langgässer, for example, published her long novel *Das unauslöschliche Siegel* in 1946 and a collection of short stories, *Der Torso*, a year later. Heinz Risse began as a writer of Novellen (*Irrfahrer*, 1948, *Schlangen in Genf*, 1951), but his inventive narrative ability has turned more recently to the short story (*Buchhalter Gottes*, 1958, *Die Schiffschaukel*, 1959); he has written: 'Perhaps one day the only remains of serious epic-writing will be the essay and the (short) tale that has been filed and compressed to the furthest possible extent'.[4] Wolfgang Borchert's fierce and unsparing impressions of the war and its immediate aftermath were best revealed in short story or brief sketch. Siegfried Lenz, Wolfdietrich Schnurre, Hans Bender, Herbert Eisenreich, Günther Grack, Rolf Schroers, Heinz Albers and a number of other younger writers have cultivated the short story and shown little interest in the traditional Novelle. For many authors the word 'Erzählung' is used for both short story and Novelle, perhaps deliberately in order to avoid raising issues of theoretical definition in the minds of readers and critics;

the term 'Erzählung' is less committing and less pretentious, at least for some authors, than the term 'Novelle'. It is indeed true that the Novelle as an expression of stable nineteenth-century German middle-class society came to its completion and dissolution with Thomas Mann's *Der Tod in Venedig* and Kafka's work, just as that society itself disintegrated after 1914; for some writers the whole concept of 'bürgerlich', as exemplified in many nineteenth-century Novellen, has become questionable. Heinz Huber writes quizzically in a short story *Die neue Wohnung*: 'Wir sind middle class (keineswegs bürgerlich, wohlgemerkt) und wissen, was uns zukommt'.[5] The word 'Novelle' itself has its associations with the idea of 'Bürgertum', and may find itself open to being looked at askance in a similar way by some people. But there have been a number of good Novellen written in recent times, and the experiences of the mid-twentieth century can be given convincing imaginative form in this medium. Nevertheless the short story has undoubtedly gained more support and has offered greater scope for experimental adventure. The Novelle tradition is certainly alive in 1960, though no important innovations within the form have been made since the end of the First World War. No attempt can be made here to prophesy the future of German prose fiction forms; however, in a period of renewed and varied literary activity in Germany, the Novelle, if not always known by this name, certainly continues to have full opportunity to make its contribution.

NOTES

INTRODUCTION

1. See Karl Viëtor, *Geschichte der deutschen Ode*, Munich, 1923.

CHAPTER I

1. See Karl Viëtor, *Geschichte der deutschen Ode*, Introduction.

2. For an interesting instance of an anecdote which at a first hearing seemed to be 'the very subject for a short story' and proved ultimately unsuitable see Paul Ernst, *Der Weg zur Form*, Berlin, 1928, chapter entitled 'Ein Novellenstoff'.

3. F. Hirt, *Das Formgesetz der epischen, dramatischen und lyrischen Dichtung*, Leipzig, 1923, p. 12.

4. Georg von Lukács, *Die Seele und die Formen*, Berlin, 1911, p. 158.

5. In the continuation of chapter 7, book 5 of *Wilhelm Meisters Lehrjahre* already cited, Goethe contrasts the importance of fate in the drama with that of chance in the novel and adds that chance may be allowed to bring about pathetic but never tragic situations. In this connection it is worth recording that in the majority of Novellen with unhappy endings the effect is rather pathetic than tragic. See in this connection Chapter VIII.

6. Friedrich Gundolf, *Goethe*, Berlin, 1916, p. 743.

7. Goethe an Staatsrat Schultz am 10 Januar, 1829.

8. Conrad Ferdinand Meyer to Félix Bovet, 14 January, 1888.

9. Friedrich Schlegel, *Jugendwerke*, ed. Jakob Minor, Vienna, 1882. Nachrichten von den poetischen Werken des Johannes Boccaccio.

10. Similar ideas, characteristic of the Romantic conception of the genre, are expressed by Schelling in his *Philosophie der Kunst*: 'Die Novelle... ist der Roman nach der lyrischen Seite gebildet, gleichsam, was die Elegie in bezug auf das Epos ist, eine Geschichte zur symbolischen Darstellung eines subjektiven Zustandes oder einer besonderen Wahrheit, eines eigentümlichen Gefühls'. Quoted in *Deutsche Literatur*, Reihe Romantik, Kunstanschauung der Romantik, p. 268.

11. Goethe to Eckermann, 29 January, 1827.

12. *Don Sylvio de Rosalva*, Ausgabe von 1772, vol. i, p. 22.

13. Schleiermacher, *Vertr. Briefe*, p. 432.

14. Ernst, *op. cit.* p. 288.

15. Ludwig Tieck, *Gesammelte Werke*, vol. xi, p. lxxxv.

16. Friedrich Hebbel, *Werke*, ed. R. M. Werner, vol. vii, p. 228

17. Paul Heyse, *Jugenderinnerungen und Bekenntnisse*, Stuttgart und Berlin, 1912, 5th ed. vol. ii, p. 68.

18. Heyse und Kurz, *Deutscher Novellenschatz*, vol. i, Introduction.

19. Fr. Spielhagen, *Neue Beiträge zur Theorie und Technik der Epik und Dramatik*, 1898, p. 74. See also the same author's *Beiträge zur Theorie und Technik des Romans*, 1883, p. 245.

20. Fr. Spielhagen, *Neue Beiträge*, p. 74.

21. As a result of his investigations into the specific character of the Novelle as a genre Hirsch arrives at the following general definition: 'Der Novelle eigentümlich ist, dass sie das Subjektive in artistischer Formgebung verhüllt, dass diese Stilisierung der Ordnung und Fülle der Welt zu einer Beschränkung auf eine Situation und zur Wahl von ungewöhnlichen Geschehnissen führt'. Arnold Hirsch, *Der Gattungsbegriff 'Novelle'* (Germanische Studien, Heft 64, Berlin, 1928), p. 147.

CHAPTER II

1. Wieland, *Don Sylvio di Rosalva*, Ausgabe von 1772, vol. i, p. 22.

2. Goethe to Eckermann, 18 January, 1827.

3. The short stories of Wieland collected under the title *Das Hexameron von Rosenhain*, an uncompleted attempt at a framework Novelle on a large scale, may be included under the type of Classical Novelle. They are however intrinsically of little merit and without profundity of thought or artistry of composition. One of the stories, *Liebe und Freundschaft auf der Dauer*, deals with the same subject as Goethe's novel: *Die Wahlverwandtschaften*. It is, however, characteristic of Wieland that he does not perceive the ethical problem involved.

CHAPTER III

1. Emil Ermatinger, *Das dichterische Kunstwerk*, Berlin, 1921.

2. The extent to which the character of the Novelle has already

changed can be estimated if the point of view of A. von Grolman be accepted: 'Es berührt diese Dinge nahe, wenn festgehalten wird, dass die altitalienische Novelle eine absolut diesseitige unmetaphysisch gerichtete und in jedem Sinne gesellschaftliche Kunstform sei'. Adolf von Grolman, 'Die strenge Novellenform und die Problematik ihrer Zertrümmerung', *Zeitschrift für Deutschkunde*, 1929, p. 625.

CHAPTER IV

1. Hermann Pongs, 'Grundlagen der deutschen Novellendichtung im 19. Jahrhundert', *Jahrbuch des Freien Deutschen Hochstifts*.
2. Ludwig Tieck, *Gesammelte Werke*, Vorbericht zur ersten Lieferung, 1828.
3. Ricarda Huch, *Die Romantik, Ausbreitung und Verfall*, Leipzig, 1908, p. 204.
4. Huch, *op. cit.* p. 207.
5. Paul Ernst, *Der Weg zur Form*, p. 75.
6. See Chapter vi.

CHAPTER V

1. Friedrich Schlegel, *Jugendwerke*, vol. ii, p. 412.
2. Complete works of Miguel de Cervantes Saavedra, translated by N. Maccoll, Glasgow, 1902, vol. vii, p. 6.
3. In view of this categorical statement of Cervantes himself the opinion of Hermann Pongs that the term 'ejemplares' is used 'in dem Sinn, dass hier exempla, Urbilder des Menschlichen aufgestellt werden, auf eine bestimmte Idee hin geformt' ('Grundlagen der deutschen Novellendichtung im 19. Jahrhundert', *Jahrbuch des Freien Deutschen Hochstifts*) seems to be untenable. Cervantes does not use the attribute 'exemplary' of his characters, but of his stories themselves. It is however true that the characters are set in a society which has a definite form of its own, that of Renaissance Spain as controlled by the authority of the Catholic Church.
4. *Las Novelas Ejemplares de Cervantes*, por Francisco A. de Icaza, Segunda edicion, Madrid, 1915, p. 208.

5. Icaza, *op. cit.* p. 168.
6. Icaza, *op. cit.* p. 220.
7. J. J. Bertrand, *Cervantes et le Romantisme allemand*, Paris, 1914, p. 482.

8. Bertrand, *op. cit.* p. 484.

9. Bertrand, *op. cit.* p. 490.

10. Ludwig Tieck, *Gesammelte Werke*, Berlin, 1829, vol. xi, pp. lxxxvii, lxxxviii.

11. Peter Kimmerich, *Ludwig Tieck als Novellendichter*, 1921.

12. Jakob Minor, *Tieck als Novellendichter*, Akademische Blätter, 1884.

13. *Die Vogelscheuche* is described as 'Novelle in fünf Aufzügen'.

14. Heinrich Laube, *Moderne Charakteristiken*, 11 Band, Mannheim, 1835, p. 407.

15. See Arnold Hirsch, *Der Gattungsbegriff 'Novelle'* (Germanische Studien, Heft 64), p. 49.

16. Theodor Mundt, *Moderne Lebenswirren*, Leipzig, 1840, pp. 155 ff.

17. Theodor Mundt, *Geschichte der Literatur der Gegenwart*, Berlin, 1842, p. 229.

18. Quoted by Hirsch, *op. cit.* p. 51.

19. Quoted by J. Proelss, *Das junge Deutschland*, Stuttgart, 1892, p. 550.

20. Heinrich Laube, *Gesammelte Werke*, ed. H. H. Houben, Leipzig, 1908, vol. vii, p. 105.

21. See Chapter vi for an account of its development.

22. Karl Gutzkow, *Gesammelte Werke*, ed. H. H. Houben, Leipzig (no date), vol. vi, pp. 102–3.

CHAPTER VI

1. Walter Muschg, *Die Zerstörung der deutschen Literatur.* Berne, 1956, p. 119.

2. Jeremias Gotthelf, *Sämtliche Werke. Ergänzungsband 4*, Zollikon-Zürich, pp. 280–1.

3. For further information on Gotthelf, cf. H. M. Waidson, *Jeremias Gotthelf*, Oxford, 1953. *Die schwarze Spinne*, ed. H. M. Waidson, Oxford, 1956, analyzes this work at greater length.

4. Quoted by F. Altvater, *Wesen und Form der deutschen Dorfgeschichte im 19. Jahrhundert.* Berlin, 1930, p. 123.

CHAPTER VII

1. *Reallexikon der deutschen Literaturgeschichte*, 1st edition, Berlin, 1925–31. Article 'Poetischer Realismus'.

2. As an example: *Das Novellenbuch, oder Hundert Novellen nach alten italienischen, spanischen, französischen, lateinischen, englischen und deutschen bearbeitet*, von Eduard von Bülow, 4 vols. Leipzig, 1834. In the 'Vorwort' contributed by Tieck reference is made to the extraordinary popularity of the Novelle at the time.

3. Adalbert Stifter, *Bunte Steine*, Vorrede (written in 1852).

4. Stifter, *op. cit.*

5. Quoted by Arnold Hirsch, *Der Gattungsbegriff 'Novelle'* (Germanische Studien, Heft 64), p. 37.

6. See Käte Friedemann, *Die Rolle des Erzählers in der Epik*, Leipzig, 1910.

7. See Käte Friedemann, *op. cit.*

8. An interesting comparison is that between Grillparzer's Novelle and Theodor Storm's *Ein stiller Musikant*. Storm's presentation of his principal character is far more sentimental.

9. *Reallexikon der deutschen Literaturgeschichte*, 1st edition, Berlin, 1925–31. Article 'Novelle' by Adolf Grolman. In the 2nd edition, Berlin, 1958– , the article 'Novelle' is by Johannes Klein.

10. Albert Köster, *Briefwechsel zwischen Keller und Storm*. Letter to Keller of the 14 August, 1881.

11. See Chapter VIII: The Novelle as a substitute for Tragedy.

12. Quoted in the introduction to Storm's Novellen by Felix Lorenz, edition published by Bongs and Co.

13. Georg von Lukács, *Die Seele und die Formen*, p. 138.

14. Emil Ermatinger, *Das dichterische Kunstwerk*, p. 114.

15. Ermatinger, *op. cit.*

16. Letter of Keller to Emil Kuh, 12 February, 1874.

17. Letter of Keller to Theodor Storm, August, 1881.

18. See Keller's own criticism of *Das verlorene Lachen* in a letter to Vischer, 29 June, 1875: 'Ich glaube, der Hauptfehler liegt darin, dass es eigentlich ein kleiner Romanstoff ist, der novellistisch nicht wohl abgewandelt werden kann. Daher vieles deduzierend und resumierend vorgetragen werden musste, anstatt dass es sich anekdotisch geschehend abspinnt, daher der tendenziöse, langweilige Anstrich'.

CHAPTER VIII

1. Quoted in Korff-Linden, *Aufriss der deutschen Literaturgeschichte*, Leipzig and Berlin, 1932, p. 180.

2. See Oskar F. Walzel, *Vom Geistesleben alter und neuer Zeit*, Leipzig, 1922. Essay entitled 'Tragik nach Schopenhauer und von Heute'.

3. An exception may possibly be made for the principal character in Kleist's *Der Findling*.

4. Bernhard Bruch, 'Novelle und Tragödie: Zwei Kunstformen und Weltanschauungen', *Zeitschrift für Aesthetik*, 1928, p. 329: 'Der Novelle ist der Bereich des Tragischen grundsätzlich verschlossen'.

5. Hermann Pongs, 'Möglichkeiten des Tragischen in der Novelle', *Jahrbuch der Kleistgesellschaft*, 1931–2. Pongs bases his claim that the Novelle is capable of tragedy on the conception of tragedy of Max Scheler.

6. See also Lessing's introduction to the translation of Thomson's tragedies: 'Und nur diese Tränen des Mitleids und der sich fühlenden Menschlichkeit sind die Absicht des Trauerspiels oder es kann gar keine haben'.

7. A similar situation, but reversed—the woman, not the man, bestows embraces upon a mistakenly recognized lover—occurs in the Novelle by Rudolf Binding (*Die Waffenbrüder*) which has not a conciliatory but a tragic ending. The situation in this as in Binding's sentimental and greatly overrated Novelle *Der Opfergang* is too 'konstruiert' to be convincing.

8. Paul Heyse, *Novellenschatz*, vol. XXI, Introduction to *Die Marzipanliese*.

9. Kenneth Hayens in his study of Theodor Fontane insists that these three works are novels. There would be more justification for claiming some of the shorter novels of Fontane, at least as far as their construction is concerned, as Novellen.

CHAPTER IX

1. 'Paul Heyses Novellen', *Auswahl für das Haus*, 3 vols. published by Cotta, Stuttgart and Berlin (no date).

2. Emil Ermatinger, *Das dichterische Kunstwerk*, p. 136.

3. Quoted by Georg von Lukács, *Die Seele und die Formen*, p. 128.

4. Compare Georg Brandes, *Moderne Geister*, 4th ed. Frankfurt, 1901. Essay on Paul Heyse (written in 1875). 'Nicht als Naturforscher, sondern als Schönheitsanbeter betrachtet Heyse das bunte Treiben des Lebens.'

5. Hans Bracher, *Rahmenerzählung und Verwandtes bei Keller, Meyer, Storm*, Leipzig, 1909.

6. Otto Kraus, *Paul Heyses Novellen und Romane*, Frankfurt a/M. 1888.

7. Otto Kraus, *Die deutsche Literatur und die Unsittlichkeit*. Quoted in *Paul Heyse* by Victor Klemperer, Berlin, 1907, p. 17.

8. Brandes concludes his essay on Paul Heyse thus: 'Man kann, sagte ein Kritiker, Paul Heyse als der Mendelssohn-Bartholdy der deutschen Poesie definieren. Er erscheint wie Mendelssohn nach den grossen Meistern. Sein Wesen ist wie dasjenige Mendelssohns ein deutsches lyrisches und sinniges Naturell mit der feinsten südländischen Bildung durchdrungen. Beiden fehlt der grosse Pathos, die durchgreifende Gewalt, der Sturm des dramatischen Elements; aber beide haben natürliche Würde im Ernst, reizende Liebenswürdigkeit und Anmut in Scherz; beide sind sie durchgebildet in der Form, Virtuosen in der Ausführung'.

9. *Briefe C. F. Meyers*, herausgegeben von Adolf Frey, Leipzig, 1908, vol. II, p. 340.

10. A writer of Novellen who approaches his historical subject matter from a point of view diametrically opposed to that of Meyer is Wilhelm Heinrich Riehl, the author of a *Naturgeschichte des deutschen Volkes*. In his *Kulturgeschichtliche Novellen* (1856) he presents incidents from the lives of unimportant but typical characters whose experiences and adventures are intended to illustrate the cultural conditions of past ages of German history. The stories, which hardly justify the title Novellen, are pleasantly told, but belong in intention and achievement to the type of fiction which the 'Professorenroman' of Dahn and Ebers made popular. More akin to the 'Renaissancismus' of Meyer are the romantic-historical Novellen of Isolde Kurz, whose *Florentiner Novellen* (1890) and *Italienische Novellen* (1895) went into numerous editions. Though she does not possess the firmness and sculptural quality of Meyer, her stories give a vivid and colourful picture of Renaissance Italy.

11. Letter to Félix Bovet, 14 January, 1888. The statement of Meyer was called forth by the following criticism of his work which appeared in the *Bibliothèque Universelle*: 'Aussi bien il semble fait pour le roman historique. Sa connaissance approfondie des sources de l'histoire, son talent incomparable du narrateur, se prêtent admirablement à faire revivre les figures du passé'.

12. See F. F. Baumgarten, *Das Werk Conrad Ferdinand Meyers, Renaissance Empfinden und Stilkunst*, Munich, 1920. I have drawn upon Baumgarten's book in my estimate of Meyer's personality and work.

13. Lukać s, *op. cit.* p. 137.

14. See Chapter VIII: The Novelle as a substitute for Tragedy. This view of the ethos of the Novelle is put forward by Bernhard Bruch, 'Novelle und Tragödie: Zwei Kunstformen und Weltanschauungen', *Zeitschrift für Aesthetik*, 1928.

15. Oskar F. Walzel, *Vom Geistesleben des 18. und 19. Jahrhunderts*. Leipzig, 1911, pp. 458, 459.

16. Unlike her contemporary Ossip Schubin (Lola Kirschner), who was at one time her rival in popularity: a more temperamental writer with a more highly coloured style. Her novels and Novellen (*Dolorata, Etiquette, Mal' Occhio*) are now forgotten.

17. See the first paragraph in his Novelle *Die Geigerin*.

18. Gerhart Hauptmann's Novelle *Der Ketzer von Soana* (1918) —a work of very great imaginative beauty, with the theme similar to that of Storm's *Renate* and Raabe's *Else von der Tanne*, of a young priest infatuated by the beauty of a girl who lives as an outcast from society—receives a sudden symbolical twist in the last few pages, which shifts its significance on to another plane of ideas.

19. I have not cited instances from Saar's later collections of Novellen because they repeat, frequently in less effective form, the themes of the earlier Novellen. They deal for preference with characters who are weak and unable to cope with the demands which life makes upon them (*Doktor Trojan, Conte Gasparo, Sappho*) or are actually vicious (*Die Brüder, Ninon, Requiem der Liebe*) and often describe the collapse of a personality in contact with an unworthy woman.

20. Frank's story traces the cause of the murder of a schoolmaster by a former pupil to an inferiority complex which the master's contemptuous treatment of the boy had set up.

CHAPTER X

1. Sean O'Faolain, *The Short Story*. London, 1948.

2. H. E. Bates, *The Modern Short Story*. London, 1941.

3. Klaus Doderer, *Die Kurzgeschichte in Deutschland. Ihre Form und Entwicklung*. Wiesbaden, 1953; and 'Die Kurzgeschichte als literarische Form', *Wirkendes Wort*, 1957, pp. 90–100.

4. Hermann Pongs, 'Die Anekdote als Kunstform zwischen Kalendergeschichte und Kurzgeschichte'. *Der Deutschunterricht*, 1957, pp. 5–20.

5. Benno von Wiese, *Die deutsche Novelle von Goethe bis Kafka*. Düsseldorf, 1956, p. 13.

6. Manfred Schunicht, 'Der "Falke" am "Wendepunkt". Zu den Novellentheorien Tiecks und Heyses'. *Germanisch-Romanische Monatsschrift*, 1960.

CHAPTER XI

1. Quoted by Mary E. Gilbert, 'Some Observations on Hofmannsthal's Two "Novellen" "Reitergeschichte" and "Das Erlebnis des Marschalls von Bassompierre"', *German Life and Letters*, 1958, pp. 100 and 106.

2. Johannes Klein, *Geschichte der deutschen Novelle*. Wiesbaden, 1954, pp. 428–9.

3. Quoted from Martin Esslin, *Brecht: A Choice of Evils*. London, 1959.

4. From a preface by Heinz Risse to an anthology of his short stories published by Reclam, Stuttgart, 1960.

5. In: *Auf den Spuren der Zeit. Junge deutsche Prosa*, ed. Rolf Schroers, Munich, 1959, p. 98. For further information on the German short story and for some examples of the genre, cf. *German Short Stories 1900–1945*, ed. H. M. Waidson, Cambridge, 1959; *German Short Stories 1945–1955*, ed. H. M. Waidson, Cambridge, 1957; and *Seventeen Modern German Stories*, ed. R. Hinton Thomas, Oxford, 1965.

SELECT BIBLIOGRAPHY OF WORKS RELATING TO THE NOVELLE

(i) General

Reallexikon der deutschen Literaturgeschichte, 1st edition, ed. Paul Merker and Wolfgang Stammler, Berlin, 1925–31. Articles: Dorfgeschichte; Novelle; Poetischer Realismus; Rahmenerzählung. 2nd edition, ed. Werner Kohlschmidt and Wolfgang Mohr, Berlin, 1958– .

AUERBACH, ERICH. *Mimesis. Dargestellte Wirklichkeit in der abendländischen Literatur.* Berne, 1946.

BASTIER, PAUL. *La Nouvelle individualiste en Allemagne.* Paris, 1910.

BORCHERDT, H. H. *Geschichte des Romans und der Novelle in Deutschland,* vol. I, Leipzig, 1926; vol. II, *Der Roman der Goethezeit,* Urach, 1949.

DODERER, KLAUS. *Die Kurzgeschichte in Deutschland. Ihre Form und ihre Entwicklung.* Wiesbaden, 1953.

ERMATINGER, EMIL. *Das Dichterische Kunstwerk.* Berlin, 1921.

ERNST, PAUL. *Der Weg zur Form.* Munich, 1906.

FRIEDEMANN, KÄTE. *Die Rolle des Erzählers in der Epik.* Leipzig, 1910.

HEYSE, PAUL. *Novellenschatz,* vol. I, Munich, 1871.

——*Jugenderinnerungen und Bekenntnisse.* Stuttgart and Berlin, 1901.

HIMMEL, HELLMUTH. *Geschichte der deutschen Novelle.* Bern and Munich, 1963.

HIRSCH, ARNOLD. *Der Gattungsbegriff 'Novelle'.* Germanische Studien, no. 64. Berlin, 1928.

KILCHENMANN, RUTH J. *Die Kurzgeschichte. Formen und Entwicklung.* Stuttgart, 1967.

KLEIN, JOHANNES. *Geschichte der deutschen Novelle von Goethe bis zur Gegenwart,* 2nd ed. Wiesbaden, 1954.

KOCH, FRANZ. *Idee und Wirklichkeit. Deutsche Dichtung zwischen Romantik und Naturalismus.* Düsseldorf, 1956.

KUNZ, JOSEF. 'Geschichte der deutschen Novelle in der Neuzeit'. In: *Deutsche Philologie im Aufriss,* ed. Wolfgang Stammler, vol. II, Berlin, Bielefeld and Munich, 1954.

LOCKEMANN, FRITZ. *Gestalt und Wandlungen der deutschen Novelle.* Munich, 1957.

LUKACS, GEORG VON. *Die Seele und die Formen.* Berlin, 1911.

—— *Die Theorie des Romans.* Berlin, 1920.

MAJUT, RUDOLF. 'Der deutsche Roman vom Biedermeier zur Gegenwart'. In: *Deutsche Philologie im Aufriss,* ed. Wolfgang Stammler, 2nd ed., vol. II, Berlin, Bielefeld and Munich, 1959.

PASCAL, ROY. *The German Novel.* Manchester, 1956.

PETSCH, ROBERT. *Wesen und Formen der Erzählkunst.* Halle, 1934.

PONGS, HERMANN. *Das Bild in der Dichtung,* vol. II, Marburg, 1939.

SCHLEGEL, FRIEDRICH. *Jugendwerke,* ed. Jakob Minor. Vienna, 1882.

SPIELHAGEN, FRIEDRICH. *Beiträge zur Theorie und Technik des Romans.* Leipzig, 1883.

—— *Neue Beiträge zur Theorie und Technik der Epik und Dramatik.* Leipzig, 1898.

TIECK, LUDWIG. *Gesammelte Werke,* vol. XI, Berlin, 1828.

WALZEL, O. F. *Das Wortkunstwerk.* Leipzig, 1926.

WEYDT, GÜNTHER. 'Der deutsche Roman seit der Renaissance und Reformation bis zu Goethes Tod'. In: *Deutsche Philologie im Aufriss,* ed. Wolfgang Stammler, vol. II, Berlin, Bielefeld and Munich, 1954.

WIESE, BENNO VON. *Die deutsche Novelle von Goethe bis Kafka. Interpretationen I.* Düsseldorf, 1956.

—— *Die deutsche Novelle von Goethe bis Kafka. Interpretationen II.* Düsseldorf, 1962.

—— *Novelle.* Sammlung Metzler, Realienbücher für Germanisten. Stuttgart, 1963.

(ii) *Special Aspects*

ALTVATER, F. *Wesen und Form der deutschen Dorfgeschichte im 19. Jahrhundert.* Germanische Studien, no. 88. Berlin, 1930.

ARX, BERNHARD VON. *Novellistiches Dasein. Spielraum einer Gattung in der Goethezeit.* Zürcher Beiträge, no. 5. Zürich, 1953.

BRACHER, H. *Rahmenerzählung und Verwandtes bei Keller, Meyer und Storm.* Leipzig, 1909.

EICHENTOPF, H. *Storms Erzählkunst in ihrer Entwicklung.* Beiträge zur deutschen Literaturwissenschaft, no. 2. Marburg, 1908.

EWALD, K. *Die deutsche Novelle im ersten Drittel des 19. Jahrhunderts.* Rostock, 1907.

FÜRST, R. *Die Vorläufer der modernen Novelle im 18. Jahrhundert.* Halle, 1897.

GARNIER, J. D. *Zur Entwicklungsgeschichte der Novellendichtung Tiecks.* Giessen, 1899.

GOLDSTEIN, M. *Die Technik der zyklischen Rahmenerzählungen Deutschlands von Goethe bis Hoffmann.* Berlin, 1906.

ICAZA, F. A. DE. *Las Novelas Ejemplares de Cervantes.* Second edition, Madrid, 1915.

JOST, W. *Von Ludwig Tieck zu E. T. A. Hoffmann.* Frankfurt, 1921.

KIMMERICH, P. *Tieck als Novellendichter in seiner entwicklungsgeschichtlichen Bedeutung.* Dissertation, Bonn, 1921.

KUNZ, JOSEF. *Die deutsche Novelle zwischen Klassik und Romantik.* Berlin, 1966.

SHIPPER, CLARA. *Der historische Roman und die historische Novelle bei Raabe und Fontane.* Forschungen zur neueren Literaturgeschichte. Weimar, 1930.

SILZ, W. *Realism and Reality. Studies in the German Novelle of Poetic Realism.* Chapel Hill, North Carolina, 1954.

WALDHAUSEN, E. *Die Technik der Rahmenerzählung bei Gottfried Keller.* Bonner Forschungen, Neue Folge, no. 2, 1911.

WEISSER, HERMANN. *Die deutsche Novelle im Mittelalter.* Freiburg i. B., 1926.

(iii) *Periodicals*

ARNOLD, P. J. Goethes Novellenbegriff. *Literarisches Echo,* vol. XIV.
—— Storms Novellenbegriff. *Zeitschrift für Deutschkunde,* 1923.

BRUCH, BERNHARD. Novelle und Tragödie: Zwei Kunstformen und Weltanschauungen. *Zeitschrift für Aesthetik,* 1928.

GROLMAN, A. VON. Goethes Äusserungen über die Novelle. *Germanisch-Romanische Monatsschrift,* 1921.
—— Die strenge Novellenform und die Problematik ihrer Zertrümmerung. *Zeitschrift für Deutschkunde,* 1929.

HEINZ, OTTO BURGER. Theorie und Wissenschaft von der deutschen Novelle. *Der Deutschunterricht,* 1951.

MARTINI, FRITZ. Die deutsche Novelle im 'bürgerlichen Realismus'. *Wirkendes Wort,* 1960.

MINOR, JAKOB. Tieck als Novellendichter. *Akademische Blätter,* 1884.

MÜLLER, JOACHIM. Novelle und Erzählung. *Etudes Germaniques,* 1961.

POLHEIM, KARL KONRAD. Novellentheorie und Novellenforschung. *Deutsche Vierteljahrsschrift* (Sonderheft), 1964.

Pongs, Hermann. Über die Novelle. *Zeitschrift für deutsche Bildung*, 1929.

—— Grundlagen der deutschen Novelle des 19. Jahrhunderts. *Jahrbuch des Freien Deutschen Hochstifts*, 1930.

—— Möglichkeiten des Tragischen in der Novelle. *Jahrbuch der Kleistgesellschaft*, 1931–2.

Ritchie, J. M. Drama and Melodrama in the Nineteenth Century Novelle. *AUMLA. Journal of the Australasian Universities Language and Literature Association*, 1963.

Schunicht, Manfred. Der 'Falke' am 'Wendepunkt'. Zu den Novellentheorien Tiecks und Heyses. *Germanisch-Romanische Monatsschrift*, 1960.

Seuffert, B. Über Goethes 'Novelle'. *Goethe Jahrbuch*, vol. xix.

Silz, W. Geschichte, Theorie und Kunst der deutschen Novelle. *Der Deutschunterricht*, 1959.

Stranik, E. Heinrich von Kleist und seine Novellen. *Jahrbuch der Kleistgesellschaft*, 1923.

Waidson, H. M. The German Short Story as a Literary Form. *Modern Languages*, 1959.

General histories of literature and general bibliographical works, which have not been listed here, will provide further information, particularly about specific authors and their work.

INDEX

Albers, H., 299
Alverdes, P., 280
Andres, S., 290–1
Anzengruber, L., 109, **122–3**
Aristotle, 199
Arnim, A. von, 50, 58, **68–71**, 80
Aubigné, T. A. d', 226
Auerbach, B., 109, **117–19**, 120, 121, 123, 127
Austen, J., 146

Bartels, A., 123
Bates, H. E., 243, 299
Bender, H., 299
Benn, G., 292
Bergengruen, W., **286–9**, 299
Binding, R. G., 279
Birch-Pfeiffer, C., 119
Blunck, H. F., 280
Boccaccio, G., 7, 13–15, 20, 21, 23, **24–6**, 28, 29, 31, 33, 34, 36, 37, 40, 43, 51, 55, 78, 81, 82, 83, 84, 87, 104, 131, 134, 180, 184, 192, 244, 295
Bodmer, J. J., 185
Böll, H., **297–8**, 299
Borchert, W., 299
Bräker, U., 111
Brecht, B., 286, 296
Bredel, W., 296
Brentano, C., 32, 58, 68, **71–2**, 75, 80, 108
Broch, H., 260–1
Büchner, G., 104–5
Byron, G. G. B., 96

Camoëns, L. V. de, 91
Carossa, H., 291–2
Cent nouvelles nouvelles, 30
Cervantes, M. de, 43, **80–6**, 87, 91, 93, 178
Chamisso, A. von, **67–8**, 103
Chrétien de Troyes, 79
Claudius, M., 107
Corneille, P., 199

Dante Alighieri, 81, 219, 221, **222–4**
Dauthendey, M., 264–5
Dickens, C., 102
Döblin, A., 261
Doderer, H. von, 274
Droste-Hülshoff, A. von, 6, 15, **129–34**, 135, 144, 149, 215

Ebers, G., 163
Ebner-Eschenbach, M. von, **233–5**, 236, 239
Eckermann, J. P., 9, 34
Edgeworth, M., 37
Eichendorff, J. von, 58, 63, 68, **72–5**, 80, 85, 166
Eisenreich, H., 299
Ernst, P., 11, 36, 70, 77, 161, **277–8**, 284

Feuerbach, L., 126
Fontane, T., 124, 201, **202–3**, 232
Fouqué, F. de la Motte, 54, **75**, 103, 157
Franck, H., 280
Frank, L., 240
Frenssen, G., 123
Freud, S., 247, 248, 271

Gaiser, G., **297**, 299
Geibel, E., 122
Gellert, C. F., 22
Gessner, S., 106
Goes, A., 293
Goethe, J. W. von, xi, 4, 8, **9–10**, 12, 17, 21, 23, **27–36**, 37, 39, 40, 43, 45, 47, 48, 50, 51, 53, 78, 81, 88, 89, 103, 129, 131, 133, 143, 147, 149, 150, 161, 184, 186, 192, 195, 225, 244, 256, 284, 295
Gotthelf, J. (Bitzius, A.), 26, 103, **109–17**, 118, 121, 123, 124, 127, 130, 152, 176, 241, 268, 278, 279, 284, 289
Grack, G., 299
Grillparzer, F., 89, **153–6**, 157, 158, 215, 218, 236, 248
Grimm, F. M. von, 187
Grimm, H., 280

Gutzkow, K., 95, 96, 98, 99, **101-4**, 127, 196, 202

Halm, F., 201-2
Hansjakob, H., 121
Hardy, T., 123, 139
Hauff, W., 56, **75-6**, 147
Hauptmann, G., 111, 153, 172, 197, 201, 238
Haym, R., 194
Hebbel, F., 12, 42, 89, 124, 137, 152, 157, 159, 194, **196-7**, 198, 241, 248
Hebel, J. P., 107, 241, 278
Heine, H., 70, 99, 100, 110
Heiseler, B. von, 283-4
Hesse, H., xiv, **261-4**, 265
Heyse, P., 13-15, 16, 17, 33, 52, 70, 101, 122, 131, 135, 148, 150, 152, 161, 171, 175, 202, **206-15**, 216, 227, 229, 230, 237, 239, 288
Hoffmann, E. T. A., 20, 26, 39, 50, 54, **58-67**, 68, 69, 71, 74, 75, 77, 78, 80, 85, 92, 151, 229, 278
Hofmannsthal, H. von, 241, 243, **250-2**, 271, 275, 287
Hölderlin, F., xi, 62, 64, 169, 263
Holz, A., 238, **242**, 253
Homer, 26, 117
Hopfen, H., 120, **122**
Houwald, E. von, 195
Huber, H., 300
Huch, R., 60, 69, **284**

Immermann, K. L., **128**, 129

Jean Paul (Richter, J. P. F.), 32, 141
Joyce, J., 248, 270-1, 295
Jung, C. G., 263

Kafka, F., 241, 243, **265-71**, 276, 287, 300
Keats, J., 192
Keller, G., xii, 5, 15, 17, 26, 55, 110, 115, 116, 124, 126, 129, 130, 136, 141, 143, 152, 153, 160, 165, 169, 173, **176-92**, 194, 198, 200, 201, 206, 207, 208, 210, 215, 216-17, 219, 226, 229, 230, 234, 236, 241, 245, 247, 261, 262, 275, 278, 284
Keyserling, E. von, 217, 239

Kleist, H. von, 5, 8, 15, 16, 17, 20, 23, 26, **37-46**, 47, 49, 51, 52, 55, 58, 61, 62, 64, 65, 66, 68, 78, 79, 84, 92, 107-8, 129, 136, 170, 197, 200, 202, 229, 241, 244, 245, 265
Klopstock, F. G., xi
Kröger, T., 122
Kühne, G., 97-8, 127
Kurz, H., 13, 208
Kyd, T., 90

Laistner, L., 209
Lampe, F., 294-5
Langgässer, E., 299
Laroche, S. von, 23
Laube, H., 94, **98-101**, 104, 127
le Fort, G. von, **284-6**, 287
Lenz, J. M. R., 104-5
Lenz, S., 299
Lessing, G. E., 196, 198, 199
Loti, P., 54
Ludwig, O., 124, 126, **144-53**, 161, 181, 188, 193, 200, 207, 209

Mann, H., 231
Mann, T., xiii, xiv, 67, 147, 153, 210, 243, 244, 245, **252-9**, 260, 261, 262, 275, 276, 287, 288, 300
Marlowe, C., 90
Maugham, W. S., 272
Maupassant, G. de, 241
Meissner, A. G., 20-1, 23
Mendelssohn, M., 199
Menzel, W., 88
Meredith, G., 189
Meyer, C. F., 8, 15, 16, 17, 26, 43, 55, 92, 121, 145, 149, 152, 161, 175, 207, 210, **215-30**, 241, 242, 244, 278, 284
Meyer-Eckhardt, V., 288
Meyr, M., 120
Molière, J. B. P., 226
Mörike, E., 71, 153, **156-9**, 207, 208, 263
Mozart, W. A., 62, 158-9
Müller, F. (Maler), 106
Müllner, A., 195
Mundt, T., 94-5, 98, 127
Musil, R., 273-4

Nash, T., 90

Nicolai, F., 23, 199
Nietzsche, F., 135, 213, 255, 256, 257, 287
Nossack, H. E., 261
Novalis (Hardenberg, F. von), 63, 89

O'Faolain, S., 242

Platen, A. von, 209, 218
Poe, E. A., 241
Ponten, J., 280
Prescott, W. H., 276
Proust, M., 248
Pustkuchen, J. F. W., 88

Raabe, W., 124, 172, 201, **203–5**, 231
Riehl, W. H., 204
Rinser, L., **293–4**, 299
Risse, H., 299
Rosegger, P., 120–1
Rousseau, J. J., 281
Ruskin, J., 114

Saar, F. von, 233, **236–9**, 248
Saint-Simon, L. de R., 226
Schäfer, W. 161, **278**, 280
Schaper, E., 289–90
Scherer, L., 76
Schelling, F. W. J. von, 54, 74
Schiller, F. von, 21, **23**, 39, 47, 48, 53, 195, 196, 198
Schlaf, J., 238, **242**, 253
Schlegel, F., **7–9**, 21, 23, 27, 34, 35, 38, 42, 65, 74, 76, 78, 80, 81–2, 83, 154, 183, 228
Schleiermacher, F. D. E., 10
Schmidt, A., **295–6**
Schnabel, J. G., 22
Schnitzler, A., xiv, 240, **248–50**, 271, 275
Schnurre, W., 299
Schopenhauer, A., 193, 195, 196, 197, 199, 255, 257
Schroers, R., 299
Scott, W., 115
Seghers, A., 295–6
Sévigné, Mme. M. de R.-C., 226
Shakespeare, W., 80, 81, 90, 193, 195, 220
Sohnrey, H., 121–2

Sophocles, 195
Spielhagen, F., 16, 17, 120, 122
Steffens, H., 54
Stephan, H., 284
Stifter, A., 114, 124, 130, **135–43**, 144–5, 166–7, 176, 188, 191, 192, 195, 200, 205, 207, 208, 215, 230, 236, 278
Storm, T., 1, 15, 26, 55, 75, 122, 130, 135, 139, 143, 148, **160–76**, 177, 182, 183, 184, 187–8, 190, 191, 193, 194, 195, 200, 201, 204, 205, 206, 207, 208, 210, 215, 218, 230, 236, 237, 255, 278, 282
Strauss, D. F., 126
Strauss, E., 30, **278–9**
Sudermann, H., 279–80

Tchehov, A., 241
Thoma, L., 279
Tieck, L., 1, **11–12**, 16, 20, 23, 39, 43, 47, 50, **52–8**, 62, 63, 67, 74, 75, 76, 77, 79, 80, 84, **85–94**, 95, 105, 133–4, 135, 141, 146, 165, 180, 183, 190, 244

Uhland, L., 118
Ungern-Sternberg, A. von, 98, 127

Varnhagen von Ense, K. A., 100
Voss, J. H., 106

Wagner, R., 253, 255
Waiblinger, W., 263
Walser, R., 264, 265, 294
Wassermann, J., 275–6
Weise, C., 22
Werfel, F., 274–5
Werner, Z., 195
Wezel, J. K., 23
Wiechert, E., 123, **281–3**
Wieland, C. M., 10, 20
Willkomm, E. A., 98
Winckelmann, J. J., 288
Woolf, V., 294, 295

Zhdanov, A., 297
Zillich, H., 280
Zschokke, H., 108, 111
Zweig, A., 259–60
Zweig, S., **271–3**, 276